The Borders Within

∴ ∴ ∴

The Borders Within

Encounters Between Mexico and the U.S.

Douglas Monroy

The University of Arizona Press
Tucson

The University of Arizona Press
© 2008 The Arizona Board of Regents
All rights reserved

Library of Congress Cataloging-in-Publication Data
Monroy, Douglas.
The borders within : encounters between Mexico
and the U.S. / Douglas Monroy.
p. cm.
Includes bibliographical references and index.
ISBN 978-0-8165-2691-8 (hardcover : alk. paper) —
ISBN 978-0-8165-2692-5 (pbk. : alk. paper)
1. United States — Relations — Mexico. 2. Mexico —
Relations — United States. 3. Cultural relations —
United States. 4. Cultural relations — Mexico.
5. National characteristics, American. 6. National
characteristics, Mexican. 7. United States — Civilization —
Mexican influences. 8. Mexico — Civilization — American
influences. 9. Mexicans — California — History. I. Title.
E183.8.M6M827 2008
327.73072 — dc22   2007039510

Publication of this book is made possible in part by
the proceeds of a permanent endowment created with
the assistance of a Challenge Grant from the National
Endowment for the Humanities, a federal agency.

Manufactured in the United States of America on acid-free,
archival-quality paper containing a minimum of 30% post-consumer
waste and processed chlorine free.

13 12 11 10 09 08   6 5 4 3 2 1

For my wonderful wife, Ann Van Horn,
and for my dear friend, trusty confidant, and
earnest tennis partner, John Shethar —
two who have made my exile in Colorado
endurable, even joyous.

∴

⁘ ⁘ ⁘

Contents

·:·   ·:·   ·:·

Acknowledgments

I have had the remarkable good fortune to receive gracious financial, emotional, and intellectual support on this project. I had a wonderful year as the Ray Allen Billington Distinguished Visiting Professor at the Huntington Library and Occidental College. Roy Ritchie at the Huntington provided me with time and space and introduced me to the remarkable array of scholars who grace the archives and the lunch area and who gave me such inspiration. Lynn Dumenil at Oxy connected me with new friends like Alexandra Puerto and Nina Gelbart and old friends like David Axeen and Norman Cohen. This manuscript is considerably richer because of all these fine teacher-scholars.

The Hulbert Center for Southwest Studies at The Colorado College (CC), under the recent directorships of Vicki Levine and Anne Hyde, has provided a home away from home and a warm and stimulating place to work. The support and input from my fine colleagues there and in the history department at CC have been truly sublime. My words are better and my concepts more developed because of the incisive discussions I have had with these talented people of good will.

I thank, too, Jimmy Santiago Baca for encouraging me to find my voice and Simon Ortiz for showing me that a sentence can be like music.

The Borders Within

Introduction

America has always understood itself to be very separate from Mexico. The border from San Diego/Tijuana, which commences at the Pacific Ocean and extends to El Paso/Ciudad Juárez, has always been "a line in the sand"—to evoke that momentous and theatrical rhetoric that William Travis allegedly pronounced at the Alamo. From El Paso/Ciudad Juárez to the Gulf of Mexico, the Rio Grande has nominally divided the two countries. As with the Mississippi River, which clearly demarcates the eastern United States from the western, America has seen rivers as authoritative boundaries. There is one place or country on one side of the border and another place or country on the other. Americans are mostly unaware of how many times America has crossed that border to invade Mexico.

Mexico has known more of the interconnections between the countries because its experience has been different. The Mexican-American War was fought on its soil, whether the place was New Mexico, California, Chihuahua, or Mexico City. Its most celebrated national heroes are los Niños Héroes, the cadets in Mexico City who tried to hold off the invading Marines in 1847 and died, in a losing cause, for the national honor. Mexico's greatest symbol of national pride, after the Virgin of Guadalupe, is the nationalization of British and American oil companies in 1939, the time Mexico successfully stood up to the colossus of the north. In the past few decades Mexico has watched American media might colonize its TV shows, movies, music, and fashion. These celebrate sexuality and blondness. Mexico has watched its husbands, sons, and daughters go to the north, many times never to return. Mexico is aware of America and the shared, usually contentious, and even perilous history of the two nations. Neither country, though, either understands or is even willing to admit how interwoven our histories are, how intertwined our economic and social interests are, how and why we are such intimate strangers. I will tell stories here about Mexico and America, ones that disclose the depth and breadth of this relationship, ones that hopefully will bring more compassion to our future discussions and actions. In this book we will explore the myriad ways America and Mexico have commingled our pasts, the various reasons and means by which people on both sides of the border deny this reality, and how it is that our futures are bound up together.

California has been both Mexico and America; it was even part of Spain once. The European settlement of California began in 1769 with the first mission at San Diego. As more missions followed, priests and soldiers, often Catalonians and serving the Catholic Church and the Crown of Castile, ministered to Indians. The most famous one, the one actually considered for sainthood and a celebrity among many California Catholics, is the famous and fabled Mallorcan, Padre Junípero Serra. He was the one, beginning with San Diego in 1769, who founded the first missions of California and in whose footsteps people, products, and culture have traveled back and forth—for centuries now—between Mexico and California.

Of course it was from this mix of Spanish and Indian that would come the mestizo, the people who would become identified with Mexico. In the first decades of Spanish California, there were only two little towns, la Villa de San José, and la Reina de los Angeles. The founders of the latter, the one that would become the stunning megalopolis, the town's first census lists as mestizo, mulatto, *negro*, and *indio*.

By most any calculation, California has become the most important place in America. One in eight Americans lives there; its economy rivals that of France; like New York once did for expansive Europe, Los Angeles and San Francisco serve as the bridge cities to the new economic dynamo of Asia; as either a paradise or a paradise lost, it has captured the American imagination, as has its creation of celebrities; it portends the future about what America will be, especially regarding those difficult matters that we have called "race" and "culture." Be they the priests or, later, the largely mestizo peoples, the ones who would call themselves *Californios* and develop the mythical rancho society in the Mexican Era (1821–1848), Spanish-speaking people were the first "Californians." Though some were from the Iberian Peninsula, and even the priests sojourned for training at the College of San Fernando near Mexico City, the first settlers of what is now the most important state in America came from Mexico.

This interwoven history of Mexico and America is absorbing both for its drama and for the ways in which the peoples of the two countries construe it and deny it. I also find this common history fascinating because I am interwoven with it. Half of my family came west to California from Colorado, the other half came north from Mexico. Books and documents about history and politics of California, Mexico, and America, conversations with people either directly on the landscape or through their printed stories, and writing these words make me smile at what has been for me—in contrast to much of the overall picture—a rather happy mixture.

Out of this mix of interests, wonders, insights, confusions, and genuine concern for the future of our two peoples has come this book. I have been a full-time college professor since 1978 and have written two other books on Indian, Spanish, and Mexican California. I teach classes on the American Southwest, twentieth-century U.S. history, and philosophies of history. This has been enjoyable work. There has been, though, some unease on my part stemming from the isolation of the ivory tower and from living away from my home, Southern California, for so long.

These stories and essays, then, have yet more significance. They are for me to meditate more about my locality, they are to explore the interweaving of American and Mexican history and society, and they are to bring insights and knowledge to the public square that have too often been sequestered away in the academy.

I will be here, then, in this book. It will take people's stories, my own included, to that public square. Some of the stories derive from the deep past of California, some of them from a century ago, and some of the stories are only recently told. All of them live in the present moment.

Helen Hunt Jackson wrote the love story of *Ramona* in 1884, but its account of the destruction of the Indians of Southern California exists in the present alongside Indian casinos. Woodrow Wilson's guns are present in the imbalance of power that characterizes NAFTA even with its rhetoric of free and fair trade. The missions of California are not simply architecture; they haunt all of Europe's and America's dealings with non-Christian peoples.

These stories spin out apart from linear time; actually, I am becoming unstuck from linear time. Writing the chapter on Woodrow Wilson, American liberals, and Mexico confirms that there are other kinds of time besides the usually progressive chronology of events that most of us learned in high school. I have come to understand something of how the indigenous people of the Americas have lived in the "mythic present," how they eternally seek return to "first things." Similarly, William Faulkner in *As I Lay Dying*, Carlos Fuentes in *The Death of Artemio Cruz*, and Gabriel García Márquez in *One Hundred Years of Solitude* have shown us that many people exist in time in non-linear ways. "What do you expect?" sighs Ursula in *One Hundred Years*: "Time passes." Aurliano admits, "That's how it goes, but not so much." I am becoming more and more that way too.

This is why these chapters occur not in linear time but rather in a way that favors a narrative structure that reflects some other sense of time. We begin with a chapter about NAFTA and what I, and many others, have called the "New World Border." We then move back in linear time to the fabled days of the California ranchos and then to imaginings of Ramona. Then we encounter Woodrow Wilson's efforts to influence the Mexican Revolution and why it is that American liberals and Mexicans, and by extension other peoples whose tribal past still endures, have such a hard time conceptualizing one another. That is a story that resonates with our fifth chapter, a discussion of the efforts of Spanish priests to missionize the Indian peoples of California. Finally, we encounter the perils and opportunities that the New World Border presents to both Mexicans and Americans. Breaking out of linear time is to me a good way to tell the stories of those who have followed in the footsteps of Padre Serra.

The stories of Indians and mission priests, of lovers like Ramona and Alessandro, of Woodrow Wilson and Mexico, of people crossing the literal and figurative borders of this challenging new world of free trade will prove significant and interesting in and of themselves. These stories of California, Mexico, and America are not just about the people but about what so many of us are thinking and arguing about—faith and devotion, love and pleasure, culture and progress, and mixing and authenticity. This blend of good history and people's stories will bring these savory and difficult issues to the public square.

For decades I have been studying history, politics, and culture. Yet I found out new and rather stunning things about America, Mexico, and myself as I investigated issues and engaged in this writing. I knew that the penetration of the market into Mexico had profound consequences but had not imagined their magnitude. I have always affirmed the importance of Native American history but had not realized how essential knowledge of Indian events is to understanding California, Mexico, and America. A consequence of the limits of my extensive education, I had assumed that Indian life in California had expired by the turn of the last century; I was not prepared to know how Indian peoples have continued into the twenty-first century. The different ways that people have related to time I have previously found to be quaint; now I comprehend how crucial time orientation is to human conduct. To say that the U.S.–Mexico border is a contentious issue only states the obvious; what has been startlingly new for me is how many different ideas there are about just what a border is.

I have sentimentalized and critiqued love and devotion; now I am more aware of their destructive capacity. I have found in my explorations an evocative term for feelings of love I have always had but couldn't name — "topophilia," or love of a landscape. Having taught about how people evolved from Mexican to Mexican American, to Chicano, to Latino in rather glib fashion obscured to me how truly changeable people are. Childish bouts of fanciful flights to genteel "Old California" blinds one to the extent to which this was a society obsessed with sex. Observations of naked tourists in Mexico and variously clothed people on the beaches of Southern California prove more than merely salacious when one realizes how dangerous and facile Western Civilization's constructions of such categories as the "naked savage" are. My psychotherapeutically oriented friends often joke about how DENIAL is not just a river in Egypt, but now I am more sensitive to what a powerful human emotion it is as I have wrestled in these pages with how resolutely so many people deny the intimacy of Mexico and America.

I set out to share some history, some insights and analysis, even do some explaining of matters I thought I understood: I found myself thrilled and surprised at these discoveries.

It is hard for many people to imagine how and why thinking about history can be transformative. I presumptuously offer myself as an example throughout these essays. There is much to wonder and agonize about: at how something like devotion can be creative, as in beautiful works of art, and how it can be destructive, as in the efforts to Christianize Indians or change Mexico and Mexicans; over how an idea or belief can be true for some people, but not true for other people, and yet continue to have truth; about whether or not love for another person really exists or if it simply derives from our own anxious cravings; about how some people have created nasty fabrications about other people based on what we usually call "race"; I have despaired about whether or not such grand notions as liberty and freedom have any meaning.

Traveling around and talking to people has fashioned many of the questions addressed here. Participating with public school teachers in seminars about California history, U.S.–Mexico relations, and the New World Border; playing in tennis leagues, golf foursomes at the public links, and beer-league softball; accompanying my children to all the usual kid stuff of day care, baseball and soccer leagues, swim teams, and now college; socializing with rich people at the behest of my college to encourage them to give money so that more Mexican American kids can have a shot at a first-rate education; going to Mexico as a *pocho* tourist (as we will see, *pocho* is what Mexicans often call Mexican Americans); all of these activities have informed the question-making process.

Teachers want to know how they should refer to their students — Chicano, Mexican American, Latino, Hispanic. After we have spent enough time to gain one another's trust, I often get the queries about why it is that their students from Mexico — and they still don't know what to call them — don't respond to their genuine efforts to help them with reading and numbers, or to the teachers' entreaties to excel, or to simply stay in school. I don't know any definitive answers to these questions, but I have brought some ambivalent insights to this book.

At these other more social occasions in more monocultural Colorado Springs I have happened, rather reluctantly, to chuckle at the statements that come after I answer the question about "what kind of name is that? Monroy?" I say that "my father's family is from Mexico and it's a nice Mexican/Spanish name. There is this little town near Portugal named Monroy and . . ." Then come the tales of these harried peoples' travels to Mexico and how they so adore how people are there. "Life is so simple there. The people just aren't so worried about everything." Or "What the hell are we going to do with all these illegals?" It's not always easy to be polite. I know that Americans find Mexico and Mexicans repulsive and attractive.

When I go to Mexico, it appears at first that I am a native Spanish speaker. Quickly, though, strong whiffs of my American accent and lack of vocabulary manifest themselves. People ask me to change pesos into dollars for them. Unlike in Spain where my pocho Spanish is endearing and I am greeted as a long-lost son (*¡de la familia de Extremadura Monroy!*), the resentment of the privilege of having dollars and crossing the border at will is palpable. Reading classical psychology has informed me that resentment is a response to envy.

Likely these ominous mixes of emotions — repulsion and attraction, envy and resentment — characterize how Americans and Mexicans feel about one another. Mexicans don't understand how it is that Americans disparage Mexican conduct and recalcitrant nationalism and then welcome them as laborers and love to go to Mexico on vacation. Americans don't understand how it is that Mexicans can so resent America and then want to come here in such huge numbers.

Likely many readers wrestle with this long list of issues, both the ones universal and the ones particular to America and Mexico. "To change in a good way, for a good life," as Simon Ortiz has put it, is the goal here. Reflection about such historical matters as the California missions, the Victorian novel *Ramona*, Woodrow Wilson's Liberalism and Mexico, and contemporary issues such as free trade and the changing nature of the U.S.–Mexico border have brought me more understanding of these matters, more peace, and more courage to have a good life and to act in good ways in the public square. Read here about Woodrow Wilson's guns and about NAFTA, and you might know more about why Mexicans resent America and then try to migrate here. The chapter on Rancho California may explain something of the attraction of Americans for Mexico, and the chapter on the New World Border will explain why the Mexican immigrants so confound Americans. Think about how California was once Spain, how Woodrow Wilson wrestled with the consequences of the massive investments of U.S. corporations in Mexico, and you will realize that globalization is not unique to our time.

Yet, ironically, such reflection convinces us all the more that there is no one truth about any of these matters. In his abstract paintings, Pablo Picasso proclaimed that a visual reality may be chopped up and then reassembled in a new and often vexing and provocative way to give a subject a look very different from how a traditional artist or a camera might record a scene or a person. Actually, Picasso revealed that "reality" has more to do with how it is perceived and assembled than with what seems to meet the eye. The same is true for the subjects under discussion here; there is no one correct description.

When one sees a beautiful mission or Mexican men pleading for work at a Home Depot or some strawberries or avocados at the market, there is much more to see and understand about the story of those things than they seem to appear. I have tried to assemble different stories, outside linear time, so that we may all see the reality of the matters differently. Our old ways of understanding issues confronting California, Mexico, and America are really ways to avoid the truly difficult. "Diversity" when it comes to religion, the missions, the public schools, the course syllabus at college; "cost-benefit analyses" to understand the value and meanings of immigration and free trade; and "progress" to think about a better future are all concepts whose effectiveness has worn thin.

The point of these redescriptions, then, is to think about matters affecting California, Mexico, America, and our lives in new ways. In some ways, this endeavor will put us back into linear time, into the mindset of progress. Yes and no. The discussion of Woodrow Wilson and Mexico will explain how there are many conceptions of time. For now, let me tell how I have heard about time from Pueblo Indian people. When Tewa speakers refer to the past or the future they use the word *geh*, which means "place." There is "past place" and "future place," and neither is very distant from "now place." This is what I mean: it's not that we have to "progress," but that redescription, re-imagining, will enable us to be in a new "place" as we think and act on shared matters having to do with California, Mexico, and America.

With some trepidation I offer these stories in essay form — ones that bare my own temptations, anxieties, and delights — to you, my readers, in the hope that I can explain some issues, that we can envision them in ways we haven't thought of, that we can have conversations via the printed word that will make for more good lives.

I have had to translate these histories and stories to get them here. Sometimes this means from Spanish to English, but mostly it means rendering the dimness of the past; the rhetoric, delusions, and insights of many of the players; and the jargon and obscurity of people who have studied and analyzed these matters into words that should intrigue readers and challenge them to think about matters differently.

There is great affection for the study of the past evident in these writings. This is because the histories here are not a series of randomly associated events — the way history has been taught to most of us. I understand history to be our relationship with the past, with *past place*. And, like all good relationships, it is one that is always growing and changing. It's not that the "facts" change, what we had to memorize in high school, though we are always finding out new things, but rather that our interpretations of the past and its meanings change. Most people have a hard time understanding the concept that the past is *mutable*, that is, *changing*, as we in the present come to have new concerns and thus interrogate the past in new ways. Most people think of the past as *immutable*, or *unchanging*.

I don't think of the missions of California the way I used to, nor of Liberalism, and certainly not of love. Indeed, I've already written on some of the subjects of this book — the missions and the ranchos of California; it's just that my relationship to these subjects has grown and changed. This is because I became rankled about various issues for one reason or another, then investigated, or re-visited, those issues in the past, and then found that the whole range of human possibilities was far greater than I had thought. The past is a very deep well from which we can draw all manner of insights. Most poignantly, by knowing something of the past we know that things we might once have thought of as immutable — political ideology, virtue, devotion, identity — are actually quite mutable. When we become conflicted about matters in the present — the universalism of American values, progress, economic expansion — we can refocus our vision of the past in order to know more of the broad range of human possibilities. Thus we build our storehouse of ideas and prospects for acting in good ways in the present.

This is the process by which we have revisionist history. I don't revise history to avoid inconvenient information or to make partisan political points but because when people in other countries reject the universalism of American values, when individual economic initiative evidences bad outcomes, when love doesn't turn out as planned, I look to the past with new questions and new perspectives.

We come to find there, in the past, that America's efforts to impose its values have usually failed and that it's not a good idea to try and do so, but that that doesn't mean that many of those values aren't quite worthy; that human pain and destruction have typically accompanied economic progress; that love and devotion are actually quite mutable; that there is no one thing to be concluded about any of these matters. When we revise the past we revise ourselves; this is how we "change in a good way, for a good life." How we, dare I say with Navajo people, "walk in beauty."

The concept of revisionist history, one that seems so natural and lively to me, is not well accepted outside of the profession. Similarly, the rejection of objectivity most people find perplexing, if not preposterous. It's not that objectivity might not be a good idea; it's that it is impossible. I can't be objective when I see a majestically recreated California mission, with bright bougainvillea and fantastic palm trees, against the beautiful blue sky, and then feel my eyes tear up as the disquiet of the Indian bones in the graveyards (usually disguised as gardens) palpate under my feet.

I can't be objective about Liberalism when I take the Enlightenment vision of a human being freed from superstition and ancestral commands and apply it to my own life and pursuit of happiness, only to have that vision painfully fail me sometimes, and to know how destructive it has been when imposed on people who treasure doing things as they have always been done.

I can't be objective when I find that immigrants from all over the world are transforming my familiar, my Southern California, in ways that I find distasteful, and then acknowledge that my father's family arrived from Mexico to Los Angeles in 1922 and monolingual in Spanish.

I can only be honest with my readers and — here's the hard part — with myself. I am, we all are, positioned to see things in certain ways. The trick is to acknowledge that, then proceed with information and other people's stories, then appreciate the situation in which those stories came to be, and then try and create some intelligent history and social analysis.

This project requires passion and imagination too. The word *compassion*, as continually pointed out in the following pages, derives from the Latin *pati*; the word means to me "to suffer with." We "suffer with" people when we know their stories. Sometimes I have read the stories and sometimes I have got them in conversation, but I have tried here to enhance everyone's *compassion* by presenting important stories from California, Mexico, and America.

Imagination constitutes we humans' most powerful means of understanding. More so than even our ability to reason. I imagine many things here: about the lives of Spanish priests and Mexican immigrants, about what Woodrow Wilson must have been thinking when he had American troops occupy the port of Veracruz in 1914, about traveling around Southern California with the fabulous Ramona.

This sort of honesty, compassion, study of the stories, and imagination is how we have, dare I say, some truth. Here are the truths that I have discovered, in large part from my study of history, and have confirmed for myself in these writings: that time is different for different peoples; that only rarely, if ever, is there a single truth about a matter; that the differences between humans derive from different social evolutions, not "race"; that we humans should not have to experience pain and humiliation; that we humans are all equally worthy of moral consideration.

There is beauty and wonder in these truths about these places whose pasts and futures are so interwoven, about California, Mexico, and America.

NAFTA and the New World Border

I've watched immigrant Mexicans file into the chapel at Mission San Luis Rey for Saturday evening mass. This is about 30 miles north of San Diego, site of the first mission of what was then called Alta California, and 60 miles south of Los Angeles, which the Spanish founded in 1781, only 12 years after Mission San Diego. The Mexicans look much like Indian people, like the ones for whom the Franciscan priests first built the mission.

Only a few of the descendants of the Indians remain on the landscape. The ancestors of these Luiseño people died and died, mostly of the Europeans' viral and bacterial infections. The founder of the mission, Padre Junípero Serra, believed that the Franciscans could create a utopia of believers joyously gathered in the promise of salvation. The vision he brought north from Mexico turned horrible as disease ravaged the indigenous people and those who survived mostly viewed the new religion and its sexual discipline with, at best, apathy.

The utopic vision of the free market and its manifestation in the form of the North American Free Trade Agreement (the famous NAFTA) does much to explain the presence of these worshipers. They have followed in the footsteps of the visionary Serra from Mexico, to the chapel of the mission that his successor, Padre Fermín Lasuén, founded nearly three centuries previously.

I don't empathize much with utopian thinking, though I will confess to having been drawn to it on occasion. I think I can understand how Padre Serra could imagine the Indians—in this case ones recently released from the grasp of the Devil—as people united in Christ, bound by the ritual of Holy Communion, and freed of corruptions of the flesh and civil society. Later, my grandfather, the one whose great-grandfather had seen the missions, would flirt with utopian thinking associated with the Mexican anarchist movement. All we had to do was get rid of clergy, law, and capital, the structures that made us, respectively, superstitious and intolerant, possessive, and greedy and rivalrous, and we could "make art out of life."

My father and I, he in the 1930s and me in the 1960s, found that Marxism and its promise of the application of reason to human society, instead of capitalist greed, suggested that "a better world's in birth." Some of my friends from high school and college were taken with Woodstock Nation, the idea that, as people fled the uptight Establishment, a new age was dawning in which human love would create a communitarian society.

It's curious indeed how the California missions, the Mexican Revolution, the Soviet Union, and the San Francisco Bay area Altamont Festival all turned into dystopias — horrid, painful, dysfunctional places.

There is much utopian thinking in discourses I hear about the free market. I hear that "all we have to do is get rid of government intervention, and we will have a self-regulating, fair system, in which anyone who wants to can succeed." It rings of getting rid of the Devil, capitalism, institutionalized religion, and uptightness, and then how everything, for those who join in, will be ideal.

Still, it's hard to know exactly why these things don't work out. People who study our close cousins — chimps, orangs, and monkeys — will likely say that aggressiveness and possessiveness are part of our simian makeup. Traditional Christians would tell us that sinfulness is included in God's package and an inescapable part of our existence on earth. (Heaven, of course, is utopia.) These are wonderful things to think about, likely best in borderlands ways: I just think that we humans have all these seedy passions and that it feels so good to express them, which makes trouble, but that not expressing them makes us angry and anti-social, which makes even more trouble.

We shouldn't reject this utopian thinking entirely. I think it's true that the communitarians of the Franciscan order and of the hip New Age derived wonder and satisfactions from being a part of something that transcended this material world.

Practical policies have their roots in utopian thinking. Surely the American New Deal and the social democracies of Europe have applied reasoned government programs to society and, while falling short of Marx's vision, have provided comfort and security to millions. And one is struck over and over again how it is that we humans, when our imaginations and activities are freed from rules and regulations and old habits, are capable of creating magnificent and wondrous things.

I take great comfort from F. Scott Fitzgerald in trying to sort these matters out. Actually, I do and I don't. "The test of a first-intelligence," he posits as "a general observation" in his unnervingly magnificent *The Crack-Up* of 1936, which he wrote from LA alcoholic and despondent, "is the ability to hold two opposed ideas in the mind at the same time, and still retain the ability to function."[1] I think of this when I think of communitarianism, Socialism, and the free market. Just because there are good and appealing aspects to them doesn't make them systems with which we should necessarily proceed in a wholesale fashion; indeed, each provides encouragement and guidance, and frustration and pain.

"And so we beat on, boats against the current, borne back ceaselessly into the past." It all makes for good stories, though sometimes they are harsh; let us commence.

This is how it was supposed to work to everyone's benefit, or at least how its boosters peddled it. NAFTA would erase the tariffs that hindered trade between the United States and Mexico. This would allow each country to sell more of its products to the other. Mexico would no longer restrict the foreign ownership of its land and industry, and this would enable capital to flow into the country, build factories, and thus create more jobs. Of course those factories would be manufacturing things once made in America, and this would cost American jobs. But, if Mexicans got more money in their pockets from their new jobs, then they could buy more products, many of which would be made in the USA, and American workers would get their jobs back. While there might be some dislocation in the short term, everyone would get cheaper products eventually.

Suffering a disadvantage against cheap labor in Asia, American capitalism would remain competitive as it countered with cheap labor in Mexico; if American cars had some of their parts made more cheaply in Mexico, then Ford and Chevy could compete more effectively with Honda and Toyota, and American auto workers would keep their jobs. If the United States would lower or even eliminate its tariffs on raw materials imported from Mexico, then American capitalists would have lower costs of production and be able to manufacture more inexpensively, again maintaining competitiveness with Asia. If Mexico eliminated its tariffs on American appliances, then those appliances would compete more strongly in Mexico against those from countries without such tariff-eliminating agreements, and Mexicans would buy more appliances produced in America than, say, Korea, whose exports to Mexico still suffered tariffs. This would more than compensate for the jobs that appliance workers would lose to parts manufactures that moved to Mexico to take advantage of lower wages there. Overall, then, American capitalists would have more sales and more profits, and American workers would experience more demand for their labor.

If Mexico lowered its tariffs on imported foodstuffs, sure some small farmers would be hurt as they tried to compete against American agribusiness, which delivers a much cheaper product. But those displaced farmers could find jobs in the new factories, have money in their pockets, and Mexicans, without those tariffs that artificially raised the price of food, could provision themselves more cheaply. In a way this would recreate the industrial history of the United States. As agricultural technology vastly increased the amount of food that industrial farms could grow on the land, and yeoman farmers were thus displaced, those very ex-farmers (or more accurately their sons) could assume the burgeoning jobs that industrial technology and consumer demand had created in the auto, appliance, aircraft, and other industries.

There is utopian thinking in all of this, the idea that such an economic arrangement (or non-arrangement, really) would be self-regulating, just, and beneficial to all who joined in. The ideal of the free market is what will relieve us from bureaucracy, war, and human want.

Two imaginative metaphors for understanding the New World Border have come to me from economists Joseph Schumpeter and Andre Gunder Frank. Schumpeter presciently named this universal capitalist process "creative destruction," a notion containing "two opposed ideas" and one not very utopian. "Capitalism," he said, "is by nature a form or method of economic change and not only never is but never can be stationary." Is it not exceedingly curious that capitalism these days is usually associated with Conservatism when indeed it has always been, if not revolutionary, at least an astounding bestirrer of societies? Schumpeter in 1942 wrote in some awe about the "industrial mutation" that had transformed "organizational development from the craft shop and factory to such concerns as U.S. Steel." And now U.S. Steel's once-enduring plants sit dolefully rusting while South Korea's, Japan's, and Brazil's send millions of tons of steel to build America's cars, buildings, and appliances. It is this dynamic of capitalism "that incessantly revolutionizes the economic structure *from within*, incessantly destroying the old one, incessantly creating a new one." We shall proceed from here in our discussion of the consequences of NAFTA and the New World Order from Schumpeter's related insight that "the problem that is usually being visualized is how capitalism administers existing structures, whereas the relevant problem is how it creates and destroys them."[2]

Andre Gunder Frank argues that while capitalism may function this way in the so-called First World, it does not do so in places like Latin America. Instead, we witness a process of "developing underdevelopment." In this scenario, NAFTA does not have the potential for creation of capital and wealth in Mexico but rather functions to keep Mexico impoverished and underdeveloped. The influx of cheaply produced trade goods, both manufactured and agricultural, means that local production will always be undercut, local capitalist enterprises will rarely be able to generate profits and more capital, and workers and farmers will be underemployed. The best they can do, then, is to supply raw materials, including labor, to the developed countries where such will enter into the dynamic capitalist system.

Such creative (though not with the missions) destruction and developing underdevelopment in our current age is evident everywhere on the landscapes of California, Mexico, and America; this will be the subject of several of the following chapters. Americans—Mexicans to a lesser extent I think—are inclined to see the consequences of NAFTA and the changing nature of the border in either/or terms. Immigration, the destruction and creation of jobs, the new faces and languages in the public schools are discussed in terms of "good" or "bad."

Indeed, Americans like melodrama—think of *Uncle Tom's Cabin*, *Birth of a Nation*, *The Godfather*, and, most certainly, my beloved *Ramona*. The New World Border, though, presses us to transcend this thinking in binary oppositions, this worldview of black and white, American or un-American, this side or that, in favor of ambiguity and paradox. The words of the most creative, insightful, and compelling artists go beyond the polarities and the melodrama in favor of uncertainty and wonder. F. Scott Fitzgerald and Toni Morrison, Bob Dylan and John Lennon, Carlos Fuentes and Gabriel García Márquez are some of the ones who have helped me see that tragedy and hope, and genuineness and awful intermingling, can simultaneously be part of the same complex of events, and that such a conception of the world is more conducive to understanding than "good" or "bad," "right" or "wrong."

Such a rejection of these customary categories might seem to lead us into an analytical and moral abyss in which we students of society simply sit in a position of bemused superiority, as I must confess to doing in some of this book. But it has been the writers mentioned above, and I would urge readers to think who such artists have been for you, who have also convinced me of the actualities of pain and humiliation. It is these realities that we must keep in our minds and hearts as we ponder the ambiguities of NAFTA and the New World Border. My challenge here is "to think of people wildly different from ourselves," as Richard Rorty puts it, "as included in the range of 'us.' "[3] This is not to put away the profound differences among peoples and cultures that we will encounter in our treatment of Woodrow Wilson's guns or the California missions and then to posit in its place some universality of humankind. Rather it is to acknowledge that more and more people, as they are, are worthy of moral consideration.

This is one way that I have come to think about American history. At its founding, American democracy only included property-owning, white males. This has been said enough already, but the important thing is that first all white men, then African Americans, then women, and then Mexican Americans came to be included via the vote. We could say, then, that they have become worthy of moral consideration. Let us include gays and lesbians, Native Americans, and even the environment as becoming more and more worthy of such regard. My appeal to you here is that undocumented immigrants, and the issue is not the franchise, should also be worthy of our moral consideration. Indeed all of us, Mexicans and Americans, are more and more bound up together as we come to acknowledge the trouble and turmoil we see every day on the landscapes of California and Mexico, and as the borders between us move or are erased altogether.

Irapuato Interlude — Watching the Change Happen

In Irapuato, state of Guanajuato, Eugenio Guerrero has auctioned off the hog farm and the pigs that have sustained his family for two generations. Fifty people worked on the farm. On January 1, 2003, Mexico, in accordance with NAFTA, ended its remaining tariffs on most agricultural goods coming from the United States. "In the United States," the *New York Times* reported, "a pig can be raised and sold in Iowa for a fifth of what it would cost to raise and sell one in Irapuato." American pork producers control at least 40 percent of the Mexican market. The same will happen with poultry production when Mexico ends its 48 percent tariffs on chicken products.

Vicente Fox and his party blamed the corruption and mismanagement of the Institutional Revolutionary Party (PRI) for the farmers' problems, and it is certainly true that the peso crisis of 1995 devastated the credit system and disabled what minimal government subsidies the Mexican government had provided. Leaders of the Mexican National Agriculture Commission note that President Bush's farm bill promises each American hog farmer about $20,000 per year in subsidies, while their country can only provide $722.

"Mr. Guerrero said he had laid off all but five of his workers. Most told him they would immigrate to the United States illegally in search of a new start." In Iowa it is very hard to find many of the state's native sons who will butcher and process pigs and chickens for $8 per hour. There are, however, workers who will jump at the jobs and who are on their way up from Irapuato. If they can outrun the *migra*, and they will eventually, they will work on hog and poultry factories keeping prices for American products low. This will keep Americans happy and enable more exports to Mexico, which will wipe out more Mexican hog and poultry farms.

Some of them will stay in Mexico. Mexican and transnational food-processing companies in Mexico can now buy cheaper agricultural goods (especially grains and meat) from the United States which, combined into their product, lowers their costs of production. Such corporations as Grupo Bimbo, Maseca, and Sigma can now export successfully to the United States, and indeed, such exports have doubled. This production creates some jobs and perhaps some of Mr. Guerrero's workers, the ones who don't go to the United States, will find jobs there.[4]

The question is will this turn out to be "creative destruction" or does it simply "develop more underdevelopment"?

It is also quite remarkable how different people tell different stories about the same thing. The Business Roundtable in its 2004 report, "NAFTA: A Decade of Growth," describes how the original vision of

NAFTA has been coming true. It tells how America's exports to Mexico have nearly doubled, and so have Iowa's, since NAFTA took effect. It tells many stories, like how "the Farmers Cooperative Company (Farnhamville, Iowa), the largest local cooperative grain marketer in Iowa, ships the majority of its grain to feed and processor markets across the western half of the United States and into Mexico." They quote the grain marketing manager about how "corn consumption in Mexico has been steadily increasing" and that "supplying that demand in Mexico has greatly benefited the company and its 4,000 producers." In other words, sales to Mexico for those four thousand corn farmers in Iowa who sell through their cooperative have increased as have, presumably, their prosperity. The statistics are good on NAFTA.

Unless you are a corn farmer in Mexico. And there are at least fifteen million Mexicans (some put the figure as high as twenty-three million or a quarter of the population) who farm corn on their milpas. Corn has always been Mexico's staple, especially in the times of the Olmecs, Toltecs, and Aztecs. Corn exports to Mexico have tripled since NAFTA. This tremendous increase in the supply has naturally lowered the price of corn in Mexico, actually "by more than 70 percent (from 732 pesos in 1994 to 204 in 2001)." According to the U.S. Department of Agriculture, which puts the matter in dollar terms, corn has gone from $5 per bushel in 1995 to $1.80 in 2000.

For those who depend on corn production for their livelihoods, this is an unmitigated disaster. Their income from corn has dropped to one-third of what it was before free trade when the Mexican government simply disallowed foreign corn into the country unless there were shortages. It used to be that the price of a gallon of gasoline equaled the price of a kilo of corn; now it's five kilos of corn. Even though cheaper corn (if valued in dollars) has entered Mexico, the drastic devaluation of the peso, among other factors, has meant that the price of tortillas has unmercifully tripled over the same time period. There is no money to supplement the diet of tortillas and beans with meat, fruits, or milk, or to take children to the doctor, or to purchase condoms. The men must leave to where there are jobs that pay real money — agricultural fields in the Imperial Valley, the car washes and restaurant kitchens of Los Angeles, Colorado ski resorts, Georgia cotton mills, Iowa meat-packing plants. The women are alone to care for their children and their aging parents. They pray that the men will send dollars back.[5]

I listen in disbelief at the soothing female voice that comes on before the PBS *NewsHour* telling us about Archer, Daniels, Midland (ADM), sponsor of the news program, telling how "our global transportation network and our facilities around the world continue to allow us to grow things where they grow best and sell things where they are needed most." And then how "ADM is resourceful in opening new markets, breaking down barriers to deliver food where it is needed most."

It's the opposite of what she says. Opening the trade doors has meant mostly hunger and separation from kith and kin for farmers in Mexico and Africa and South America. All that corn and wheat and beef and beans that come flooding in devastate the price that can be got for their own relatively inefficiently produced crops. It is calamity for a *ranchito* when the cheap corn comes from the north, when this new competition drops the price below what a Mexican corn grower needs to survive. It's the irreducible actuality of pain and humiliation. The small farmers of Mexico are delivered a *chingazo*, a cruel blow, destruction that so far has been far from creative.

And it happens in the cities and towns. Producers in Guadalajara, Mexico's second largest city, feel the effects of NAFTA. There, small workshops made things like bricks, leather gloves, and shoes both for local sale and on a contract basis for retail stores. These shops provided jobs and incomes for primary breadwinners and opportunities for aspiring artisans. American tourists have found these wares attractive. Mexican tariff policies previously protected them against cheaper imports. Free trade allows stores to import these usually Asian-made products from the United States at prices substantially below those the small manufactories can offer. In fact, once one store does it, then they all must lest they lose competitive advantage. An outcome, then, is that more and more people in Guadalajara must move to where the jobs are — the United States. Young men there talk about Watsonville, Chicago, Los Angeles, Iowa, as if they were part of Mexico.

Actually, ADM and other such multinationals posit as economic science a notion that is quite value laden. In the early nineteenth century, David Ricardo advanced the idea of "comparative advantage," a principle routinely taught to undergraduate students in introductory economics classes and one that has informed prescriptions about NAFTA. The idea here is that each country should produce those products that they do most efficiently and best. If the people in a place have iron ore and coal, they should produce steel; if they have good soil for grapes, heat, and fog, they should produce wine. The prices for products in which one enjoys "comparative advantage" will naturally be lower, more can be sold and more money got, and then that money can be used to buy other products that somebody else produces most cheaply and efficiently. We can see this process at work: the United States enjoys comparative advantage in agriculture and information technology; China in cheap, disciplined labor; Venezuela in oil, etc. Each should emphasize what they do well and trade accordingly. This theory underscores ADM's rhetoric about how we should "grow things where they grow best."

It could be "creative destruction," but maybe it is something else. Latin American thinkers on these matters have put forth the notion of "developing underdevelopment." In America and Europe, capitalism had what we might call a "take-off" phase. Small manufacturers eyed great opportunity, put capital and labor together, and then created goods for a lively market. In the United States, government, most efficaciously the Republican administrations of the post–Civil War era and under the leadership of capitalists who (correctly) conflated their own interests with those of the nation's, saw fit to assist capitalists by passing protective tariffs, a tax, in other words, on incoming goods. Having artificial advantage in the marketplace, American steel and textiles, especially, could thrive — capitalists made big profits and put to work lots of workers — while British and other European manufactured goods languished in their home ports, overpriced now because of the tariffs.

Think, in this context, what is happening to Mexico's "take-off" indusries. Free trade means that they must compete with advanced American, and Asian, producers without the protections of tariffs, exactly what enabled American industries to "take off." The history of Latin American capitalism has repeated this motif of a capitalist class mostly interested in its own quick profits through trade, rather than long-term development through such strategies as tariff protections. (Actually, their use of tariffs didn't really work either, for deep political and cultural reasons.) This is why they will not only remain "underdeveloped," but why it is that NAFTA and free trade "develops" that underdevelopment. Instead of "take off" they have destruction of their local markets, and their workers, who are often more like artisans than proletarians, are cut loose to migrate to the slums of Mexico City or the packing plants of Kansas or the hotels of Las Vegas.

This then, actually, is the big question: whether or not this process will result in "creative destruction" or continue Latin America's experience of "developing underdevelopment."

There is another irony, besides the fact that free trade destroys the livelihoods of small farmers in Mexico and elsewhere, about this idea of comparative advantage: sometimes a country, for whatever reasons, will decide not to produce something — indeed they might even criminalize its possession — for which its people express a market demand. This prohibition will give another area comparative advantage in the production of that desired, but perhaps illegal, trade good. This is the case with marijuana and cocaine.

Because the United States artificially inflates the free-market value of psychoactive drugs by criminalizing them, other producers in places where such production is not against the law, or the law is ineffectual, can and will produce them. Indeed, this is about the only arena of agricultural production that I can think of where Mexico enjoys comparative advantage over the United States. (Colombia, because of climate and geology, enjoys comparative advantage in coffee, but world supply greatly exceeds demand, meaning that the coca leaf is much more profitable.) Thus it is that Mexican farmers find it to their comparative advantage to produce marijuana. Much like a tariff, America's drug laws create a protected zone for Mexican and Andean farmers, and Mexican and Colombian distributors, to produce and distribute a commodity at an advantage. And that participation in the cocaine trade is one area where young men in Mexico will find some opportunity. The unrelenting power of the market, and unctuous governmental activity in it, calls forth such economic activity.

The inexorable American demand for drugs means that plenty of money can be made in the drug trade and that the demand will be consistent. Of course, just how much money the drug trade generates is hard to calculate, but for the mid-nineties, Mexico estimated gross revenues at $30 billion, and the United States estimated profits of $10 billion, per year. Oil grossed $7.4 billion in 1993. Because the drug trade is such a good business in Mexico, more people will want in on all the dealings, especially the police and the politicians, because it actually is quite illegal in Mexico to produce and distribute these commodities. Drug traffickers can either try to slip product across the border — a bad choice if they have a large load or want to avoid confiscation or getting shot — or they can pay police authorities not to enforce the law, a much wiser choice.

The plots are stunning, none more so than those of the stinking Salinas administration (1988–1994), the very one that ushered in NAFTA. There was the chief anti-drug prosecutor, Mario Ruiz Massieu, who sold posts to prosecutors and police commanders along the border for up to $1 million, and then got more kickbacks. The dirty cops and lawyers got their investment back and plenty more. On and on it goes: $1 million to the commander of the Federal Judicial Police; $500,000 to Mexico's Deputy Attorney General; and . . . It can even look like we were winning the war on drugs: lots of drugs are confiscated at both sides of the border and people are arrested—except that it's the guys and product that are the rivals of the cartels paying off the various law enforcement agents.[6]

In the state of Sinaloa, the youth idolize Chalino Sanchez, emigrant to Los Angeles and martyred singer-songwriter of *narcocorridos*. Sinaloa, along the Pacific Coast, has become the center of the Mexican drug trade; it has always been a place of family feuds and masculine mayhem. The men are *valientes*, tough guys who will never back down from a fight. Chalino had to leave his home state after he gunned down a man who had raped his sister. He picked some crops around California, then went to Los Angeles, washed some cars, dealt some drugs, served some time in Tijuana, and then rose to incredible heights singing *corridos*, the traditional Mexican folk ballads that celebrate a folk hero or event.

The *raquitas*, the racks of audiocassettes, at car washes, stores, and especially the swap meets sold scads of recordings that celebrated drug traffickers, womanizers, and unpolished tough guys: valientes like him. He even got into a shoot-out with an audience member in Coachella. American style, he was becoming a celebrity. In 1992 he returned home for a concert in Sinaloa's capital, Culiacán. After the show he was spirited from his car and, with his comrades, assassinated.[7]

Newspapers continue to tell us about "three men shot to death with assault rifles" in Sinaloa and elsewhere. The next day "police found five more bodies in a Lincoln Navigator, which had apparently been armored, and two more bodies were found just a few yards away." It's all about drugs and money.[8]

Mexico has always had a high murder rate, one much higher than America's. But, "when a Mexican kills—for revenge, pleasure or caprice —he kills a person, a human being," as Octavio Paz, who we will meet in our discussion of Woodrow Wilson, explains. "Modern criminals and statesmen do not kill: they abolish," he continues, and, in a depiction reflective of what happened to Alessandro and his people, "they experiment with beings who have lost their human qualities." Ramona, who learns a similar lesson from her life with Alessandro, has heard from Señora Moreno, her adoptive mother, about the Americans: "Every day there comes the news of their murdering each other for gold. Mexicans kill each other only for hate . . . or in anger; never for gold."[9] Now Mexicans, 150 years after America conquered Mexico's far northern frontiers, kill for money, like Americans.

It's a mess everywhere: In Kannapolis, North Carolina, law enforcement agents stopped a car with 27 pounds of methamphetamine. Most of the meth in Georgia and the Carolinas seems to originate in Michoacán and California, and this stuff had been driven from Southern California in a car from Atlanta. From Española, New Mexico, to Dalton, Georgia, to New York City, more and more marijuana, cocaine, and heroin are arriving under the umbrella of the trade and immigration routes. "From 1994 to 2000," reported the *New York Times*, "the number of Mexican citizens jailed in the United States on federal drug-trafficking charges nearly doubled, to 8,752 from 4,394.[10] Until 9/11, the plan had been to eventually open the border to truck commerce. Imagine the drugs that will be coming in when this scheme gets back on track.

Again America and Mexico are so bound up together, this time in the matter of drugs. As with the Mexican-American War, the two sides are rather uncomprehending of one another. America blames Mexico and Colombia for the drug problem. This is simple psychological denial of the fact that this is a problem of domestic origin. Mexico and Colombia are furious that this American demand for drugs has resulted in the rapid and nasty multiplication of political and law enforcement corruption in their countries.

Americans do not understand that forces in this country—so many people beg, borrow, and steal in order to buy cocaine, and a few make enough in the first place—are responsible for the creation of this very rich, very violent, and very powerful class of narco-criminals who have penetrated every fiber of economics and politics, and the very social fabric itself in Mexico and Colombia. And it is true that illegal drugs from Mexico have destroyed families and communities across America. With free trade bringing more and more containers and trucks full of legitimate goods, with more and more communities of immigrants providing cover and couriers, and with consistent demand for drugs, the situation will only get worse.

There is more curious irony in the whole matter as well. One of the great talents of the American system has been its ability to put aside its oratory about the virtues of limited government and free trade in favor of a strong national state that can build irrigation projects and transportation systems, subsidize industry and agriculture, intervene militarily where American capitalism's interests are threatened, and bring its might to negotiate treaties that favor American producers.

From the 1930s through the 1960s, Mexico's rhetoric profiled a program of state-supported capitalist development. Mexico's capitalists did not succeed like America's. The corruption of the ruling party, lack of capital and initiative, and, some would say, the weight of *México profundo*, have meant that Mexico has not capitalized irrigation projects, industry, agriculture, or transportation anything like the laissez-faire United States. Thus it is that the American government and taxpayers subsidize the agricultural products that swamp the Mexican market and wreak such havoc.

The U.S. government gives corn farmers over $10 billion per year. World Trade Organization (WTO) and NAFTA bylaws do not count this as an explicit subsidy because the payments are linked to the amount of land a farmer has and past output, not current output, which would be a violation of principles. Nonetheless, such payouts certainly enable and encourage American farmers, and of course most of this money goes to big agri-business, to advance their technology and expand their production. If they sell at near or even below their actual cost of production, American farmers can still prosper because they get a government check. When Mexican farmers sell below world market price, they face calamity.

This is what all the dissension was about at the WTO meetings in Cancún in September 2003. Brazil led the charge against these subsidy practices along with other countries whose small farmers cannot compete against the technologically advanced and subsidized behemoths we call the American farms. People in those countries leave their farms for the already overcrowded and impoverished cities or migrate across borders for work. Proving once again that foreign policy derives from domestic politics, the farm block in Congress made sure that America would not budge in its subsidies for farmers.

All over the world, poor people are on the move because of these sorts of policies that are made in faraway places. On January 1, 2005, the WTO's quotas that limited the tonnage of clothing that countries like China and India could export to the United States and Europe expired. Because China could only export so much, what remained of clothing manufacturing in the United States received some protection and the quotas also created some shelter for the establishment of clothing factories in places like Honduras, Mexico, the Caribbean, and even Kenya. Big retailers in the United States will buy product where it's cheapest — from China with its comparative advantage of low overhead and worker discipline — and not these other countries. As clothing factories close, workers will be on the move, and for reasons they cannot control and mostly do not understand.[11]

In El Salvador, because of negotiations that ended its terrible civil war, employers must pay textile workers at least $5.04 per day. The quotas limiting China, where the daily wage is much lower, meant that some clothes would be sewn in El Salvador. Upon the removal of the quotas, the South Korean owners of OrientalTex Company closed their Salvadorean factory, an episode repeated over and over again. China is cheaper and more efficient. The women workers in El Salvador don't understand. They move, maybe to the United States. They leave their families. Older siblings must then leave school to care for the young.

In Africa the situation is worse; there is no place to move to. There, when they are fired from wage jobs that have gone to more efficient producers, they must sell their only possession with any value on the free market, their bodies. AIDS spreads. Free-market ideologues say that "this isn't punishment for those countries that are losing jobs"; rather "it will make them aware that they have to shape up," as one German "expert on the quota system" put it.[12]

Imagine what having "to shape up" means for peasant societies like Cambodia, Honduras, Lesotho, ones with only a modest minimum wage and a modicum of protections for their workers. They are supposed to become like Communist China. This is how the free market is dictatorial and cruel.

What we have here, however, is a well-functioning system, if we factor out the human cost. America has several troubles when it comes to the economy. Too much money goes overseas to buy oil, electronic consumer goods, clothes, and cars. This balance of payments deficit, about $763.6 billion dollars in 2006, is a consequence of many things, among them capitalists' failure to invest in American factories and the availability of cheap labor overseas, the sophisticated and efficient transportation infrastructure to transport materials and finished goods around the world, and Americans' insatiable desire to consume and own stuff. Unfortunately, selling all these agricultural goods puts only a small dent in this dangerous deficit. Indeed, it's pretty much all America can offer for sale to Japan. Next, American farmers, agribusiness and the remaining small ones both, get to prosper because the government helps them export through its subsidies. In the U.S. Senate each state including Montana, Wyoming, and the Dakotas — none of which has over a million people — get the same representation as California and New York. This over-representation of farm states will assure that the farmers will continue to get these benefits from the federal government.

One of the accomplishments of the New Deal, unionization, World War II, and the economic boom of the post-war years was that American workers, at least the white ones but even some blacks in the north and Mexicans in urban California, came to make enough money to buy the products of one another's labor. It is also true that there was no meaningful competition for American steel, cars, appliances, and television sets: this was because our bombers had flattened German and Japanese factories and England was worn out. But really, consumer demand, what with a working class who had money in their pockets — unprecedented in world history — fueled American capitalist production in the decades after World War II. Few capitalists have understood that high wages and full employment can actually be good for the system because such creates reliable markets.

In order to maintain such a dynamic system, capitalists must invest in technology that keeps producers competitive with the rest of the world — and remember that the war-ravaged countries of Japan, Germany, and South Korea all have NEW factories — and pay decent wages. Through neglect and American capital's disinclination to invest in new and modern equipment, America doesn't really make things like it used to but mostly provides technology, services, and agricultural goods. The jobs are divided between high tech, management, and the professions (like doctors, lawyers, and money managers) which pay well on the one hand, and then service jobs like fast food, restaurant and hotel cleaning, car washes, gardening, unskilled construction, and megastore sales which all pay under $10 per hour on the other hand. It's hard to find people who will do these jobs enthusiastically.

Agriculture is not just about work in the heat but has a political history, one in which politicians have made decisions with considerable significance. Large farmers persuaded the New Dealers to exclude field and packinghouse workers from the benefits of the National Labor Relations Act (NLRA) (1935), an elision of titanic consequences for both the United States and Mexico. Agricultural workers did not partake of this appreciation of labor, which the NLRA brought to industrial workers through its support for unions, and have thus remained low-wage, Mexican that is.

Think for a moment here of strawberries. They're tasty, nutritious, and an appropriately stylish and appreciated addition to virtually all meals. Much better for our arteries to eat strawberries for breakfast than doughnuts. And when in season, they cost less than a dollar a pound. Here are some interesting statistics: it takes 3 person hours of labor to harvest an acre of wheat, 75 hours for an acre of broccoli, and 2,150 person hours of labor to harvest an acre of strawberries. The delicious red berries, like all of the fruit and vegetable crops that health-conscious people increasingly demand and expect, require much more intensive labor than field crops such as wheat and corn. Work in the strawberry fields is intermittent and pays only about $5,500 per year.

The average life expectancy of a Mexican farm worker in the United States is 49. It's the dehydration, sanitation, stooping, the pesticides. Agricultural labor takes a Mexican facing calamity in the small village and gives him life. Then over time such travail, and by extension the free-market system that has brought him north, takes his life. This is the opposite of utopian; it is two opposed occurrences happening at once.

This is what I mean by how this is all a quite functional system: the new world economy, of which NAFTA is only a part, uproots people from their small villages, puts them in motion, and, in the case of NAFTA, draws them to where they are needed.

Colorado Interlude — Watching the Change Happen

In Colorado I've had several interactions with roofers, including the installation of two new roofs, one in 1983 and one in 2004. In my upscale neighborhood, it is always apparent when somebody gets a roof — not only are there trucks and tar, there's music blasting from car radios. I recall clearly the scene from 20 years ago: blond, scraggly-haired youths chuffed on the roofs listening to Metallica and Arrowsmith while they hammered down shingles and spread hot tar. I even remember chatting with one of these young men about work and life and his comment about them, as he said, "it's hard to get even a little ahead." He wanted just a little bit more than the bare minimum. This was not work anybody wanted to be doing. Now it's different.

Just recently, after contracting with the owner of the local company, a crew of Mexicans showed up on my roof. I went up to make sure that we were all on the same shingle about what was going to be done. I quickly realized that while I could discuss a number of things in Spanish, roofs were not one of them. (I didn't even know what a "scupper" was in English, let alone how to say it in Spanish.) Later I went up and brought bottles of soda and ice. I asked them where they were from. "De México," one replied as if I should have known, which of course I did.

"Sí, ¿pero de donde en México?"

"De Chihuahua," said one, and I pushed to see if what sociologists said about "sender communities" was right.

"¿Del mismo lugar?" I asked, wanting to know if they were all from the same town.

"Sí, de Parral," said one, and another added that they were all from the area just outside of Parral apparently known as "Jiménez."

I knew before I asked what the answer was to my next question about whether any of the six were cousins. Three of them were.

I asked them what their families did in Chihuahua. "Rancho," several responded at once. It was getting more textbook-like all the time.

"¿Ganado?" I asked figuring they had some cattle.

I was right again: "Poco de ganado y otras cosas." I envisioned a marginal life on a small, inefficient landholding, one with too many children.

"¿Es difícil hoy dia la vida en un rancho?" I asked in likely incorrect Spanish.

"Sí, claro, porque en México es muy caro todo." "Everything is expensive in Mexico," one was explaining, with the word "caro" reiterated by several others. I knew that it was expensive to buy things in Mexico if you only had pesos, and if the importation of beef unprotected by tariffs had ruined what they could get for their "poco de ganado." Life for rural Mexicans is rarely simple.

"¿Les gustan a Colorado?" I asked, predicting that indeed they liked it here.

"Cien dólares por día," exclaimed one, with the others smiling in accord. "Y mucho trabajo."

They didn't all make that much, but the Mexican foreman, who didn't want to have anything to do with an inquisitive pocho like me, made more. I was seeing here the way it works, how transborder migrants come to do so much of the work. One hundred dollars a day sounds like a lot of money, but I need to point out that my amigos, as we called one another, worked 10 to 12 hours on my roof. Let's call it $10 an hour; that's $20,000 per year, if one works steadily, which no roofer in often-inclement Colorado does. Few scraggly-haired white kids will do that kind of work, at that pay, for very long, and certainly not for 12 hours a day. That $20,000 gets a lot of pesos and goes a long way back in Parral. If three brothers get that kind of work, they will make $60,000.

This is what I mean by the idea that this is a "well-functioning system." The New World Border drives them from their ranchitos in Parral; roofing contractors get steady labor; my neighbors and I get cheap roofs; the little ranchos in Chihuahua get an influx of good dollars; I don't know what the scraggly-haired American youth get. Maybe jobs at Wal-Mart. Colorado Springs has a lot of meth labs.

I didn't need to ask if they went back to Parral in the winter when work was slower, because I knew they did, but I did ask, "¿Es difícil cruzar la frontera?" Of course I knew the answer to that one too.

Most all of them nodded emphatically as one said about the difficulty of crossing the border: "Es difícil porque de la migración, la migra. Ahora tienen helicópteros, caballos, motocicletas y todo." It was hard to imagine my new amigos running through the desert with horses and motorcycles after them. But they were kind of chuckling because, obviously, they were here, making a hundred dollars a day, and drinking Pepsi on my roof while the migra was still at the border chasing people with all their equipment.

They had no comment when I told how my father's family had simply walked across the border at El Paso in 1921.

Again, the system functions. Our congressional delegation rails about undocumented Mexicans and votes for lots more money for the Border Patrol. The good citizens of Colorado feel like something is being done to stem the tide of threatening Mexicans when they read about the helicopters, motorcycles, and all the other high-tech stuff at the border. And they still get cheap roofs.

The scene on the roof also reveals the variety in the immigrant experience. It's hard to predict what will become of my *amigos* on my roof. That they were smiling suggests that for them their move to the north was succeeding. In Mexico it is assumed that young men will act independently of their families, that they will have adventures, that they will avoid family responsibility if they can. My amigos were clearly doing all this; if they sent money back that was no doubt a boon to the family but it was not as important to them as having this adventure in the north, a place where there was work, money, and cheap food.[13] They were away from the drudgery and poverty of life in Parral. They would work hard to make sure that they could stay or to make enough money to go home with some security and a bit of prosperity.

In Parral these young men no doubt had patterns of family aid and support to which they felt variously obligated. Likely fleeing these sorts of obligations made the trip north more attractive. I wonder what it must mean that they are away at planting and harvest time in Parral, that they are not there for aging parents, that there are few young men left in Jiménez who can repair a roof.

Praying for remittances does not necessarily call them forth. Their sisters, wives, and mothers no doubt came to have hugely expanded responsibilities. Care of the children and the elderly would be theirs alone now, as would not only cleaning but household maintenance. If money didn't come from the north, then they would likely have to rely on relatives or take on extra work. In this way migration north would come to be a good idea for them too. They could reconstitute the family and make their men responsible. They will work hard too.[14]

This is what migration is all about for most of the Mexicans who have recently come to the United States. *Trabajo*, "work," is what most everyone I've talked to says. One time in the fall of 2004 I called for a taxi. Yellow Cab didn't pick up where I was (a largely Mexican neighborhood), and they gave me another number to call. Everything was in Spanish; the cab came (late), no meter; the driver figured fares by looking at his odometer. I was in the Third World.

Later, driving through a prosperous part of Pasadena, I asked him what he thought of all these people from all over the world in Los Angeles. I'm not sure I understood what he said about that, but he did say that they, like him, were here because there is *mucha oportunidad*. I asked, "¿Es fácil conseguir empleo aquí?"

"Sí, para los que quieren trabajar. Algunos no mas quieren tomar. En México [he was from Puebla] trabajo muy duro, pero," he paused and shrugged his shoulders, "pero nada."

Here in the north he could find work and get some money for it, and it was his view that anyone who wanted to work could get a job, though some just wanted to drink. Nodding his head, "hay bastante trabajo."

Over and over when I talk to people comes the word *trabajo*. Trabajo. Trabajo. Trabajo. This is what life is about. It may not be good by many standards, but compared to Mexico where he worked so hard but for "nada," it was certainly an improvement. In Puebla his family had lived in a house that was made of "palos con basura" — sticks with trash stuck in. I'm quite certain that he had little idea about why the price of their tortillas had tripled since *La Crisis* of 1994 and why those who farmed corn in Puebla only earned about $400 for their crop, one that cost them between $460 and $520 to produce.[15] Only that "trabajo muy duro, pero nada." Again, life is not simple for common Mexicans.

People from Mexico hunger for work; they hurt for work. For work that pays real money. The dollars are what stand between people and calamity. This aching is why they work so much harder and more eagerly than others in the job market, why they get the jobs. Why it is that getting trabajo is the end goal.

The media (which is supposed to inform), politicians (who are supposed to lead), and academics (who are supposed to develop knowledge and educate) have all failed when it comes to the matters of immigration, free trade, and drugs. The media only presents isolated articles in which the connections between trade practices and immigration, drug demand and political corruption, are rarely made. Politicians rely on focus groups to tell them what will sell themselves to the electorate. Academics only talk to other scholars, or they are dismissed as "liberal."

Americans, then, don't understand how the "creative destruction" of NAFTA and free trade, and the corruption and weakness of Mexico, combine to develop underdevelopment and put people and drugs on the move. And why, then, Mexicans, like the guys on my roof, will work so hard. Newspaper headlines say things like "U.S. Immigrants Finding Work; Native-born Losing out."[16] People blame the immigrants.

In a report that has garnered some attention, the Center for Immigration Studies concluded that "in fact, an analysis of the latest Census Bureau data shows that between March of 2000 and March of 2004, the number of adults working actually increased (by 2.3 million), but all of the net change went to immigrant workers." Moreover, "the number of adult natives holding a job is nearly half a million fewer." The study even broaches a nasty little secret regarding the statistics about unemployment in America, namely that the unemployment rate only includes people actively looking for a job. Those who are too discouraged or otherwise unable to work don't count, like the "1.2 million working-age natives (who) left the labor force (in just the last year), and say that they are not even trying to find a job."[17]

Adding and subtracting job numbers can be misleading, of course. It's hard to calculate such matters as the number of American households that can have two incomes because a *niñera* from Mexico or El Salvador takes care of the children and cleans the house. (It is even harder to calculate how many marriages have been saved because an immigrant woman takes care of the children and cleans the house, but we can be sure that the number is substantial.) Plenty of the areas of the economy — construction and retailing are two — have seen expansion because immigrants perform effectively so much of the unskilled, low-wage work, which in turn facilitates the pursuits of skilled American workers. And there is the argument that immigrants do the work no one else wants or will do.

All of these matters are much more complicated than the apparently complex calculations of number crunchers let on. Many resorts that used to be staffed (think skiing and table waiting) by American youth off from college or the summer no longer are because land values have so skyrocketed that no one can live near the places unless they are rich. Thus the workers live in trailer camps and take a long bus ride everyday to work. American youth will not do this. Ultimately, though, Americans know that hard work for low wages is for chumps.

Cleaning hotel rooms, washing dishes, mopping floors, and cleaning toilets in offices late at night, butchering hogs and chickens in rural Arkansas, toiling in the hot fields, are not the things that "Americans" do. Once, when there were high wages in the meat-packing plants, Americans would kill and process the animals, but remember they were the children of the immigrants from Eastern Europe, like Jurgis in *The Jungle*, who wouldn't stand for the abuse their destitute parents suffered and so formed the unions that got those high wages.

Recall that the only time that "Americans," like the Joad family in *The Grapes of Wrath*, would do agricultural labor was when the calamity of the Dust Bowl pushed Oakies and Arkies to sufficient desperation that they would do work that disparaged immigrants have always done in the fields of California. Or that blacks would pick cotton and follow the crops along the Southern Atlantic coast. They did so only under conditions of actual slavery and then when slavery times had not completely been over, when Jim Crow, arbitrary arrests for vagrancy at picking time, and the sharecrop system compelled them to work. The whole legacy of racism, slavery, and segregation has now translated into the impossibility of large numbers of blacks working in subservient positions, as maids, dishwashers, or pickers, under whites.

In May 2005, Vicente Fox, guilelessly defending the presence of Mexican immigrants in the United States, stated that they "do work that blacks won't even do." People had a tizzy and he had to apologize. Nobody was willing to say that, in a powerful way, he was right. White Americans in general will not do harsh or boring jobs for minimum wage as a career; now African Americans in general will not do them either, and now there is neither whip nor starvation to compel them to do so. If slaughtering animals or working in the fields paid $25 per hour (about $50,000 per year), then maybe Americans would do that work.

Can we really expect employers—who, historically, have generally preferred Mexicans over African Americans[18]—to hire those whom the media and many politicians have made into the most vilified sector of the population—young black males—to greet customers in fast-food restaurants or bus tables in restaurants when there are tens of thousands of non-threatening people available from south of the border who ache for trabajo?

I speak some harsh truths here. The ideology of hard work has never been enough to compel sufficient numbers of people to do shit jobs for little money. That some agreeable person seemed willing to do such labor, and received a pat on the head for it or a turkey at Thanksgiving, has validated the fable of the willing, low-paid worker, except that no one knows where this person is anymore. The only ones who seem at all content to be doing such labor are those for whom such labor stands between them and calamity. There is no such person on television—not on MTV, reality shows, sitcoms, or anything. If you are from the middle class or above, there is no such person that you know, unless they are working for you.

Mexico has needed people who will work hard and invest money in the economy. Another thing that Americans refuse to understand is that, while certainly the United States does a favor for Mexico when it functions as a safety valve by soaking up some of Mexico's unemployed and then having them send money back in support of families and economic and political stability, Mexico does a huge favor for the United States when it sends north its most productive laborers. Any country's most precious natural resource is its young, hearty, eager workers, and when it comes to hard, physical travail, that means its men aged 20 to 40. In other words, the ones who should be building an infrastructure of irrigation and transportation projects, growing food and constructing homes, digging mines and making steel, have come to the United States to rub on cars, pick strawberries, butcher hogs and chickens, clean buildings, install roofs, bus tables, install sprinkler systems on golf courses, and maintain people's yards. Its young workers constitute one of Mexico's greatest gifts to America. It's another example of how the power and wealth imbalances of the United States and Mexico develop one country and underdevelop the other.

Mexico has always hoped that they would come back, not just with dollars but with Yankee know-how. In the 1920s, during the first Great Migration north, the Mexican consulate sponsored all manner of *festejos*, Mexican patriotic celebrations, in order to maintain the allegiance of Mexico's emigrants. In the 1930s Mexico welcomed back the *repatriados*, those who returned either voluntarily or were deported during the Depression when demand for Mexican labor collapsed. The national government embarked on a program of state-sponsored economic development, hoped that these workers would bring to the cause of Mexico's economic development the work and time discipline thrust upon them while in jobs north of the border.[19]

Some of this Yankee-learned ingenuity does return to Mexico, though perhaps it is better understood that what they bring back is "the Creed," which we will encounter in future chapters. People like Andres Bermudez—who snuck across the border in the trunk of a car, went to California, and eventually made lots of money growing tomatoes— bring back to Mexico a sense of the rule of law, individualism, the work ethic, and a strong sense that humans can effect change. Perhaps it is this latter notion that Mexico needs the most. This "Tomato King" is running for mayor of Jerez in Zacatecas. Said one naturalized American, "Someday, I want to come home to Jerez. But first I want people like Andres to come and make things better." Another, Fort Worth furniture salesman Martin Carvajal, is running for mayor of Apulco, also in Zacatecas. Bermudez campaigns to "make Jerez more like America."[20] This is what Mexico has been powerfully ambivalent about since the time of the Revolution and with good reason: it is going blond.

Transnational migration makes cultural insularity impossible of course, as we will discuss in the following chapters. I watch Univisión and Galavisión to try and keep my Spanish up. There are fairly good news shows (it's quite remarkable how little news we get about matters of great importance in Latin America on English-language TV), dopey game shows, hot dancers on music shows, and pathetic imitations of American trash talk shows. But the stars are so often blond, especially the women. Watching shows produced in Mexico or by Mexicans in the United States, one would think that it was a xanthic country. Well, OK, they aren't all natural blonds, the male newscaster aims for the Latin lover look, and the people in the audience and those being interviewed on the trash talk shows emphasize the Indian phenotype, but this is a statement about values and hierarchy, indeed.

I wonder what the "blonding" of Mexico means. Surely it comes from the influence of *el norte*. These are matters that will unfold as we continue our stories of Mexico and America. Is Mexico a mimetic nation? Is this another flight from the deep Indianness of Mexico?

For now let me add how this amplifies my amazement at American local news. At least one of the anchors is usually Asian and the other an Anglo male, the sports guy is African American, and a "Hispanic" usually gets in there too. So if you watch the news you'd think Mexico was a fair-skinned country and America was a racial polyglot.

Only the future will tell who or what brings more Americanization to Mexico—people like Andres Bermudez, blond pop stars, or the West Side Kansas Street gang. Maybe they have been deported or maybe their families brought them back, but "over the years," as Sam Quinones reports, "a kind of gangland minor leagues has emerged across Mexico, a pre-NAFTA export mimicking LA's big show." In places like Zamora, Michoacán, kids who learned to be gangbangers in the United States have returned to re-create the West Side Kansas Street (South Gate), East Side Wilmas (Wilmington) in Michoacán, and the thousands of Mara Salvatruchas (various LA street gangs) who menace Honduras and El Salvador. ("Mara" is a Salvadorean word for "gang" and "Salvatrucha" translates roughly as "Salvadorean guy.") In LA these youths learned to steal (there's very little to steal in Zamora), obtain, and consume "withering quantities of pills, marijuana, glue, cheap mescal, and nonfilter cigarettes." The transnational *cholos* mimic American culture, but not "the Creed." Along Avenida Juárez, named for Mexico's most revered president and liberator from the French, cholo gangstas strut along in their Dickie pants, "poor and barely literate . . . , a rootless, Walt Disney urban nightmare of tantalizing glitz and violence."[21] They terrorize people and make Mexican mothers and fathers ashamed and afraid of their children.

Recall, too, all those arrested for drugs in el norte, and those who "no mas quieren tomar," in the words of my amigo in the bandit taxi. They go to American prison. There, whatever networks they may have had with their family or people from their village are severed and new bonds are forged. It is a scene beyond nightmarish, beyond dystopic; it is the horrible world of the prison gang where one's only hope against rape and blood-letting is affiliation with one of subsets of the Mexican Mafia or La Nuestra Familia. A young man enters prison because he did something stupid or desperate or merely unthinking. Maybe he lost a job and someone offered him a thousand dollars to drive a drug shipment to another state; maybe the allure of American commodities (Japanese electronics made in China) became too strong and he burglarized a car; maybe he was just always a *pendejo* and he delivered a chingazo to a paisano in a bar.

One Mara Salvatrucha, arrested for the murder of a prison guard, when asked why he was deported from LA, simply said "I went a little crazy there." First-timers in prison have usually done something witless like this. What happens, though, is that jail turns them into hardened criminals. Loyal to the gang, sociopathic towards everyone else, utterly excluded from real work, the ex-cons bring the psychopathic prison culture onto the streets of Los Angeles.[22] If they are illegal aliens, they are deported and they bring that same culture back to their hometowns in Mexico and Central America.

Understanding why one becomes a Mara Salvatrucha (or MS-13 as they often call themselves) requires us to have some sympathy for the young man or woman (or boy or girl), but the overall situation is utterly unsympathetic. Gruesome assassinations of informers, shakedowns and robberies at both the U.S.–Mexico and Mexico-Honduras borders, the massacre of 28 Christmas shoppers on a bus in San Pedro Sula in Honduras, the everyday menace in such barrios as Ilopango in San Salvador, all characterize the activities of MS-13.

In El Salvador an estimated thirty thousand belong to either the Maras or to such other gangs as M-18. Tens of thousands more afflict Honduras and the other countries of Central America. From Virginia to Texas to their original home in Los Angeles, there are another ten thousand in the United States.

No one can deny that unemployment (recall how textile plants are moving to China) and the consequences of the fact that 20 percent of Salvadoreños have fled the country for the safer confines of the United

States in the past two decades, which leaves families disorganized, create fertile grounds for the growth of youth gangs. But Deputy Citizens' Security Minister Rodrigo Ávila claims that the deportation of nearly twelve thousand Salvadoreans is "at the core of the matter. Gangs here now copy the whole LA gang culture, the way they talk, the clothes they wear and the absolute ruthlessness," he claims. When deportees arrive back in El Salvador where job possibilities are desperately scarce and, if they came to California as children, they don't speak much Spanish, they have little else to do besides join the counterpart of their LA gang in El Salvador. This reign of terror has produced the controversial Operation Super Firm Hand, which gives the police all manner of dubious powers, ones reminiscent of the terrible times of the civil war that sent so many north in the first place, to stem the tide of this imported gangsterism.[23]

This is the way we learn about these things from the press, the liberal press no less, which acknowledges the social causes of gangsterism. A friend of mine introduced me to a friend of hers who operates a clinic that removes tattoos. She in turn introduced me to Nestor "Tricky" González (not his real name—he's undocumented), an ex–Mara Salvatrucha who had the large "M" removed from the left side of his face and the large "S" removed from the right. He still had a lot of tats. He told how one day when he was seven, his relatively prosperous grandparents had been having a family party. Men in uniform—he doesn't know if they were government or revolutionaries—came and started harassing them. In front of Nestor's and his cousins' eyes, a soldier put a gun in his grandmother's mouth and blew her head off. Then they shot the grandfather. Four years later, he and some friends left for the United States, the place that had been sponsoring the violence in Guatemala in the first place—he to find his mother who had left for the United States before, and the others because there was nothing else left in Guatemala.

Nestor wound up in South Central LA sleeping in alleys and asking for his mom. Soon he began robbing people to buy food from the push-carts whose owners had also come from Central America. He needed shoes, but he jacked people "not to buy expensive shoes, only Nike Cortez, fifty or sixty bucks."

MacArthur Park, just west of downtown and where I did the paddle boats as a boy in the 1950s, is now Central America. In order to protect themselves from the dominant Mexican gang, the 18th Street Gang, Salvadoreños formed the Mara Salvatruchas, and plenty of other Central Americans joined. Nestor and his hommies have been in and out of jail, and many of them have stories like his. I asked him if he thought there were really bad guys in MS and he said they "gotta lotta people who are really crazy. Guys who were in the army. The sergeant says 'kill anything that moves' in the town. Some of these guys are in MS." He continued that "lotsa guys in MS seen lotta people killed in their country. Lotta these guys are really messed up."

Social science can tell us much about the horribleness of the Mara Salvatruchas, but to really know about them, you need to know the stories of them, like Nestor's, of which we will hear more later.

The New World Border will bring more of America to Mexico just as more of Mexico has been coming north. American culture will travel in the baggage of Andres Bermudez, who energetically faces the future with optimism and a belief in humans' abilities to improve life, and the West Side Kansas Street gang, who are without hope or a future. I am not optimistic about which part of American civilization Mexico and Central America will mimic most.

Visualizing the dividing line between the United States and Mexico, and then thinking about how each side names and understands it, will reveal more about how Americans and Mexicans understand such cultural exchange. From the Pacific Ocean to El Paso/Ciudad Juárez, there is a line drawn in the sand, a product of the Treaty of Guadalupe Hidalgo and the Gadsen Purchase of 1853 between the United States and Mexico. Then from El Paso/Ciudad Juárez to the Gulf of Mexico, the Rio Grande divides the two countries.

A line in the sand will not provide much of a natural barrier, and building an effective fence is really not viable and, even if it were, would be too reminiscent of the vulgar and odious Berlin Wall. Rivers are poor boundaries because they form one ecosystem; they do not divide the landscape so much as provide a valley in which the two sides form one whole. Indeed, the dwellers along the river apparently dividing south Texas from Coahuila and Tamaulipas are all one people and part of one economic, social, and natural terrain.

And it is important to think about some words when we think about what pretends to keep separate Americans and Mexicans. Americans refer to "the border"; Mexicans to "la frontera." This is a good example of how words cannot really describe something precisely. The *Oxford English Dictionary* gives us several senses of what a border is: "A side, an edge, a brink, a margin; a limit, a boundary," and "the frontier line which separates one country from another," and "a continuous bed which forms a fringe round a garden area." A "frontera" is variously defined, but Spanish dictionaries refer to "el extremo o confín de un estado o reino."

Americans think that the border should be a barrier much like a fence around a garden to keep animals out, or a sports stadium where people come through only if they have a proper admission ticket. America is like the compelling spectacle in the stadium in which there are only so many seats; Mexico is the teeming crowd outside wanting in. If you are inside with your ticket, citizenship in other words, you can leave the stadium for a quick visit to a bar for some shots of tequila, a lap dance at a strip club, or some stealthy hits of marijuana. This is what Americans have always done at Tijuana (TJ) and Ciudad Juárez — slipped out for booze when it was Prohibition or one was too young for American bars; for whores when a girlfriend or wife wouldn't put out, or when it was really a young brown boy who caused arousal; and, of course, now Mexico is American's primary dealer. That Mexico seemed always to oblige in these surreptitious transactions legitimated Americans' vision of the turnstile at the border.

The more lyrical word, *frontera*, shapes a very different vision in our mind's eye. This frontera is not only a "border," a "confine," but a "place" that the extremities of each country share. Thus it is that la frontera is not so much like a stadium but more like a provincial park where everyone can bring a picnic and come and go as they please. Or adapt, or mimic, what they see there. There is always peril in the provinces, and like a person's limbs, the extremities are the most exposed to danger. But people often like a frontera, and Americans will think of their own word "frontier" and know that it is not improper to be there, either to picnic or work, and to bring things back and forth like money or DVD players. Americans and Mexicans, then, conceive of the very thing that divides the two countries in very different ways.

The Mexican side may seem the most sad, but it is the most consistent. The Mexican government has printed up a million illustrated handbooks about how to cross the border safely. It, of course, discourages people from crossing the border, but then warns of heat prostration, the dangers of streams and rivers, and the unscrupulousness of smugglers. These booklets are handed to migrants.[24] Mexico knows that without emigration of its surplus population and repatriation of dollars, it will face yet more calamity. Each emigration represents not just family hardship and heartbreak, but national failure.

The American side is correspondingly contradictory. Americans expect that their government will work to maintain a "border," and this is a fair assumption: any nation-state must safeguard its people and maintain social order. Unbridled immigration threatens jobs, schools, and Americans' sense of the familiar. But a government must also help its people prosper and meet their needs for food, clothing, shelter, and even some leisure: thus it is that in order to have cheap food and time to work and play, Americans have come to rely on huge numbers of people crossing the border. Governments under capitalism must also facilitate the accumulation of profit, which is central to investment and growth; profit in service industries and agriculture come in good part from low wages. These are the things that governments must do to maintain their legitimacy.

In a perverse sort of way, the Border Patrol functions quite well in the matter of supplying America's labor needs. "Tijuana is like a dam," Luis Alberto Urrea says, "and it's beginning to groan before a tidal wave of human flesh." So many of the people behind that dam are feeble, hapless, aged, resourceless who, lemming-like, have come to border towns desperate to cross over to a place where they imagine they can be fed and housed. Militarizing the border and making transit a dangerous, indeed brutal, undertaking creates an unnatural selection process that unmercifully sifts out the weak and useless and fiercely supplies those people American employers will want — the energetic and the hardy.

Thus it is that the American government must simultaneously allow hearty immigrants to cross the border, because areas of the economy and family prosperity depend on it, and give the impression that it is not allowing people to cross the border, because people fear for their jobs and schools: it must do two opposite things in the case of emigration from Mexico to sustain legitimacy. And there is the matter of government policies, such as NAFTA, that actually work simultaneously to increase both wealth and comfort for some Americans as well as the number of illegal immigrants, which increases unemployment and discomfort for others.

We wind up with what Peter Andreas has called "Border Games." The Immigration Reform and Control Act of 1986 (IRCA) and the Immigration and Naturalization Service (the INS or "la migra") are not really about maintaining steadfast the defense of the border against allegedly variously dangerous immigrants, let alone solving the genuine problems that migration present, but rather are about appearances. It makes for good election-year politics to promise constituents that their jobs and schools will be protected, that border communities and ranches will not be used as dumping depots by the smugglers of migrants, and that undesirables will not be in our midst. At the same time there will be low-wage workers in hotels and agriculture.[25]

The Immigration Reform and Control Act threatened employers with sanctions, expanded the Border Patrol, and offered a program to legalize the status of many who were already in the country. None of this worked. Making employers check documents, and many kinds were acceptable, simply fostered a massive expansion of the forged papers industry. Making the border more difficult to cross meant that more died in the heat of less-patrolled areas and that, instead of people going back to Mexico in their customary circular migration pattern, they stayed north of the border. Legalizing more immigrants, which had intended to fulfill the American demand for cheap labor, meant that those "receiver" communities in the United States would be safer to harbor yet more of their illegal compatriots from south of the border. In other words, what IRCA claimed that it would do—give integrity to the border and stem the number of undocumented immigrants—actually resulted in the opposite.[26]

But IRCA and the buildup of the INS and the Border Patrol do give the impression of a government and its agencies heartily protecting the American people. This is more of what I mean by the idea that the present situation is a "well-functioning system." There are still plenty of workers coming over to butcher animals for our meat counters, harvest crops, mow yards, hammer on roofs, and clean dishes and hotel rooms. The expansion of NAFTA, the population explosion, and the worsening economic and political situation of Mexico will guarantee that. At the same time, government laws, policies, and expenditures give the impression that the border, and think back to our discussion of that word, will remain under control. The statistics are awesome all around:

The Business Roundtable and other advocates of free trade can point to the increase in exports of hogs, corn, and shoes to Mexico since the passage of NAFTA.

This process will separate more small farmers in Mexico from their place and send them north.

The Border Patrol, which bases its budget requests on the number of apprehensions of illegals and drugs, will get more money and positions the more of them they catch. Their militarization of the border will select out the useless in favor of the heartiest of workers.

When the emigrants do get across, at least some of them will send some of the money they earn back to Parral and Irapuato where it will save families from calamity, buttress marginal village economies, and take heat off corrupt local and national Mexican governments.

In the United States, meat packers and strawberry growers will have ready workers, restaurants and hotels will be cleaned, niñeras and house-keepers will enable two-income families and save marriages.

Ministers, politicians, and the police can blame Mexico and Co-lombia for the drug problem and not have to pay attention to the so-cial forces that create addiction, and avoid admitting that pleasures can come from drugs.

As American capitalists attack the American standard of living by crushing unions and exporting jobs, demagogic politicians will pander to people's fears and disappointments and direct their anger at powerless people — immigrants and especially undocumented ones.

Constituents will feel gratified when they read about the militariza-tion of the border and go to Wal-Mart, where the night-cleaning crews have been undocumented Mexicans, where they can buy cheaply both the products of American agribusiness and their Mexican workers and those of low-wage foreign factories and sweatshops. Wal-Mart is great, immigrants are bad.

Academics will have more subjects for study and get more research grants.

A system functioning as well as this one is not likely to do anything except continue to reproduce itself.

And cause more pain. In one weekend in August 2004, a dozen corpses were found on the north side of the Arizona border. They died of heat exhaustion and dehydration trying to avoid the Border Patrol and all that new technology that my amigos on the roof had been telling me about. In the past decade nearly three thousand have died trying to cross, and the death rate is increasing. When one part of the border is tightened (San Diego and El Paso/Ciudad Juárez), people go where it is looser (the Arizona desert), and much more dangerous. The temperature is over 100 degrees, and the smugglers often simply shoo people out of the vans and point them north. One cannot carry enough water to make it safely.[27]

Tijuana Interlude: Watching the Wound Get Worse

I'd heard about the disaster that Tijuana has become; I'd been there in about 1970 when it had a population of about fifty thousand. Nobody knows for sure how many live there now, maybe two and a half million. I went again in 2006 and managed to stay at the Casa de Migrante, a Catholic charity house for those in the crossing process.

Away from the official crossing point, one can stand before a massive fence separating Tijuana from a no-man's-land, which itself abuts massive steel and concrete bunkers. On the fence are crosses memorializing those who have died trying to cross; each has the casualty's name and state of origin, though some merely note *desconocido*. True to the sociological literature, most are from the stricken interior of Mexico. The fence has also been painted with murals commemorating migration and has slogans such as "la frontera es una llaga abierta."

There is no shortage of such metaphors for the border: "an open sore," in this case; an open wound (*una herida*), in another; the dam poised to burst.

There is tragedy in the street names in downtown TJ, ones that reflect the cruel ironies of Mexican history since the revolution. There are *calles* named for Miguel Hidalgo (instigator of the independence movement against Spain in 1810), Benito Juárez (president and leader of the resistance against the French, 1862–1868), Negrete (leader of the local resistance against William Walker, the filibusterer who tried to take more Mexican territory after the Mexican-American War), Emiliano Zapata (great hero of the peasant masses during the revolution and assassinated in 1919 by the victorious Constitutionalists), Plutarco Elías Calles (a leader of the Constitutionalists), and Juan Serrabia and Ricardo Flores-Magón (both Anarchist leaders of the Mexican Revolution). Each of these is celebrated for their efforts to free Mexico from foreign domination. Ruefully, I think of these men's aspirations for Mexico and what the New World border has done to them. There is even a calle named for "Artículo 123" of the Mexican Constitution. It guaranteed the eight-hour day (and the six-day week), minimum wage, collective bargaining, and the right to strike. All of these have been waived for the foreign maquiladoras along the border.

It's the human magnitude that most strikes me. Tijuana is no longer simply the place to where Americans traversed to transgress Protestant morals. That's still there, but it is now much more of a place to which Mexicans go hoping to transit to the United States. On the way to Colonia Fausto González (named for the owner of the dump), one sees hundreds of people swarming over the trash. Half the people in the *colonia* "trabajan en la basura"; they work picking up bits and pieces of aluminum, plastic, cardboard, anything that can be exchanged for a few centavos. And wait to cross.

I go to a small community center there where children are cared for while their parents go to *la basura*. The little children get some tutoring too. There is love and dignity in the trash.

I go to Colonia Maclovio Rojas on the outskirts of TJ and meet people who are simply not down with the whole New World Border program, *gente* who, indeed, live with the Mexican Revolution. I know what I'm getting into when I'm walking into a sparse courtyard where the fence is painted with murals and the slogans "la tierra pertenece a los que trabajan" and "tierra y libertad." Emiliano Zapata lives at Maclovio Rojas and in Chiapas. His present-day followers believe that the "land belongs to those who work it," in "land and liberty," and not in the dictates of the free market. The denizens of Maclovio Rojas think that the colonia should belong to them (they have paid some money for it and have some disputed legal documentation) mostly because they work it and improve it. The state wants to sell this upgraded land to foreigners to build another maquiladora. There are also real politics in Tijuana.

Mostly there are desperate poor people there.

Yet they continue to come. Tijuana fills with people dying (literally all too often) to get over. Thousands pick through its trash dumps; thousands of criminals come from all over Mexico to prey on the weak and vulnerable, especially the Indian migrants. The groan one hears and even feels there is yet another apparition of the New World Border, of border towns bulging on the south side of the border with people pushed from their villages, yearning for the peace and stability they think they'll find in the north, aching for trabajo, just wanting something else besides the disaster of what so much of Mexico and Central America have become.

Some Americans put water out for people so they don't die; others shoot at the migrants. It's like how some are so eager to give poor mexicanos a job and others are trying so desperately to keep them out. And like how some want to exclude the children of undocumented people from schools and then in the schools there are special programs to teach them English and skills. Crazy gringos are hard to figure out.

Indeed, on the surface it is hard to compute these matters. In 1994 California voters passed Proposition 187, the so-called "Save Our State" ballot initiative, which sought to deny education and social and health-care services to undocumented people. The courts, bureaucratic lethargy, and common sense have largely blocked the measures, but we see here many Californians, Mexican American ones included, express their ambivalence, some would say hypocrisy, about the immigrants who feed them and give them life.

This matter is related to the "Paradise Lost" theme, indeed that we are headed toward dystopia, that we often see in writings and musings about what has happened to Los Angeles and California, and whether or not we witness there a harbinger of what is to come to the rest of America.[28]

Is this "paradise lost" because immigrants are overrunning it? Because poor, non-English-speaking immigrants have crowded out from the schools children who don't need to learn English but need the skills to get into the University of California, and because wealthy Chinese and Iranians have so driven up home prices? Is this "paradise lost" because no longer can any immigrants come here and find blue-collar jobs and a reasonably priced house to live in and then send their children to public university? Is this "paradise lost" because the homeless and the criminal, the detritus of de-industrialization and the New World Economy, clutter up the landscape and threaten safety? Is this "paradise lost" because ill-tempered, fearful, bigoted populists voted for Proposition 13, which ruined the property tax base for funding state spending on schools and everything else, except prisons? Or has "paradise" simply been so attractive that so many people have come here that it is now impossibly over-crowded, the freeways so much so that no one can get anywhere? Or is this "paradise" theme just so much hype? The millions who have done all the work and got little for it, and I'm referring not just to super-exploited immigrant workers but all the way back to mission Indians and Ramona and Alessandro, might agree with that last premise.

It is the case that life in California, especially Los Angeles, is certainly different now. Ask any native of the place. There were halcyon days for fledgling middle-class families like my own. There was space and cheap property; endless water and open freeways; good schools, good social services, and good jobs, even for blue-collar people. California was the place where, if you were in one of the groups included in the paradise paradigm, you could grow up in the warm and affirming milieu of pleasures like kissing with Ramona on the beach or in the car with Wolfman Jack on the AM radio.

California was the place where anyone, almost, could go and re-make themselves. It was a place where decentralization and the freeway system meant that one could avoid, even be safe from, that terrible and terrifying creation of northern racism and discrimination — the black ghetto. It was the Watts Riots of 1965 that made those who thought they lived in some kind of paradise say, "oh my, them."

Now California is crowded and dangerous. This is the "paradise lost," and what is so disconcerting. Really, this "paradise" has been as real for some as it has been a mirage for others, and mockery for yet so many.

My experience with history — informed reflection about the past which reveals the complexities of human motivation, agency, and possibilities — has helped me escape "either/or," "good or bad," and "right or wrong" styles of thinking about matters of the New World Border, indeed many aspects of the world. Most everyday journalism and almost all political discourse provides "news" that sensationalizes, simplifies, and excludes information that would complicate or contradict what people perceive to be true and good, that might explain the relationship between NAFTA, cheap strawberries, and immigrants in their midst.

Most people respond to the so-called "news" through the lens of their emotional associations, their sense of right and wrong, and presuppositions that they have developed from schools, TV, and religion. They know that entering into the United States without proper documentation is against the law. They know that the children of undocumented immigrants crowd up the schools and that they pay taxes for those schools and may well wind up having to spend more money to send their own children to private schools.

It should be becoming more and more apparent that the New World Border condition means that the sort of thinking to which most in Mexico and America have been accustomed, this thought pattern of moral and legal absolutes, has gone the way of the old version and comfort of "the border." One side cannot be so easily separated from the other. In a New World Border way of thinking, we would realize that the presence of Mexican immigrants, legal or not, is not random, inexplicable, or malicious.

The situation has to do not so much with the criminality of Mexicans as it does with the actions of economic and political elites on both sides of the border. The notion that undocumented Mexican immigration should simply be criminalized and the children tossed from schools —the easy conclusion using the simplistic and sensationalist ways of politicians, preachers, and TV news personalities—is not as simple as it would appear. Nor is the notion that federal legislation decriminalizing undocumented immigrants, and more teachers and diversity programs in the schools, will make everything OK. Neither will restore the Paradise Lost. Free-market thinking will only distance it further.

No one is inclined to think in utopian terms anymore. Maybe this is realistic, but it makes it hard to imagine a better future.

Instead it's about holding several opposed ideas at once. NAFTA increases the prosperity of some, ruins the subsistence of others, brings more immigrants to the United States, sends more gangs and drugs across the border, enhances the quality of life for many natives and many strangers, burdens schools and hospitals, and binds countries together in ways that will become all the more astounding.

And in the short term it is about including immigrants from south of the border in our sense of who is worthy of moral consideration. Mexicans and Americans are so bound up together that there is no other ethical or practical course.

Yet people on both sides will continue to blame what they don't like—immigrants; de-industrialization and NAFTA; desperation and criminality; cranky, scared voters; a population exceeding what the ecosystem can bear—when indeed the harsh truth is that all of these things come into play, and they are, obviously, inter-related. Amidst all the creative destruction, itself a notion containing two opposed ideas, we can only "retain the ability to function" if we enhance not only our "ability to hold two opposed ideas in the mind at the same time" but our ability to hold many opposed ideas.

Bienvenidos to the New World Border.

Zorro, Cows, Indians, and Dons

Re-creating Californio Rancho Society

When I was a little boy, the cinder block wall in the back yard of our house had a lot of chalk "z's" on them. This had nothing to do with some genetic predisposition toward graffiti art. I would prance around in my mask and cape and, with my chalk-tipped sword, imitate Zorro. Every week I would watch on black-and-white TV and marvel at his ability to escape the rotund and greasy Sargent Garcia and to bring definitive justice to someone who had been done wrong. As both Don Diego and Zorro he was such a gentleman, and I liked his fancy drapes.

On the TV show everyone lived well and in pretty houses. It was California as paradise. Our house emulated that, in a way. It was in Laurel Canyon in the 1950s when there was open space there. Many of the men in the neighborhood were building their own houses; I even did some hammering myself. They were not professionals, and the houses were a hodgepodge of shapes and styles. This was California as paradise too.

In my class photographs from Wonderland Avenue Elementary, there are two African American kids, two Mexicans, and one Asian. Most of my classmates were also *hijos del país*, kids born in California. Several of us were born in Queen of Angels Hospital. My best friend and I had birthdays two days apart and first saw light at Queen of Angels.

Some people say that Los Angeles was originally named el Pueblo de Nuestra Señora la Reina de los Angeles (The Town of Our Lady the Queen of the Angels), but most likely it was simply la Reina de los Angeles. Either way, that I was born in that particular hospital makes me all the more an hijo del país. Many of the streets around there — Alvarado, Figueroa, Micheltorena, Sepulveda, Echeandia, Pico — were all named for the people you will meet in these stories of California before it was America.

Participating in some of the festivities during the California ses-
quicentennial, in a hotel room in, appropriately enough, Monterey, I
found re-runs of Zorro on the cable offerings. It had been colorized.
Don Diego's *chaleco* was now salmon colored. I was taken aback.

And there appeared barely any women and no Indians, another
definition of colorized.

As the credits rolled I noticed something else that no six-year-old
would have. None of the actors, except for Don Diego's father, had
Mexican names. They were all gringos including, thankfully, the
corpulent and blundering Sargent Garcia. I choose not to make a big
deal of the fact that one of my childhood heroes was now known to
me as a gringo in an unmanly orange chaleco.

There is all this fantasy about "Old California," but I knew someone, who knew someone, who knew someone who had been to the
ranchos and the missions in the 1830s. It was my grandfather whose
mother died when he was young—his *abuela* raised him—and it
was this grandmother's father, of the mellifluous name Francisco
Sotomayor, who traveled from Sonora to Alta California. He was a
wagon master who journeyed back and forth between Sonora and
New Almaden (near present-day San Jose) transporting quicksilver
in leather bags back to the mines of Sonora for the processing of
gold. He commuted on the el Camino Real—the very one on which
traveled Padre Serra as he visited those first missions that he founded
—passing missions and ranchos on the way.

Sotomayor had seven sons, several of whom rode shotgun on the
"recua" and actually fought Indians in Southern California, the very
ones we shall hear about in this essay. One of the sons, Francisco el
segundo, deserted his father and this dangerous life one time when
they were in San Francisco. It was one of Francisco el primero's two
daughters who raised my grandfather, and whom my own father
actually remembers, but only dimly, meeting.

I wonder if my ancestor, Señor Sotomayor, ever attended any of
the fiestas at the ranchos of the dons. At least he would have con-
versed with some of the dons, likely about the Indians. I can imagine
what he would have seen of the Indians and heard expressed his and
the dons' disgust, rage, and fear about the peoples whose lifeways
they, the padres, and the soldiers had so disrupted. In the little pueblos of Los Angeles and San Jose, he would have seen Indians who
had experienced the tragedy of unsuccessful missionization: they
would be doing most of the work but interspersed with dubious

pleasures; some few would have remained dedicated to the missions; those who had never come in to the missions would be in league with those who had fled and would have been robust, dangerous, and terrifying. To know their stories, and to attend a fiesta, I would eagerly, and fearfully, join the *recua*.

Certainly, this was a dangerous border crossing for Francisco Sotomayor as he too journeyed in the footsteps of Padre Serra from Sonora to Alta California. It is tempting to compare the Indians to a sort of border patrol, and of course there are plenty of morbidly humorous comments made about the failure of Native American immigration policies. Suffice it to say for now the obvious: there has long been commerce between California and Mexico and crossing borders into California has been dangerous for a long time.

There are other issues that Zorro and the Californios raise, ones about visions of justice, pleasures, and the meaning of life, and about the creation of the self.

Civic, business, and antiquarian organizations began in the 1890s to extol Californio society with various "Fiesta Days" celebrations. Typically including floats depicting fanciful scenes of old California, local businessmen riding horses and dressed as *caballeros*, and always presented as "Spanish," these gala rituals, these invented traditions, provided Americans an opportunity to romanticize the non-market social relations of the people whom they had summarily replaced on the landscape of California. For the festivities of May 1903, the *Los Angeles Times* told how the city wore "too commercial an aspect during eleven months and three weeks of the year," but how during Fiesta Week "it needs now but a slight imagination to garb all Broadway's pedestrians as peasants of Andalusia."[1] Not Mexicans, but Andalusians.

When people write the history of a place, they often consummate a name for it. "The Old South," "Colonial New England," "The Wild West," and "Spanish California" are several good examples that come to mind. When they name the place, they often define it: "aristocratic and genteel," "industrious and middle class," "masculine and violent," and "gracious and generous" are phrases that have come to define the above-mentioned places. When people define a place, they also possess it, or they give possession to certain people. Plantation owners, Puritans, cowboys, and Spanish dons, then, become the possessors of these fabled places in spite of the fact that they all lived with a good number of

Indians, some had slaves who outnumbered the white people, and others lived with, and often were themselves, mixed-race people. Each could be named otherwise and thus have different owners; we will name the Rancho Period in California in yet other ways.

Every generation has had some sort of exposure to Zorro and, by extension, to the dons and ranchos of California. Whether it was the 1940 film starring the swashbuckling Tyrone Power, the television serial in the 1950s, or the most recent *Zorro* with Antonio Banderas, where Zorro saves thousands of enslaved Indians working in a fantastic gold mine, most everyone has had the opportunity to fantasize about life on a genteel California rancho. And about visions of quick, personal justice. We usually think of this Rancho Period of California history as dating from Mexican Independence in 1821 to the American Conquest in 1848. It had its origins years earlier and, in some places in California, lasted until the 1860s. These were the first people to call themselves "Californians," Californios actually, and they were Mexicans.[2]

They were a people who began utterly inauspiciously; forged themselves places upon the landscape, sometimes as owners of great landed estates but usually as simple ranchers; created a singular identity for themselves out of their relationships to priests, Indians, lower-class immigrants, Americans, Mexico, and cows and horses; battled the Indians; faded into physical obscurity in the political economy of California; and then participated in their mythical re-creation as gracious masters of a lost pastoral paradise. Their story portends much about the unfolding of California history, about the state's changing political concerns, and even about the contingencies and exigencies of human existence.

Mexico in the nineteenth century, like America, sought to forge a nation out of a variety of regions and states. Neither country succeeded either completely or without trouble: things fell apart horrifically in the United States in 1861, and Mexico could not unite to defend itself either in 1846 when the Americans invaded or in 1862 when the French did.

Both new nations had to finish the conquest of the indigenous peoples of their lands. America vanquished at mid-century the Arikira and later the Sioux, the Navajo, the Apache. Mexico tried to defeat the Yaquis in the north and the Mayans in Chiapas. Mexico had much less success than America, including in California. There, in the 1850s and 1860s, Americans achieved what Mexico could not in the matter of the Indians, and in monstrous fashion.

This is the context for understanding just who these first self-defined

Californians were: they were a regional variety of Mexican culture. Interestingly enough, unlike New Englanders, Virginians, or residents of Guadalajara or Mexico City, they did not have several hundred years of historical development out of which they might evolve something we call "culture." What Zorro's family was trying to do, and what the Moreno family had done in the novel *Ramona*, was to make something of themselves besides rustic frontierspeople. One thing they didn't do much of, actually, was fight with swords.

From the earliest travel accounts to *Ramona* to "Zorro," the recreations of Rancho California demonstrate how our relationship to the past is always growing and changing, and rarely in a linear fashion. History is best appreciated not merely as the "facts" but rather as the meanings that people derive from it at different times and for different purposes.

The first Americans who wrote about California did so to vindicate their imperialist pursuits, and they judged negatively those they considered generally inferior. Said one Anglo American of California in 1831: "By all accounts it is worthy of more wise and more enterprising masters than those to whose rule it is subjected . . . if populated it would be perhaps the most delightful country in the world. How many Countrymen of mine who are jostling one another for room at home might live happily in those fertile but uncultivated plains you describe."[3]

Paradise identified; paradise doomed.

Then, confined within their system of isolating market relationships, Anglo American chroniclers made of the Californios that for which they so yearned: gracious gentlemen and ladies who acted graciously and solely out of considerations of honor, solicitousness, and faith towards one another and their subordinates. And they made of them Spaniards.[4]

With their own narratives often as the sources, Hubert Howe Bancroft, the most renowned but now picked-upon of California historians, lapsing from his nineteenth-century Positivism in favor of legend, celebrated the previously maligned traits of the Californios in his fanciful *California Pastoral* (1888): "And so they lived, opening their eyes in the morning when they saw the sun; they breathed the fresh air, and listened to the song of the birds; mounting their steeds they rode forth in the enjoyment of healthful exercise; they tended their flocks, held intercourse with each other, and ran up a fair credit in heaven." By 1900, Anglo Californians came to lament the passing of the Californios (and the missions) but to attribute their passing to their own shortcomings.

When the Americans told the stories of "Old California," they reflected their own optimism and faith in progress and technology, and their negative judgment of peoples deemed non-progressive. Alfred Robinson's famous *Life in California* (1846) explained how "the early Californians, having lived a life of indolence without any aspiration beyond the requirement of the day, naturally fell behind their more energetic successors." The acclaimed works of Josiah Royce and Charles Nordhoff similarly sympathized with the Californios, savored their prosperous and genteel lifeways, and condescendingly criticized their lack, in Nordhoff's words, "of the energy and ingenuity of civilized life."

For people who think in terms of progress and linear time, such as these commentators on Californio life, such a construction of history legitimates the conquest of California. If history leads to more and more progress, if productive energy is what either God, or evolution, or fate will reward with success, then Californio society was in the way of history and progress. The natural unfolding of progressive history is what caused the acquisition of California, not Yankee military might.

My purposes here will be to use the Californios to ruminate on matters of historical identity, the uses and limits of leisure, and legal and extra-legal justice, and on the matter of sex and with whom and how people engage in it.

Land and Liberty

The beginnings of the Californios were much less auspicious than any of the expansive re-creations would suggest. While Franciscan priests struggled to Christianize the native people at the missions, a competing idea of civil society — that people could unite through bonds of property, law, and citizenship — came to California in the baggage of the first two governors, Felipe de Neve (1775–1782) and the former military comandante Pedro Fages (1782–1791). These forceful men feuded incessantly with Padre Serra and then with the later Franciscan leaders. In part, their conflicts derived over who should control the newfound bounty of Alta California and, in part, over these great ideas of what should organize society and what the future of New Spain (Mexico and the former provinces in the present-day United States) should look like: religious communities or secular, civil towns.

To further his conception, Neve ordered the founding of two pueblos, one at San Jose in 1777 and the other in 1781 along the Río Porciúncula, where the old village of Yanga-na had been, Nuestra Señora de los An-geles. The Mission Road (paved today and tenanted with mostly Asian shopettes) connected the pueblo, named for the Queen of the Angels, with the Mission San Gabriel, named for the archangel who announced the good news to Mary that she would bear the Son of God. The mission sits by the river of the same name. The rancor would increase between those associated with the vision of a civil and secular Los Angeles and those who would see its future in terms of spiritual utopia.

Indeed, it was as if proponents of these two great ideas — of the spiritual and secular societies — had found a barren place where their visions could be played out and the aboriginals' supposedly nondescript existence could be replaced with something sublime. On the side of civil society, Governor Neve issued a *reglamento* in 1779 directing the found-ing of pueblos (towns). In it he codified the proper ordering of a town regarding house lots, pasturage, a proper plaza, and how "the settlers shall nominate by and from themselves the public officials that shall have been arranged for." It was with these ideas in mind that Pedro Fages suggested that the area along the Río Porciúncula "offers a hospitable place for some Spanish families to join together as neighbors."

Eleven families who had journeyed from the interior of Mexico marched from the Mission San Gabriel on September 4, 1781, to the site the governor had selected. There are divergent stories of the ceremony that Neve conducted, but we do know that the mission fathers blessed the new *pobladores* and that they were a mix of mestizos, mulattos, and Indians, though one claimed to be Spanish. With pasturage, cows, and seed, they were to be independent economically and politically. Indeed, each patriarch described himself in the town records as "queda avezin-dado en el pueblo." *Avecindarse* means "to join as neighbors," and this is the word that helps us understand the fundamental social relation in the new Pueblo de los Angeles and the rest of Californio society. And there the settlers proceeded to do with many of the Indians as the rest of Spanish America so famously did — they worked them, corrupted them, and married with them.

In 1784, the Rosas brothers of el Pueblo de los Angeles, Carlos and Máximo, who were of Indian and mulatto descent, both married gentile Indian women (who had to be baptized for the occasion). The two women of Yanga-na and Jajambit *rancheras* were both probably familiar with pueblo life. In 1796 another Rosas married a neophyte from San Gabriel, as had a number of other pobladores. Those few soldiers from Santa Barbara and San Juan Capistrano who married Indian women, as Spanish policy encouraged, mostly moved to Los Angeles before the turn of the century. After 40 years of missionization, a very few Indians were selected to leave, marry other "nuevos cristianos," and join the pueblo.[5]

On and on went the diatribes of the friars about "the residents [who] are a group of laggards . . . in those pueblos without priests." Imagine the righteous indignation when Padre José María Zalvidea fumed from San Gabriel about Los Angeles in 1816: "That [pursuit] to which everyone dedicates himself is to go about on horseback, put in grapevines, hiring a few gentiles for this purpose, teach them to get drunk, and then take jars of *aguardiente* ["firewater" or brandy] to Christian Indians."

More than just a tirade against the civil settlements, Zalvidea's words portended much about the final outcome of those Indian peoples whom missionization assaulted. The Indian peoples of the California coast from the San Francisco Bay area to the south responded in different ways to the Spanish incursion. Ultimately, though, the Spanish presented them with "a time of little choice," as Randall Millikin has put it. "People's loss of faith in the feasibility of continuing their traditional ways within the context of a new reality" meant that with "both dread and hope" they had to abandon their old ways, usually by moving into a mission. Unlike those in the interior or the far north of California, ones out of reach of the Spanish and who maintained their tribal integrity for much longer, members of disease-ravaged villages or ones that emigration to the missions had disarranged, often attached themselves to the pueblos or presidios. As regards Indians near the pueblo of Los Angeles, "the Indians underwent social disintegration precisely because," as George Harwood Phillips put it in his path-breaking research, "they had become tightly integrated into the pueblo's economic structure." Disease and cultural unraveling pushed them from their villages, and the dubious opportunity of becoming the primary labor force for the town pulled them in. Indeed, "what little progress is being made," reported Padre Señan about the pueblo, "must be credited to the population of neighboring gentile rancherias and not to the settlers. The Indians cultivate the fields, do the planting, and harvest the crops."[6]

In 1784 Pedro Fages, now governor and adversary of the mission strategy for the settlement of California, granted lands to veterans he had commanded as captain of the San Diego Presidio. He explained to his superiors in Mexico:

That the cattle are increasing in such manner, that it is necessary in the case of several owners to give them additional lands; they have asked me for some *sitios* which I have granted provisionally, namely to Juan José Domínguez who was a soldier in the presidio of San Diego on the river below San Gabriel, to Manuel Nieto for a similar reason that of La Zanja on the highway from said mission . . . and to the sons of the widow Ignacio Carrillo that on the deep creek contiguous to the foregoing.

More than a response to the increase of the retired soldiers' herds, these provisional grants entitled these *inválidos* to use land as a reward for their service to the Crown. Californios ultimately came to assume the permanency of these ambiguous concessions, and they fatefully began the process by which many of them would replace the missions and missionaries as the grandees of the frontier California landscape. Fewer than 20 grants were awarded before the birth of the Mexican Republic in 1821.[7]

About half of these were located within one hundred miles of the little pueblo of Los Angeles, a few were near Monterey, and all of them were imprecise in the actual terms of the boundaries and of the grantees' tenure: most included the phrase *más o menos* (more or less) in the description of the confines. Before trade began to flourish with Yankee ships in the late 1820s and before the end of the missions (1834) would free up an Indian labor force, rancho life was quite coarse. In one of the famous *recuerdos*, José del Carmen Lugo recalled the rustic beginnings of such grand domains as Rancho San Antonio near Los Angeles granted to his father (an ex-soldier from the Santa Barbara Presidio): "The house on a little ranch was of rough timber roofed with tules. It rarely had more than two rooms." People slept on cots or "beds of cottonwood or poplar, lined with leather." The presence of "sheets, blankets, coverlets, pillows, and so on," depended on "the resources of the owner."

Regardless of social standing, everyone lived with scads of fleas. The Indians in the days before the Europeans had simply torched their grass huts every few months and then built new ones as the fleas smoldered in the charred remains. Anyone who has ever lived in California with a pet knows about the endurance and fertility of the fleas. Imagine the place with all those cows and horses, and all those dogs who feasted on the offal, and no bug bombs. "The fleas, bugs, and other vermin, which infested our miserable lodgings," testified an American traveler in 1846, "had caused me a sleepless night by goring my body until the blood oozed from the skin in countless places."

The number of ranchos doubled in the decade after Mexican independence, and they actually began to compete with the missions in production of trade goods, and even more intensely for the devotion of the Indians along the southern coast. As early as 1795, Fray Vicente Santa María noted how the Indians were "fond of the Pueblo of Los Angeles, of the rancho of Mariano Verdugo, of the rancho of Reyes, and of the (rancho of the) Zanja." Preferring the easier life of the rancho over the discipline of the missions, the Indians went about "clad in shoes, with sombreros and blankets, and serving as muleteers to the settlers and rancheros."[8]

It was not simply as laborers that the Indians served the Californios. As they emerged from their modest beginnings at the presidios, the largely mestizo and sometimes mulatto grantees came to refer to themselves as *gente de razón*, or "people of reason." This self-conception can only be understood in the context of its opposite, those *sin razón* or "without reason," Indians that is. Originally the Spanish Inquisition created this concept, most certainly associated with childish inability to distinguish right from wrong as regards theology or deeds, to explain and release Indians from culpability for heretical actions. Positively defined in Mexican California, the phrase gente de razón came to refer to anyone who was Catholic and Spanish-speaking, and who renounced instinctual behavior in favor of service to work, community, and the Crown.

Negatively, it came to contrast a resident of California with anyone who behaved like an "Indian," or how an Indian was imagined to be. The Californios' self-serving construction of the Indian bore little resemblance to the complex spiritual and productive lifeways that the natives had developed over time but derived from the Indians' degradation in the missions, or from those outside the missions who resisted, often with violence, further encroachments on their lands and livelihoods.

This notion, not what Indians' facial features looked like, formed the primary caste distinction in Alta California. The mulatto and mestizo Don Pío Pico, or the mestizo Governor José Figueroa, or one like Don Manuel Domínguez who was so dark that he was banned from testifying in court after the American Conquest, were all considered de razón. Sín razón were the Indians tyrannized in the missions, raiding in the wild, or in disarray in the pueblo and, later, both the uncouth lower-class immigrants known as *cholos* and the vulgar American trappers who wandered into California.

While the emergent Californios valued the efforts of the padres to make the neophytes de razón, they came to see only futility and fault in the mission compounds. Pressure mounted against the despotic missions, which were obviously failing to transform the Indians, which occupied so much land, and which seemed most intent on monopolizing political and economic power in the territory. "It is just that twenty-one mission establishments possess all the fertile lands of the peninsula," complained Mariano Vallejo, "and that more than a thousand families of gente de razón possess only that which has been benevolently given them by the missionaries." According to Peruvian-born criollo[9] Juan Bandini, "indeed the system of these missions is the most appropriate to retard their [the Indians'] mental development," and "the missions extend their possessions in one continuous line although not needing the land for their crops and herds." The pressure of the gente de razón combined with the waxing and waning faith of Mexican elites in liberal ideology to secularize the missions. This process, which Governor Figueroa initiated in 1834, set the stage for the blossoming of Californio society. Now, with the missions converted into mere churches, stripped of their estates and control over the Indians, the most fertile lands and thousands of laborers were freed from what Figueroa called "monastic despotism."[10]

The administration of Governor José María de Echeandía (1825–1831) had marked the introduction of Liberalism in Alta California. "When he arrived in California in 1825," Angustias de la Guerra Ord commented, "he came speaking of the republican and liberal principles which filled the heads of Mexicans in those days." This actually inflexible and quirky man encouraged study groups in the north that excited several young men — most notably José Castro, Mariano Vallejo, and his nephew Juan Bautista Alvarado — about these ideas of liberty and equality. According to Alvarado, Echeandía's encouragement of the ideas of the Enlightenment and of education for all fostered "the true principles of republicanism and liberty" among these young men, concepts that directly and profoundly challenged the reigning beliefs emanating from the missions.[11]

Much as in America with slavery and its legacy of racism, in Mexico the role of the Indian in its caste-based society confounded the liberal vision of "life, liberty, and the pursuit of happiness." Upon independence, Mexico initiated its Plan de Iguala, which, while bound up with rivalries between various factions, sought to solve the Indian problem with one sweeping measure: the new Mexican Republic simply declared everyone born there a citizen, Indians and all. All communities were to set up to be democratic and enjoy the Rights of Man, and private property was to prevail, which the largest landholder in Mexico — the Church — naturally opposed.

Indian people revolted against the imposition of the private freehold and the challenge that political and economic competition presented to their communal land-tenure system and spirit world. Revolts of the Yaquis and Tarahumaras in the north only proved to many that Indians were incapable of enlightenment or, worse yet, that they remained loyal to Spain. In the 1850s, the several Laws of the Reform sought to break up Indian communes in favor of private property and commercial farming. These efforts of Mexico's most famous and revered president, the enlightened Zapotec Indian Benito Juárez, resulted in more revolt and, once made into private property, the alienation of Indian lands to European and American capitalists.

The rule of law enables this practice of liberty and freedom. Being able, in other words, to act, think, and produce in, ideally, good ways without the restraints of autocrats and arbitrary decrees relies on people voluntarily submitting themselves to the rule of law, which, importantly, they must see as legitimate, and this law, then, guarantees their liberty and protects them from those who might do them harm.

This system derives not from ideology and rhetoric but from the conduct of daily life. That, in turn, has most to do with history and the evolution of culture: neither Indians nor Californios had been prepared for this sort of liberty and freedom. Indians along the coast of California and many places in Mexico had indeed been freed up from their lands and disconnected from their spirit world, but the outcome was not liberty but disarray. The place in time that the Californios occupied prescribed hierarchy based upon sex and body deportment, fealty to the Church, and deference to prominent families. Imported oratory was not about to change these standards.

Californios were, above all else, de razón, people who had renounced instinct. José Antonio de la Guerra, actually an ally of the missions, ex-commandant of the Santa Barbara Presidio, and then grandee of the area and father of the previously cited Angustias, recited how "the Holy

Father . . . gave man reason in order to understand, appetite in order to love, liberty in order to work with merit . . . He gave faith to govern reason, charity in order to guide and balance his appetite, and grace in order to strengthen his liberty." These mellifluous words express the views of an elite and may or may not have been taken to heart by most of Californio society. We will see, though, that not much of Californio society practiced these sonorous values.

Liberalism was certainly not for Indians. "Equality before the law," explained Figueroa, "taken to such extremes, would throw society into upheaval."[12] In the Californios' view, secularization would not make of the Indians free and independent citizens, something for which the missions had not prepared them anyway. Of course, Indians would be scofflaws; having had no hand in the formulation of the laws nor seeing the civil authorities as in any way legitimate, the Indian peoples of California, missionized or not, did not submit themselves to Spanish, Mexican, or American laws, which made them appear all the more unreasonable. Seeing the natives as sín razón contradicted Liberalism's concepts of liberty and equality but was essential to insure and to justify that the ex-mission Indians would remain in the lower caste and subservient. Thus it was that the Indians figured in such important and complicated ways in the Californios' lives: contrasting their lives with Indians would reassure them that they were de razón; the ill-fated Indian participation in the despotic missions proved the latter's utter failure; and quickly the Indians would become the actual producers on the great ranchos.

Californios and Indios

While we behold many of the compelling manifestations of life in the Rancho Period in these descriptions, one of the bases of Californio society has only dimly emerged here: this was a society based on the work of others. These became halcyon days as recalled in the recuerdos and in the later histories because men who presumed entitlement to the service of women and especially people of color mostly chronicled them.

By the water holes and the corrals where the herds lingered, Indian laborers lived in their *rancherías* (settlements) in *jacales* made of tules and sticks tied together and stuck in the mud, or else they lived in the *indiada*, or servants' quarters. Some of these natives had attached themselves to ranchos after the secularization of the missions, others had entered service on the ranchos as their remnant indigenous societies crumbled under the Spanish onslaught, and some few others had even been captured in the wild and given over to the rancheros for what Carlos Híjar called "training."[13]

Life on the ranchos did not require the discipline characteristic of the missions; labor on the ranchos was hard but not consistently demanding, and no one worked very diligently anyway. For their labors they received food, clothing, or perhaps a few hides, which they so often traded for drink. Central to the construction of Californio society was the continuing destruction of California Indian society. Those were, after all, Indian lands, which the missions had appropriated for the Spiritual Conquest, upon which the cows and horses now grazed. Yet those very Indians did so much of the work, whether the tending and slaughter of cows; the building of palatial homes and digging of ditches (the *ayuntamiento* of Los Angeles prescribed labor on the public ditches for Indians convicted of drunkenness); or the washing, cooking, sweeping, and serving of pampered guests under the direction of the doña.[14]

Having an Indian to work for you was not limited to the wealthy. Extrapolating from the censuses of 1836 and 1844 for Los Angeles, Michael González calculates that "there would have been at least two peones for each of the 86 households who needed workers." The work relationship no doubt would often be informal and transitory, but *angeleños* generally lived with some intimacy with the Indians who had attached themselves to the pueblo. Similarly, the smaller ranchos, the majority, had an indigenous laborer or two.[15]

It's more difficult to know about Indian life on a rancho. At Rancho Petaluma, north of San Francisco in Sonoma County, hundreds of Indians worked for the Vallejo family. We can know from the archeological record that they continued to use chert and obsidian for flake tools and arrowheads, that they decorated their clothing with glass beads, and that they integrated metal containers, utensils, and sewing items,[16] but it is harder to know about their spiritual practices, their sense of retrospect about their past lives or prospect about their future ones, and their conversations as they labored for the Vallejo family. It will come as a surprise to those who only reflect upon artifacts, or who think that the end of the ranchos meant the end of the Indians, that near present-day Petaluma several Pomo speakers still re-tell the old stories of Coyote that their grandmothers told them, ones that "put a point across about how we were to behave in the world." Maidu, Miwok, and Pomo people, whose ancestors likely worked at Rancho Petaluma, are relighting the fires at Roundhouse ceremonies and re-creating the dances.[17] There are still these stories and ceremonies, yes, it's just that I want to know what they talked about during and after work at the rancho, what was in their hearts, or if their souls felt at all at peace.

Californio society relied on the Indians to confirm their own mastery of instinctual behavior. In 1824, Chumash people of the missions Santa Barbara, Santa Inez, and La Purísima revolted. Mostly the nastiness of the soldiers sparked the revolt, but carnality reigned when the mission-ized Indians "exchanged their women for those of the gentiles, without distinction as to married and unmarried women."[18]

It is not for us here to discuss matters of sexual virtue and vice or the consequences of involuntary sexual repression but rather to emphasize the dread and trepidation with which the gente de razón would have seen such an episode. Think about how modern people armed with psycho-analytic theory or romantic notions about escaping the confines of bour-geois monogamy, or opponents of imperialism and monotheism, would think about such an episode, and then imagine exactly the opposite — that is how nineteenth-century Spanish Catholics would have thought about the event, this multi-faceted spectacle of rebellion against God and Christian morality. It's not just that they would have found the behavior of Indians abhorrent, which they did, it's that they were so concerned as mestizo people — a mix of Spanish and Indian — that they were them. An interesting twist in our narrative of racial thinking, no doubt.

Once freed from the missions in the years after 1834, except for a few who remained in the dramatically diminished mission compounds, the Indians remained resolutely, in the Californio mind, sin razón. Missioni-zation had usually only succeeded in destroying the intricately forged old ways, replacing them with, at best, a tenuous new sense of discipline. Secularization all too often left the Indians without much social organi-zation, a situation that the gente de razón all too indulgently exploited. For too many Indians around the pueblos and presidios, the harsh truth is that drunkenness and vice most apparently manifested the shock of European supremacy and visibly demonstrated to the gente de razón that the Indians remained unsalvageable.

Those who avoided conquest, groups such as the Cahuilla to the east of Los Angeles or the Yokuts of the San Joaquin Valley, roamed the interior and often raided and terrorized what the Californios regarded as their outpost of civilization. Perhaps even more wicked in the minds of the gente de razón, Indians who fled the missions after secularization often banded with these peoples still "in the wild." Recall here de la Guerra's felicitous words on the meaning of de razón: none of them he would have applied to Indians. Thus their irredeemable nature not only ordained their servitude, but qualified Indians to serve as caricatures of everything that the de razón thought they were not. Ascendant Californios, often mestizo, were, in other words, gente de razón because they were not Indians.

The presentation of women's bodies most dramatically represented the differences between gente de razón and Indians. "En aquel tiempo," declared Juana Machada, "las indias no se vestían sino llevaban una cubierta de pieles de conejo para cubrir sus vergüenzas."[19] That Indian women wore a loincloth of rabbit skins does not tell us much of significance. But that these *pajales* were not considered "dressing" and that they covered what Machada called their "shamefulls" reveals much about the role of dress in creating and maintaining distinctions between the peoples of California and about Californios' ideas about what was disgraceful and repulsive.

That they grabbed so much land after secularization meant that Californios would continue to contest with Indians "in the wild" for those lands to which Indians still laid claim. Furthermore, with lands available for hunting and foraging always receding, these Indians reasonably and fittingly saw cows and horses grazing upon their lands as legitimate quarry for their subsistence. As would be the case in the American period, law and justice would be quite at odds; indeed, "law" can very much be seen as the means of injustice for Indian peoples. The secularization of the missions, the granting of ex-mission lands to Californios, and then the criminalization of Indian trespass on those lands all happened via the Mexican legal system. It would be preposterous to expect that Indians would thus adhere to Mexican law, and easy to see how they would always be outside the law and, in the eyes of the gente de razón, lawless.

These factors produced a constant situation of raiding and revenge between Californios and the Indians who still ranged free. This was one way in which the Californios forged a collective identity — they were a people whom hostile forces besieged and from whom their incapable parent, Mexico, could not rescue. Brutal fights with the Indians resolutely shatter the peaceful, genteel pastoral imagery of Californio society.

Historical perspective facilitates an awareness of how the Indians' desperation derived from the consequences of coercive missionization and how their violent actions resisted invasion and conquest. Californios understood the Indian raids as criminal acts and proof of de razón virtue for protecting civilization from, in Governor Alvarado's words, "bárbaros infieles" (barbarous infidels).

The governor received a letter in 1839 from Señor Arguello in Los Angeles exclaiming how "the number of Indians who have run away to take up criminal pursuits is so great that the entire southern district is paralyzed." The San Diego area most spectacularly experienced the Indians' desperate fury. Raiders, erstwhile occupants of the lands, plundered most ranchos there at one time or another in the late 1830s, and rancheros periodically evacuated to the town for safety. In 1837, Rancho Jamul, home to Doña Eustaquia de Pico (mother of Pío and Andrés) underwent the most sensational episode in Indian-Californio relations. Attackers assassinated Mayordomo Leyva and several defenders and kidnapped Leyva's two daughters, who were never seen again. This widely related story of the time melodramatically trumpeted the threat Indians posed to the gente de razón, especially to Californio society's most prized and guarded possessions, its females.[20]

Disease — such as the devastating epidemics in the San Joaquin Valley of 1833 (likely malaria) or the smallpox catastrophe of 1837 in Sonoma — killed far more Indians than swords or guns in all periods of California history, but this is not to say that many Indians did not meet death at the hands of raging caballeros. British voyager Sir George Simpson could not help noticing when he visited in 1841–1842 how "the Indians of all tribes are, from day to day, rendered more audacious by impunity. Too indolent to be always on the alert, the Californians overlook the constant pilferings of cattle and horses, til they are aroused beyond the measure of even their patience, by some outrage of more than ordinary mark."[21]

At these moments, for which such incidents as that at Rancho Jamul had been contributing tinder, Californio gente took leave of their reason and the rule of law and exploded into violence against people they called, among other things, *bestias* (beasts). Typical of retaliations against Indian raids throughout the Americas, the peaceful natives suffered the wrath of the righteous avengers. No Zorro would come to save them. In 1839 José Palomares of San Jose retaliated for what he called "the murder of gente de razón." He surrounded an Indian sweat lodge and torched it: "Men, women, and children were there in confusion [and] from one moment to the next, one heard more and more the terror and screams of pain." Late in 1845, José del Carmen Lugo arranged an ambuscade in league with his allies, Temecula Indians under the leadership of Juan Antonio, near a pillaged Lugo family rancho near San Bernardino. He claimed that he ordered his men "to fire only at the fighters because they were the chiefs and came only in the middle of the main body." Still, "we made a great slaughter, and falling upon them from the rear killed many of them." "On reaching Aguanga we amused ourselves killing some three Indians who continued fighting," he related. "Perhaps a hundred Indians perished."[22]

This is another reality of the quick, personalist justice that we associate with Zorro and Rancho California.

You see, we could name this not as the "Rancho Period," but as the "First Indian War Period." (The era of Ramona would be the Second Indian War Period of California history.) Who would that put at the center of our concern and consideration?

There are other profound ways in which the Californios intensely reflected the rest of Mexico's wrestling with Indians, namely the issue of what I have come to call "the Indian without and the Indian within." Think of all these things that the Indians represented to the Californios — servants and raiders, foils and relatives. Then recall that most of the Californios were mestizo, part Spanish and part Indian. The Californios were themselves part of what they so degraded, despised, and feared. Rancho California has mostly come to us through versions of Zorro, *Ramona*, Fiesta Day parades, postcards of Old Town San Diego and Olvera Street. All of them, except for *Ramona*, utterly exclude these several matters of the Indian in favor of casting the Californios as Spanish. Religion, clothing, work, sex, violence — it was all about the Indian without, but there was that same Indian within.

Just WHAT were Californios obliterating when they senselessly slaughtered Indians?[23]

So many Indians died in the Spanish and Mexican periods, and then even more in the American Period; some few remained loyal to the Church and continued on the landscape as "Mission Indians"; others, those in isolated areas of California, such as the Pomo or Maidu people of northern California, maintained some tribal integrity on their rancherías; many of those who fled the missions and then drifted from the ranchos joined their brethren still "in the wild," who themselves were being pushed further and further into harsh lands of the interior; others have lived in small neighborhoods such as Piru between San Fernando and Ventura, and 1,600 Juaneño people await federal recognition in Orange County, though the state of California affirmed their status in 1993; Luiseño bands such as Pechanga, Soboba, and La Jolla have used their casino money for cultural revitalization, and you can visit them on the Web; yet other individuals, especially in Southern California and experiencing several generations of mixing, became part of that grand project of Mexican culture, the making of the mestizo/a. There is no single story to tell of the California Indians.

Liberty and Indian Lands

The Colonization Act of 1824 and a supporting reglamento of 1828 intended to encourage immigration to the far northwestern department, but it was secularization of the missions that actually made the civil settlements, especially the rancho, the dominant economic and social institutions on the California landscape. In the 13 years between secularization and the American possession, the Mexican governors of California made a stunning eight hundred grants, mostly to Californios. It would appear that individuals simply applied to the governor for a grant, and in the context of Mexico's eagerness to fill the land with loyal citizens in light of the apparent designs of the United States and other nations for the prize of California, millions of acres were simply given away to earnest settlers. Actually, intense political intrigue had positioned only certain people to benefit from the largesse.

In the first place, the male children born to the original settlers and presidial soldiers, *hijos del país*, had successfully asserted control over the affairs of California. In the context of the new republic's regional disunity, economic distress, and political instability, Mexico became the errant mother or, as Governor Alvarado put it, the "stepmother," of California. And, as in New Mexico, Mexico wanted to collect revenues from its province, but neither would, nor even could, send troops to fight Indians. Increasingly, the hijos del país came to understand themselves as Californios, and recent immigrants as *mexicanos* and *extranjeros*. California became their *patria*, and Mexico an increasingly alien place. Actually, this sort of alienation from the new republic is a very Mexican activity in the mid-nineteenth century.

This sentiment crystallized in the Manifesto a la República Mejicana, a series of documents that Governor Figueroa assembled and which were widely circulated in California after 1834. It affirmed regional control over disposition of the ex-mission lands and California's territorial sovereignty — an interesting problem should, say, England or the United States attack California. This emerging consciousness provided the separatist climate in which the Californios stormed against governors Mariano Chico and Nicolas Gutiérrez who had both been sent from Mexico in 1836 by the centralist, conservative government. The former arrived with his "niece," who was obviously his mistress, and the latter with a coterie of Indian concubines. Their reigns had much to do with arguments over Liberalism and then federalism versus centralism, issues that raged all the more fiercely in Mexico just like the United States contended over federalism versus states rights. Particularly decisive, in late 1836, Juan Bautista Alvarado, leader of the insurgency against Chico and Gutiérrez and an hijo del país, assumed the governorship of California.[24]

As the momentous and decisive war between the United States and Mexico loomed, it is worthwhile to think about how parallel the two countries' histories had become. Threats of secession accompanied tendencies toward centralization of authority in the national capitals. Both wrestled with the matter of whether or not the authorities of family, church, and property should rule or whether everyone should vote. Mexico outlawed slavery in 1829 but maintained other systems of servitude. Indian peoples continued to resist either conquest or assimilation. Both countries relied on military force to attempt to defeat indigenous people who apparently stood in the way of their material and social progress. Indian lands represented opportunity for people of both the American and Mexican frontiers.

Inconsistent with some of the images of graciousness and indolence to which the introductory passages of this narrative introduced us, once the missions were closed up, the gente de razón swarmed over the mission lands, ones technically held in trust for the Indians, just as energetically as did the flies over the cowpies in the mission pastures. The governors of California appointed the hijos del país as commissioners and *mayordomos* of the ex-mission lands and of the Indians, to the great advantage of the Californios. "Of the administrators of the missions," stated de la Guerra Ord, "some were incapable, others without morality, and some, a very few, were men of good faith who did everything possible to conserve the properties." Mostly, the ex-mission lands became the property of hijos del país who grabbed them with little or no attention to Indian rights to those lands, or attention to the Indians' rancherías on or near the sprawling expanses. Liberalism, then, came to mean that Californios had rights to control private property and that no federal official could hinder or restrain them.

If they weren't thinking about Indians regarding land and work on the ranchos, the Californios were thinking about family. José Sepúlveda received from his father — the government-appointed administrator of San Juan Capistrano — a grant of mission lands in 1837, and then two more leagues in 1842. In that year ranchos el Niguel and la Cañada de los Alisos went to in-laws of the Sepúlvedas (there were many Sepúlvedas among Southern California rancheros; those of Rancho Palos Verdes are the most famous), and the previous year saw the granting of Rancho Trabuco to Santiago Argüello, after he too had been administrator of ex–Mission San Juan lands. Tomás and Bernardo Yorba were sons of former Sergeant Antonio Yorba, who in 1809 had received Rancho Santiago de Santa Ana, and who was one of the grandest of rancheros. Tomás received the only grant from San Juan lands not made to family members of administrators.

When Indians, or priests acting for them, contested the grants, civil authorities almost always ruled in favor of the gente de razón. When Bernardo Yorba petitioned in 1834 for a grant of ex–Mission San Gabriel lands, for example, a priest from the old mission denounced his efforts to the Los Angeles town council, claiming (properly) that the land belonged legally to the mission Indians. The ayuntamiento proclaimed the virtues of Bernardo's enterprise and validated his claim.[25]

Life on the Ranchos

Several factors converged to beget a particular style of life on these fabled ranchos. The availability of land and Indians to work on it, both resulting from the spoliation of the missions, along with trade with the Yankee ships, a seigneurial mindset, and a fecund environment, all combined to produce a particular society. Like all hoofed beasts, cows transform grasses, and these grew readily on the warm coastal landscape of California into protein for carnivores and omnivores. Later in the century, one Anglo traveler would see at San Gabriel "herds of cattle, lying down, as if oppressed by surplus food." The routine slaughter of a few cows could amply feed everyone attached to a rancho. In these most majestic days of the ranchos, the cows' only exchange value, though, derived from their hides and tallow.

We can only know approximately what quantities were loaded on the American and English ships and exchanged for manufactured goods from the North Atlantic — perhaps a million and a quarter hides and sixty million pounds of tallow between 1826 and 1848. Yet it should be easy to imagine the lifestyle that the trade for cows raised on the nearly half-million acres belonging to the de la Guerras in the Santa Barbara area, on the nearly quarter-million acres of the several Yorba families, or even on the seventy thousand acres that Joaquin Estrada occupied in Monterey County. The Lugo and Avila families probably grazed between forty thousand and twenty thousand head respectively, and in the north the grandee of Sonoma County, Mariano Vallejo, husbanded twenty-five thousand cows, twenty-four thousand sheep, and two thousand horses on his nearly three hundred thousand acres. The several dons of the Pico family claimed seven hundred thousand acres.[26]

The dramatic size of some of these ranchos should not obscure the fact that most Californios occupied modest-sized ranchos. Then, too, many of them labored as ranch foreman or as artisans in the pueblos. The hides that these Californios of the middling sort either raised or with which they were often paid allowed them a lifestyle that received little remark from outsiders who called them "middle class," if they had land, or "greasers," if they did not.[27]

History, place, and culture, though, resolve what sort of society a particular group of people will create from their productive endeavors. The dons did not transform the bovine produce of the land into anything resembling "capital," that is, the sort of machinery or land that would generate more profit and wealth. Instead, they sought trade goods to facilitate a particular style of life. With the Yankee traders aboard ship or those who had set up mercantile shops in the towns, they bartered hides and tallow, typically for "the cheapest rebozos for the Indian women . . . [and] pieces of 'Indian cloth' " to clothe their laborers, and for such luxury goods as silk dresses, laces, necklaces, muslin pants, window glass, metal knives and forks, furniture, and even books for themselves. From the hides and tallow, New England manufacturers made candles and shoes, even cheap ones for sale to slave plantations.

We see here how American economic elites thought in terms of generating "capital," that is, productive machinery that could generate yet more goods and profit, while Mexican landed elites in California set their sights no higher than on exchange of goods. What they bought served not merely for comfort, but for show.[28]

The meanings evoked in the word "seigneurialism" best represent the society that evolved from those rough beginnings on those first ranchos. Affirmation of social standing, not the mere accumulation of goods and capital, motivated the Californios' aspirations for land, production, and trade. Payment in kind and the relations of reciprocal obligation attached the poor — the landless — to both the wealthy and the middling sort — the landed. Notions of honor bound wives to husbands and children to parents. Fealty to the Church brought about good behavior. This was not a liberal society.[29] People exist in relation to the spirit world, their families and enemies, politics and ideologies, labor, and their desires for pleasure. Each of these became remarkable manifestations of the Californios' seigneurialism.

José del Carmen Lugo — son of one of the first soldier grantees, Antonio María Lugo, who received in 1810 Rancho San Antonio situated in present-day Los Angeles — told how "everyone was expected by the government to fulfill the obligations of the Church. Everyone except for the sick . . . had to attend mass on Sundays and other days of obligation." In Lugo's recollections everyone confessed, learned church doctrine, and received the sacraments. Lugo recalled how for the wealthy "the praying of their devotions" — which he claimed began upon awakening at 3:00 a.m. — initiated a family's day, and the nightly praying of the rosary concluded it. A saint's day, for example, provided an occasion for the expression of faith, exuberant festivities, and community solidarity.

Carlos Híjar recollected that in Santa Barbara, on the town's patron saint day, preparation would begin well in advance. In the morning, a solemn mass would be celebrated, followed by the ringing of bells and the firing of cannons. In the afternoon would be a bull fight (actually people and a bull chasing one another around an arena), or a bull-and-bear fight. (This was one of the most curious and unique customs of the Californios — pitting a bull against a captured bear and cheering the grisly outcome.) Dancing and drinking brandy (at least for the men) would last several more days.[30] The authority of the Church remained strong in Mexican California, despite the wavering intrusion of Liberalism. Their celebrations of faith glorified not only God but the Californios' communities, affections, and affectations.

Virtues and Vices

Family life for the land-owning elite—the ones who set the standards in these matters—took place firmly within this seigneurial mentality. Ideally, respect and honor prevailed between the patriarch and the rest of his family. Customarily, women and children submitted to the will and judgment of men, but a father was reciprocally obligated to consider his charges' needs and wishes as he directed the family and production. José María Amador, recipient of a vast land grant in present-day Santa Clara and Alameda counties, described explicitly how he conceived of Californio men in the early Rancho Period, and implicitly the ideal type: "In the years before 1830, the men were of good habits with few exceptions—without prejudice there were cases of prostitution, drunkenness, games of chance, and abandonment of families—these things existed but scarcely."

Everyone, everywhere seems to glorify the past. Amador seems to forget about when in 1785 Eulalia Callis sued to be released from her marriage to Governor Pedro Fages. "It is the case," she fumed, "that I found my husband physically on top of one of his servants, a very young Yuma Indian girl." At the urging of Nicolas Soler, assistant inspector of the presidios, the two reconciled.[31]

Bancroft tells the story of a soldier who had ruined a girl and refused to make her his wife, was confined in a fort in irons, and forced to pay her $50 out of his savings in the *fondo de retención*. As a little town like Los Angeles grew, so too did the number of complaints that people brought to the *juicio de concilio*, or conciliation court. In 1843, "having caught my husband in flagrante delicto with Nicolasa Carreaga," Marta Reyes asked the court to banish his lover, the *amasa*. Francisca Perez, claiming that another woman had "caused my husband's infidelity and refusal to support me," made the same request the next year.

Courts acted harshly against women adulteresses and when violence accompanied infidelity. In 1842 Ramona Vejar told the alcalde[32] that "my husband, Tomas Urquides hits me because of Dolores Valenzuela [with whom he] has been living . . . for more than two years." Witnesses corroborated her story and that Urquides had fathered a child with Valenzuela. The judges banished Valenzuela and her child to a *casa de honor*, but only reprimanded Urquides and fined him 10 pesos.

It was not just, in 1829 or 1830, "that a soldier of the Monterey company was holding illicit relations with a woman and her daughter at the same time, and that the latter was pregnant by him," or "that the soldier was made to marry the pregnant woman," but that after their trial "the man and the woman . . . were compelled to kneel near the presbytery, in full sight of the public, bound together by the neck with a thick hempen rope, and having before them a washtub filled with green grass, representing the manger of a stable, to signify that the man and woman had been living like beasts," and that "Father Abella delivered remarks from the pulpit relevant to the subject . . ." Justice came not from Zorro, but as in a Zorro story, "the couple afterward lived happily together."[33]

There was also quick, personalist justice in Los Angeles in the case of two lovers, María del Rosario Villa and Gervasio Alipas, in 1836. Villa had left her husband, Domingo Félix, in favor of Alipas in 1834. Félix and the courts sought reconciliation, but Alipas stabbed Félix to death as the faithlessly reunited marrieds left the reconciliation meeting. After the body was found, a group of 55 gente de razón grabbed the couple, shot them to death, and displayed their bodies in another display of Zorro-style personalist Californio justice. They did so not just for vengeance but because, in the words of their declaration, "immorality has reached such an extreme that public security is menaced and will be lost if the dike of a solemn example is not opposed to the torrent of atrocious perfidy." Nothing could be worse than Sra. Villa, "that abominable monster who cruelly immolated her importunate husband in order to give herself up without fear to her frantic passions."[34]

The censuses of 1836 and 1844 listed 13 and 35 women with "MV" after their names indicating that they lived "malas vidas" (sinful lives). These and many other instances indicate that such breaches of public decency happened regularly and that the culture and civil authorities considered them sufficiently deviant to punish them, however erratically. Actually though, as Miroslava Chávez-García has shown, these sorts of castigations translated into an illegitimacy rate lower than in other places in Latin America, actually about half that of Mexico City. Such policing of the lower class enforced morality relatively effectively. Honorable men protected women and did not treat people who were de razón disrespectfully, mostly.[35]

Juan Bautista Alvarado, the first hijo del país to become governor, maintained his mistress in an adobe house on Dutra Street in Monterey. He had five daughters with her, whom he acknowledged by giving them his last name. He had at least one other child outside of his marriage, the product of a liaison in Los Angeles, and Pío Pico stood as godparent for it. "Generally speaking Alvarado was sober, taciturn, without affection, generous and gentlemanly in his behavior but occasionally he drank spiritous liquors," said a Chilean friend of the governor. Then "he lost all judgment and no power could keep him within bounds. He . . . destroyed everything he could lay his hands on — not until after the excess prostrated him did he recover his senses — he then, ashamed of himself, remained for a long time secluded in his house, thinking over his business and attending to his family." He was too drunk to attend his own inauguration and even his own wedding, for which he sent his half-brother as proxy.[36]

Other elite men led similarly profligate lives. Bernardo Sepulveda had six children with his wife, María Verdugo, and five with his mistress, Josefa Dominguez. Teodosio Yorba had eight children with his mistress, Ynocencia Reyes, but only one with his wife Maria of the famous Lugo family. (After his wife's death, Teodosio married Ynocencia.)[37]

Unlike the executed adulterers, the passions of these men did not represent aberrant behavior. Instead, their actions reinforced racial and sexual hierarchies, maintained the nuclear family, and did not threaten patriarchal control of women, children, and servants.

Californio men guarded nothing more closely than their daughters' honor, which, by extension, meant their families' honor. Lugo described a scene at once arcadian and suspicion-filled: "The boys (slept) in the outside porches, exposed to the weather, and the girls in a locked room, of which the parents kept the key, if there was any key." Other recuerdos confirm this practice, which paralleled the surveillance of neophyte females at the missions. Richard Henry Dana, whose comments about Californio manners and morals must be approached with distrust, did note that while "the instances of infidelity are much less frequent than one would at first suppose . . . , the very men who would lay down their lives to avenge the dishonor of their own family, would risk the same lives to complete the dishonor of another." Apparently, the rituals of seduction and revenge prevailed much less among Californio gente de razón than they did in New Mexico, yet we see here the complex association of patriarchal authority, prevarication about the renunciation of instinct, women's virtue, family virtue, and vice and faith among those who set the moral tone in California.[38]

Marriage took place firmly within the considerations of the family's fortunes. The recuerdos differ slightly on the thoroughness of parental

prerogatives regarding marriage. Híjar claimed that "these arrange-
ments took place only between the fathers of the children, and they tried
hard to keep them from learning of their plans." It could be, though, that
for some sons if a fancy arose at mass or a fiesta, they could usefully
make their preferences known.

The cleaner the blood, the greater the distance from instinctual deportment. Thus those without Indian blood, and indeed there were some
few, strove to keep their families that way, and those gente de razón with
Indian blood, quite apparent even in many of the leading families, sought
to distance themselves from it in various ways. On the day of her birth in
1777, the parents of María Antonia de Lugo promised her in marriage to
Ygnacio Vicente Vallejo, and at the time of menarche, when she was 14,
she married the ex-soldier, who was 40 years old. No Zorro to the
rescue. The reasoning behind this utter care about marriage emerges
when Vallejo, immediately after his marriage, petitioned for a decree of
legitimidad y limpieza de sangre, or "legitimacy and cleanliness of
blood." The decree, granted after 15 years, affirmed that the Vallejo
name had been untainted by Jewish, African, Indian, or any other non-
Christian blood. The intense concern was not lost on the three daughters
issued from this marriage, two of whom married Euro-Americans and
the other a Frenchman.

Similarly, the five legitimate daughters of the shamelessly womaniz-
ing and frequently besotted Governor Juan Bautista Alvarado, nephew
of Vallejo, all married Anglo Americans.[39] Marriage, in other words, was
quite bound up with racial thinking: it was one way that racial ideology
and ritual practice converged. Fearful of any association with putatively
naked, licentious, and alcoholic sin razón, Californio parents guided, or
even determined, their children's marriage partners not only on account
of property concerns but to guard closely "the blood."

Californio history, then, is not just about Indians, land and liberty,
and trying to be genteel; it's as much as anything about who is going to
have sex with whom.

Among other elite families matters proved more difficult. That most
prominent family of the south, the Picos, had running through their veins
the blood of Africans and Indians, and quite apparently so.[40] Another
grandee of the south, Manuel Dominguez, in the American Period could
not testify in court because of his Indian phenotype, in spite of the fact
that he was a signer of the new state constitution. In these cases we are
witnessing the other half of the Mexican raciological coin.

In Monterey, for example, between 1773 and 1778, 37 percent of marriages were interracial, mostly soldiers and Christianized Indian women. The Church encouraged this in part because it believed that all souls were equal in the eyes of God and in part to confine the soldiers' sexual energies to marriage. After that, the rate declined to about 15 percent.[41] What is so intriguing, in part because of its apparent contradictoriness, is that consciousness of "race purity," of being "pure Spanish," existed side-by-side with the practice of officially sanctioned race mixing. The Spanish priests' famous disregard of Indian phenotype — usually attributed to the Iberian Peninsula's history with the Moors — but huge disquiet over their nudity and idolatry, also figures into this cognitive mix. (Another obvious contradiction must be pointed out here: Iberians, Celts, Romans, Carthaginians, Sephardic Jews, Basques, Visigoths, and Moors have all peopled the Iberian landscape, making the notion of "pure Spanish" a curious one.)

Parents, especially fathers, could long for the days of "respect and obedience of children towards their parents in those times," as de la Guerra Ord put it, "because paternal authority was unlimited and did not cease even after the children married or even when they had their own children." A Frenchman who traveled to California in 1827 even noted how "seldom does one see a child of either sex sitting at the table of his father who, more often, eats alone, served by his wife, sons and daughters." Such decorum undoubtedly restrained behavior but did not necessarily preclude affection; fathers built toys and furniture for their infants, and relatives exchanged locks of their children's hair.[42]

"Riding on horseback and lounging lazily around is the gamut of their days," Juan Bandini told of the men in 1828, "and the women bear all the responsibility of the house." The men's recuerdos sang the praises of women for their labors: "A woman of the house," noted Lugo, was always in charge of milking cows (though it took several male servants to hold their feet and another to milk) "so that the milk would be clean and neat." "Women and the Indian servants under the direction of the former," he continued, "made *asaderas* [a sort of curds], cheese, butter, and a mixture prepared to be eaten with beans." To these tasks, Híjar added that they "busied themselves with their domestic duties, cut the wood necessary for the meal, sowed in their gardens the seeds indispensable to the household, using the hoe, pick, shovel etc., and went to the streams to wash under an arbor which they themselves made." An American traveler, Edwin Bryant, affirmed that "while the men are employed in attending to the herds of cattle and horses, and engaged in their other amusements, the women (I speak of the middle classes on the ranchos) superintend and perform most of the drudgery appertaining to house-keeping, and the cultivation of the gardens."[43]

Women, often Indians, did the healing. Eulalia Pérez, the Hispani-cized Indian who guarded the virtue of the neophyte women at Mission San Gabriel, recalled "María Ignacia Amador . . . She knew how to cook, sew, read and write, and to take care of the sick — she was a good *curan-dera* [healer]." The climate and the abundance of the land meant that people did not get sick much, but when they did they went largely to Indian practitioners who treated them with local herbs. The record indi-cates that treatments for arrow wounds were especially sought.[44]

The men rode horses. That this was a "cow and horse culture" refers to more than the primary trade goods and the means of herding them. Being *a caballo*, on a horse, meant that one was literally socially ele-vated, a caballero. Lugo affirmed that "no Indian who was not a vaquero was permitted to ride a horse." Dons not only supervised the herds and their Indian tenders on horseback, but raced other caballeros. Horse racing, and betting lavishly and sometimes destructively on the outcome, provided the outstanding pastime for the men of California.[45]

Indian raids confounded the relationship between horses and status. They not only developed a taste for horse meat, but they rode them as well: the Indians were now *a caballo* too, an elevated position not of eminence but of menace.

Not only the horse but the all-important matter of dress ceremoni-ously displayed the hierarchies of Californio society. The representa-tive *chaleco*, or men's waistcoat, and the short-sleeved and voluminous gowns of the women, along with their gilt-laced pantaloons, sashes, and necklaces and earrings for the ladies, were all purchased with hides sold to the Yankee traders. In the recuerdos, Californios' descriptions of their clothes ring with pride and lament for the lost days. In the later fanciful writings about "California pastoral," dress symbolized that which was so elegant and genteel.[46] In the Rancho Period it symbolized the aspira-tion of elite Californios — the affirmation of their status. Such was the goal of life and work on the ranchos grand and middling: tallow and hides and subsistence foodstuffs brought a prosperity that one displayed on one's body; a home in which to guide, protect, and sequester one's wife and children; and horses and clothing to project clearly one's dis-tinction both from the repugnant cholos, and from the dreaded, frustrat-ing, and frightening Indians.

The famous fiestas that the dons sponsored rendered more than diversion. These highly ritualized occasions gathered all elements of Californio society into a public spectacle in which elites wore their finery, supplied abundant food and copious drink, and danced with elegance. In other words, they displayed their wealth and status to their Indian laborers, the common folk, and themselves. "All the town was invited to participate," marveled Alfred Robinson about a de la Guerra family (into which he would soon marry) wedding in Santa Barbara, "when old and young, rich and poor, lame and blind, black and white, joined in the feast." A Californio recalled how they would "kill a calf a day" to feed the guests, another how "they served there wine in abundance," and another relished wine and brandy "without limit." Lugo recalled with gusto quite an array of dances and the etiquette of who would dance with whom: the elderly proceeded to the floor first, and young men and women never danced, according to Lugo, "without first having received permission" from their parents. The dances carried on with these formalities, and they did so often for several nights in a row, often a week if a daughter's wedding provided the occasion. Certainly such decorum waned as the old folks retired for the evening, and as the wine consumption waxed.[47]

The fiesta simultaneously bound the society together via the dispensing of food and drink, especially to the poor, at the same time that it proclaimed the prevailing hierarchies and glorified the status of the big man giving it. Those who appropriated the bounty of the land shared some of it with those who produced so much of it. Caste distinctions prevailed when people danced, or drank or courted, but everyone, at least in the first decade of the Rancho Period, mixed in the splendid amusement. It appears, though, that as California drew both more American merchants who quickly became prosperous, as well as more troublesome cholos, the fiestas of *la gente escojida* (the select) became increasingly exclusive.[48]

Californio society was a very personalist one; that is, people related to one another by means of an elaborate series of primary, personal relationships. This included the Californios' fabled and genuine hospitality. The recuerdos and the travelers' accounts all marvel at the eagerness with which "they literally vie with each other in devoting their time, their homes, and their means to the entertainment of a stranger," not to mention a friend, family member, or godparent. Upon the arrival of a guest, "the men would proceed to kill a calf to eat, a calf which they had run down and lassoed from the road, without noticing whether or not it

was theirs. They only were careful that the beast was fat and not tame."
This constant exchange bound society members in yet more webs of
reciprocity: "They all treated each other as cousins," noted Híjar (and
this also explains how they could connive so easily to control all of the
ex-mission lands); "they considered themselves as members of a single
family." Even the poor received donations of beef. Such generosity eased
considerably any social tensions which these tremendous disparities of
wealth might have created.[49] The Californios' munificence also reveals
how in this culture the more a man gave away, the more he increased his
social stature, which was, after all, a principal aspiration of these ex-
soldiers cum grandees.

It's all the opposite of Protestant capitalism: people gave away rather
than accumulated; money did not become capital but rather a means to
affirm status through display; Californios got to heaven through the
intermediary of the Church; they may have talked of individual liberty
but for the Californios not the prodigal son, but the dutiful one, the one
who would do as his father had done, would be the excellent one; sub-
mission to the patriarch on the rancho and the maintenance of racial and
sexual hierarchy displayed virtue; law could never have the regulatory
power of clan and the handshake between caballeros. This is more proof
to me that one can reject one's culture in favor of a new one, Liberalism
for instance, but you can't escape it.

This personalism also explains the passions of the Californios' legendary squabbles. It was not just that liberal ideas did not resonate
so positively in the south, or that the *abajeños* (literally "lowlanders")
were jealous of the preponderance of political power that the less-
populated north held, but rather that the regional leaders understood
one another to have violated family solidarity. Political differences were
personal affronts. The numerous revolts of the Californios (most notably against Governor Micheltorena, whom Mexico sent in 1842 to re-
establish authority) and violent schisms resulted in near–civil war in
1845. Pío Pico had been appointed governor and the capital moved to
Los Angeles, while his *arribeño* (literally "highlanders") enemies, military commander José Castro in Monterey and Mariano Vallejo from
Sonoma, controlled the north.[50]

It doesn't take much to realize that the Californio society and lifestyle that many people might desire, myself included, is largely the fantasy image of latter re-creations. Such constructions tell more about
people's yearnings than about the Californios. I will say that I love fiestas

and conversations, wine and barbequed meat. But it is especially the non-market social relations and leisure of the fanciful Californios that look particularly good these days when most everyone must be a real estate investor to have a nice place to live and then a compulsive earner of money — or a two-income family with a Mexican niñera — to afford it. How nice it would be to have time to drink wine and converse about something besides property values, to have relations with people based upon honor and trust, to have a Zorro to treat with injustice.

What we've seen here is that Californio society might have aspired to such gentility, and certainly evidenced traces of it, but it mostly wasn't these ways. Mostly it was a society based upon dishonorably dispossessing the Indians of their lands, having them work, and then having unmerciful and brutalizing fights with those who resisted. I suspect that many conversations had to do with abhorrence for the Indians both in their degraded state in and around the pueblos and ranchos and as the constant threat that they posed as they raided on their former lands. On many beautiful California nights, it would have been hard to sleep.

The study of history has annulled my childhood daydreams of an Old California paradise and personalist justice.

Then, too, study of the Californios has explained some things to me. Quite apparently the people of this era established the predominant ideas about who should work in the heat raising the food, cleaning domiciles, and doing the scut work of construction. What the missionaries began with their efforts to civilize the Indians by teaching them European-style labor, the Californios codified on their ranchos. In the nineteenth century's Second Indian War, when the Americans devastated even those Indians of the interior who had resisted Hispanic domination (one of the subjects of our next chapter about *Ramona*), came the Chinese, who were legally banished in the 1880s, to do the hard work. The new grandees of the land, the Americans, searched about for replacement and quickly found it south of the border. As we will be seeing as more of the stories of America and Mexico unfold, Mexico dolefully supplied the service and agricultural workers for California for the entire twentieth century. The fundamental notion of such labor in California and increasingly the United States — that dispossessed, powerless people should do it — derived from Mission and Rancho California.

To be so refined may not be so fun. I grow more convinced that in at least one powerful way Californio society paralleled nineteenth-century Victorian American society. All the while each declared that they had renounced "instinctual behavior," each was actually preoccupied with the sex act. Whom their children would do it with, how much the lower classes were doing it, displaying publicly those who did do it as animals in a manger, keeping their daughters from doing it, and whom the husbands were doing it with when the wives wouldn't do it, ceaselessly obsessed Californios and Victorians. Fathers locked their daughters up to insure that they would not have the wrong sons-in-law and that the daughter would be a sexual prize, a virgin, when she married. Such "purity" distinguished the socially elevated from the lower classes, but then, with sexual restraint the design for upper-class women, men went off and did it with Indian women, or Irish or black women on the East Coast, which meant that sex was all the more repugnant for upper-class women.

We hijos del país of the 1960s, usually blamed for the moral decay of America, need to be appreciated for challenging this Victorian/Californio legacy.

Such matters of the labor system and of sex are not what have usually defined Californio society, nor, really, have the wrestling over being mestizo and the wrangling over centralized versus state and territorial power. Yet these matters are what make Rancho California so Mexican. These stories of Rancho California define it as Mexican. It is curious indeed — some will find this threatening and others gratifying — that if it has been a Mexican place, then there is some potential for it to become one again, or maybe that is what is happening at this place in time.

Defining California history has much to do with California in the present. If California is the entrepreneurs who built San Francisco and Los Angeles in previous centuries, Disneyland and the pristine suburbs of the 1950s, the Beach Boys and Ronald Reagan of the 1960s, discos, gays, and AIDS of the 1970s and 1980s, then maybe it is a (flawed) paradise being overrun by immigrants. But maybe it has been a Mexican place all along, one where Mexicans are returning to the place of their ancestors, the Californios, the first self-defined Californians. In this way, when we have a living relationship to the past, when we re-define the past, we are engaged not only in discovery but in creating the present and the future.

This now-great metropolitan center of Los Angeles has its genesis in the religious and the civil, the sacred and the profane, but its growth and troubles and strengths have been about the issues associated with mixing. In this place where God and Church once dictated authority in the mission, and Holy Communion bound neophyte and Christian together, where neighbors (*vecinos*) had voluntarily entered into a civil arrangement in the cause of settling the place for the Crown and for production of subsistence, there has been at once conflict and accommodation, and separation and mixing.

And perhaps this is the Californios' most complex legacy we Californians have inherited — the simultaneous solidity and fluidity of identity. Californians then and now, mostly without realizing it, issue a challenge to those who maintain biological — "racial," that is — explanations for who people are and why they act the way they do. Californians evidence fascination with their bloodlines and continually contest over who's who because it can be such a fluid categorization. In 1840 and 1900, one could be the offspring of an Indian and a Californio, Mexican, or Anglo and be essentially Indian if she lived on a ranchería, or a place such as one of the Juaneño villages, with her mother; or he could be a Mexican if he lived with his father's Mexican family; or half-breed if he was let loose in one of the polyglot, often unfortunate, neighborhoods of a city. Such a person might live in an enclave with people who were mostly "Indian" but, especially during times of terrible fights with Indians, opt for the relative safety of being "Mexican," but then switch back when things calmed down. The social context and historical moment, then, has more to do with identity than biology or "race."

After some indeterminate number of generations, many of the descendants of this first great mixing would be essentially Hispano-Americano, neither Indian nor Iberian in culture but a hybrid, a mestizo. This was the great idea that, out of the wreckage of Spanish imperialism to which the Catholic Church had attached itself, came from the variously sanctified and base mixings of the Americas: the stunning idea that people were not one thing or the other, nor even some cross between two civilizations, but some new *mestizaje*, some new way of being altogether. This mixture has been one of the great tensions — sometimes creative, sometimes confusing — in Los Angeles and the other great Latin American cities of the New World.

There has been barbarism in this regard as well. We will soon be visiting the unthinking destructiveness of the California missions, we have witnessed something of what we might call the First Indian War Period, and we will soon know the even more horrible Second Indian War Period when we meet with Ramona and Alessandro. This is what Carey

McWilliams called "the Indian in the Closet," and what Palemón Zavala Castro from the other side of the border, referring to the Yaquis, called "El Indio Cajeme," or "the Indian in a Box."[51] In these cases, fluidity was rejected in favor of strict racial definition of Indians as "other," as people separate and unworthy of moral consideration. The conquest of the Indians, these "others," and how Mexico and America have come to feel these places are theirs, illustrates yet another way the two countries share a common history, this sequestered, hushed secret of what became of the Indians.

Thus it was that along one river did the vision of a society united by the One True God in the Mission San Gabriel contend with the town only a few leagues distant along another river, one motivated by the vision of an enlightened civil society. Both depended on the Indian. Some readers might want to know that, while the two rivers flow separately to the sea, the two places quickly and unalterably mixed into a world-famous city, the very one that arguably portends our urban future.

The Californios have bequeathed us an uncertain heritage, but one which we should engage. It's the competing truths again, the "ability to hold two opposed ideas in the mind at the same time," that will best equip us for the future of the New World Border. "And so they lived," with apologies to Bancroft, "opening their eyes" to the modern world but entangled in the gratifying bonds of the old; they believed in reason and gentility, and practiced lust and passion; they bought goods in the world market, the very one that would ruin their ranchos after the Americans came; they guarded their families, and alternately treated hospitably and raged against "each other, and ran up a fair (debit) in heaven."

Indeed, Californio society poses questions about the end purposes of life: labor or leisure? Familial conviviality or personal choice? Reciprocal obligations or the individual prerogatives of Liberalism? Racial hierarchy or biological and cultural mixing? When does economic vigor become conquest and domination? These are all weighty matters about which the Californios press us to reflect. Let us revel in this ambiguous legacy and the New World Border with the unfulfilled values of the Californios, the ones José Antonio de la Guerra penned: the values of charity, not vilification; of grace, not meanness and blaming; of reason, not fear; of liberty, to choose a better future; and faith, that life can be better.

Ramona, I Love You

Love for a landscape, what we might call *topophilia*, derives not so much from how a place looks but rather from our interactions with the place and the stories and songs we create to record our recollections and emotions associated with the place. It is the stories that bring a landscape to life for me and make it beautiful. Beauty is never simple: for a landscape to be alive, its stories must be alive, and things that are alive are always growing and changing. Sometimes the stories change in ways that nourish our emotional longings and fears. Sometimes the stories make for a fantasy heritage that dishonestly obscures what people actually did in history, and sometimes the stories hide ugly things about what happened in the place. We all have our stories. I will tell you now my tale of love and landscape.

When I was 17, a senior in high school in Los Angeles, I got the family Volkswagen as a combination Christmas and birthday present. It was a '64 with those little taillights and a 44-horsepower engine, but more important, in it I learned my first lessons about love. Furtive sex in the back seat, you might be thinking, but no — it was just kissing and listening to small tastes of Joe Tex, Percy Sledge, Solomon Burke, and Eddie Floyd, and large quantities of the Temptations, the Rolling Stones and their idol, Otis Redding, on the AM radio. Yes, readers, I'm referring here to Wolfman Jack's broadcasts from south of the border on station XERB. Those of you who never knew the Wolfman and XERB, skip it; you had to have been there. I can't convey in words this scene, driving around Hollywood late at night listening to the Wolfman, coming to know that one's little world is neither what it seems, nor all there is in life. This is the utopic vision of Southern California as paradise.

These were such fabulous songs of heterosexual love and devotion. Joe Tex sang "Show Me a Man Who's Got a Good Woman" and how you need to "Hold on to What You've Got"; Solomon Burke sang "Cry to Me"; Eddie Floyd, so full of thunder and lightning about his love that he told us how to "Knock on Wood" to keep it. Sam Cooke's "Bring It on Home to Me" remains the most perfectly composed and executed song I can imagine. But then there was nothing like the Temptations' "My Girl," and, well, when Percy Sledge came on with "When a Man Loves a Woman," it was the only time there was quiet in the car; my friends and I just called the song "Whenna," and we listened in awe. Back then I thought, in this little world of R&B love on the Volkswagen AM radio, that Otis Redding's eloquence about the need to "Try a Little Tenderness" would solve any love problems that I might encounter.

This is still the music I listen to, and I still think about love in many of these ways: I'm still awestruck as soon as "Whenna" comes on what is now the oldies station. It's just that love hasn't seemed to work out so easily, and not even Otis's "Pain in My Heart" or the Stones' "Heart of Stone" has made the disappointments OK. I, and I will be presumptuous and say "we," need more metaphors about love than these precious and sublime songs to find satisfaction. When I say "we" here I must say right off that I speak as a heterosexual man. I won't pretend here to write about other kinds of love, though I treasure talking about love with all manner of lovers. I will say, perhaps with some presumption, that these are good songs for all of us: what can I say but that I was a heterosexual teenager when I first heard Otis Redding, the Temps, and the Stones on the AM radio in Los Angeles and thought I knew something about love.

Partly out of nostalgia for this place, for Southern California, I have read and reread the magnificent novel *Ramona*. Helen Hunt Jackson, a peculiar Victorian woman from New England, moved to the West and became interested in California Indians. She wrote her story about the man-made catastrophe of the California Indians — the horrible, dystopic narrative — and about the tragic love of the two protagonists, Ramona and Alessandro. Through her tale, I have learned a new song of love, one from 1927: "Ramona, I hear the mission bells above / Ramona, they're ringing out our song of love / I press you, caress you, and bless the day you taught me to care / To always remember the rambling rose you wear in your hair /

Ramona, when the day is done you'll hear my call, Ramona, we'll meet beside the waterfall / I dread the dawn when I awake to find you gone, Ramona, I need you my own."[1]

I must disclose something right away because it is the absolute precondition to understanding all that I have to say in this essay: Ramona, I love you. I've read your book several times now, and I've seen the movies of you too. Not as Loretta Young or Mary Pickford do I love you, and maybe not even as the beautiful and revered Dolores del Río (whose movie rendition of Ramona remains inaccessible), but as the character in the book. I only love you when I read about you.

I must say too that my love for your book character combines with a fair dose of topophilia, the love for our place, our Southern California. This is our land, Ramona, where we were born, where flora and peoples from all over the world have replaced the indigenous plants and humans, where diverse people have mixed their love and their blood.

I know to be true several things about all this: there are so many reasons why I feel this way, and I will reveal them soon. You are worthy of all of our love, yet it is the accidental emotion to take from your great novel. When Helen Hunt Jackson wrote your book, I know that she did so to call attention to the plight of your real love, Alessandro, and his people, the Indians of Southern California. To fall in love with you is to miss the point of the story, much like simply affirming the need for the inspection of meat-packing plants after reading Upton Sinclair's *The Jungle*, when, after all, he intended us to be pro-union and Socialists. This brings me to another issue that I will address shortly: what is it about humankind that they tend to misread such great novels and, instead of being roused to action or even mere indignation, personalize the stories and respond in such narrowly self-centered ways?

Me, of all people, to confuse the meaning of the novel. I wrote a whole book detailing, with scrupulous indignation, the disgraceful and shameless destruction of the California Indians at the hands first of the Spanish and then the Americans. It even criticizes *Ramona* because it "ignored the complexities of the mission and rancho periods." Many of the fanciful and unprincipled things said about the missions I discussed in the book's first chapter derived from the Ramona-esque vision in which, as I stated with disdain, "it appears that the humble and innocent Indians were treated with heavenly and blessed kindness as they received civilization."[2]

The writer about California that I admire the most, Carey McWilliams, doesn't much like Jackson or *Ramona* either. He wrote that the crumbling missions "exerted a potent romantic influence on Mrs. Jackson's highly susceptible nature" and that what she knew about California Indians "was second-hand and consisted, for the most part, of odds and ends of gossip, folk tales, and Mission-inspired allegories of one kind or another." "It was this novel," he concluded, "which firmly established the Mission legend in southern California," and which, in the hands of grasping and tawdry tourism boosters, instigated "a Ramona promotion, of fantastic proportions."[3]

Entrepreneurial Fanfare

Maybe it didn't have to be that way, though. Twenty-five years after the novel's publication, a celebrant of "Ramona Country" could congratulate Jackson on her research and attest to her portrayal of the Indians' plight as "a work of essential truth." "She saw scattered Indians, like sheep without a shepherd, worried and pillaged by wolfish Americans, driven from house and home, abused, lied to, vitiated, corrupted and cursed by the white race," George Wharton James affirmed in 1909.[4]

But yes, it probably is true what McWilliams said about *Ramona* and the mission legend in California. James also rhapsodized about how "the loving power the Franciscans held over the Indians was well understood by Mrs. Jackson," and how "*Ramona*, in its references to Missions and padres, is so true to life, so true to their spirit, that it can be used as an auxiliary textbook with great advantage to those who wish to gain a true conception of the Franciscans and their work." In her *California and the Missions*, Jackson cites the "verbal testimony" of "old Indians who recollect the mission times in the height of their glory. Their faces kindle with a sad flicker of recollected happiness, as they tell of the days when they had all they wanted to eat, the *padres* were so good and kind."[5] *Ramona* really is, then, a combination of outrage over the treatment of the Indians, the sentiments of a "California Pastoral," the fables of the missions, the white woman's burden, and a spectacular and tragic love story. Strong and compelling stuff indeed.

It was out of this entrepreneurial fanfare that came the desecration of the beautiful Ramona and the transmutation of Jackson's intended message. Ramona and Alessandro's wedding place — entirely fictional, unlike other locations in the novel — came to be located at the run-down

Casa Estudillo in Old Town San Diego through a combination of popular lore and the efforts of the owners of the Hotel del Coronado around
1910. As it is still presented, as it was displayed in the picture postcards
with the recently planted palm trees and imported agapanthus from
Africa and the begonias from South America in its garden, "Ramona's
Marriage Place" has spoiled, if not blasphemed, Ramona and Alessandro's love.[6]

Then, too, there are such matters as the controversy over the ersatz
"Home of Ramona" that diverted people away from the novel's intent.
There can be little doubt but that the Rancho Camulos, between Ventura
and San Fernando and home of the del Valle family when Jackson visited
it briefly in 1882, served as the model for Señora Moreno's fictional
house, the one in which Ramona was raised. Yet, in the decades after the
publication of the novel, Rancho Guajome, indeed closer to the Mission
San Luis Rey that figured importantly in the lives of Alessandro's people,
became "Ramona's Home" once land developers and nostalgia marketeers found the story useful. The boosters even insinuated that Helen
Hunt Jackson wrote *Ramona* there, when in fact she wrote the whole
thing in the Berkeley Hotel in New York City. Real estate developers and
railroad companies captured the story of Ramona and used the compelling myths it contained about the halcyon days of old California to sell
house plots and train tickets to newcomers. Thus it was that people
uprooted from the Midwest could find rootedness in California as they
adopted the captivating myths of the new place, stories that *Ramona*
helped generate. To this day developers use whimsical Spanish names
with ersatz Mediterranean architecture that recall Californio society to
sell real estate. Thus it was that the Americans came to venerate the
Californios, even emulate the unreal lifeways of these people whom they
had only recently displaced from the landscape. The nostalgia myths
consequently work to transform the landscape even further — to make
Southern California even less like the way it was before the Americans
came or like the Southern California Helen Hunt Jackson invented.[7]

I have taken visitors to all of these places. The missions San Luis Rey
and San Diego, Old Town San Diego with Ramona's "Marriage Place,"
Rancho Camulos where we dined outside surrounded by orange groves
and palm trees, even the recently sprouted wineries of Alessandro's by-
gone domain of Temecula all enchanted them. I told them a little about
what really happened at all of these places, about the paradoxes and contradictions of the story of Ramona, and about all of the undocumented

Mexicans who these days do the work that the Indians did in the novel. I couldn't bring myself to sully the legend too much, however. Or maybe there was something in me such that I just didn't *want* to spoil it—for them or for me. These make-believe images were once popularized by millions of postcards printed for both tourists and potential real estate customers. The cards of the "Marriage Place" and other Ramona locales that I acquired in antique stores I have rather reverentially placed in a display book. My topophilia waxes maudlin and profound: I wish I lived there.

I have, in other words, tried to dispel the myth in one place— *Thrown among Strangers*—yet perpetuated it in others and then reveled in it as I imagined myself living in this foolish fantasy of halcyon days gone by. (Anyway, I could not take care of such a home and garden by myself any more than Señora Moreno could take care of hers without a squad of gardeners—then Indians, now illegal Mexicans. And it was such hired help—which will become clear shortly—that started all the trouble in *Ramona*.) Certainly, Ramona's tale is one of myriad entice-ments. Mostly, people have understood and used the story and its char-acters in ways that have much more to do with their emotional, eco-nomic, and social purposes than with anything Jackson intended.

An old tourist brochure, "The Story of Ramona's Marriage Place," stumbles deafly and insularly upon this matter: "Yet all this [meaning old California] would be forgotten and unnoticed . . . were it not for the fact that way back in 1884, that charming and gifted woman, Helen Hunt Jackson, gathered in Southern California the material around which she wove *Ramona*, a story so beautiful, and so throbbing with love and life and sympathy, that it sent a thrill around the reading world."[8] The tour-ist tract has no mention of that which was Jackson's point, the outrages against the Indians, but reminds us of the potency of love stories, of stories in general, and their power to keep both the glory and the seamy underside of the past before us.

Landscape of Fire and Blood

Living in the actual story Jackson told in *Ramona* would be terrible. She meant to make us sick to our stomachs and angry over the treatment of the ex-mission Indians of Southern California and to make us under-stand the lawlessness of the Americans and their occupation of Califor-nia. Alessandro tells how "I have no home; my father is dead; my people are driven out of their village. I am only a beggar now" (171).[9] He understands that the perpetrators were "Americans—eight or ten of them. They all got together and brought a suit, they call it, up in San Francisco; and it was decided in court that they owned all our land. That was all Mr. Rothsaker could tell about it. It was the law, he said, and nobody could go against the law" (172). And "he said the judge had said he must take enough of our cattle and horses to pay for all it had cost for the suit . . ." (173). Alessandro concludes with the drastic prediction that "these Americans will destroy us all. I do not know but they will presently begin to shoot us and poison us, to get us all out of the country, as they do the rabbits and the gophers" (178). And that is exactly what happened, in the novel and in real life.

Jackson, of New England Protestant stock, minced no words in her condemnation of the Americans: She has the gentle and guileless Ramona say, "There is no hope. They have power, and great riches. . . . Money is all that they think of. To get money, they will commit any crime, even murder. Every day there comes the news of their murdering each other for gold. Mexicans kill each other only for hate, Alessandro, —for hate, or in anger; never for gold" (230). Indeed, if Helen Hunt Jackson is to be believed, her country people acted like lawless, murdering thieves in their treatment of the Indians of Southern California. And this is something that the historical record quite utterly bears out.[10]

Jackson contrasts the Americans with Ramona and Alessandro and describes the interior of their humble household in the Indian village of San Pasquale: "Below [Ramona's statuette of the Madonna] hung her gold rosary and the ivory Christ; and many a woman of the village, when she came to see Ramona, asked permission to go into the bedroom and say her prayers there." And "with the money from the first sheep-shearing, and from the sale of part of his cattle, Alessandro had bought all he needed in the way of farming implements,—a good wagon and harnesses, and a plough" (241–42). The Indian and his half-breed spouse are the good Christian plowman and housewife; in fact, it was a model Victorian marriage. But into this paradise came the news: "The Doctor said the land did not belong to Ysidro [the Indian captain who had let them farm on land at San Pasquale] at all, but to the United States Government; and that he had paid the money for it to the agents in Los Angeles, and there would very soon come papers from Washington, to show that it was his" (248). Then another man would come: "Alessandro had not been plowing more than an hour, when hearing a strange sound, he looked up and saw a man unloading lumber a few rods off. Presently he came toward him, and said roughly, 'Look here! Be off, will you? This is my land. I'm going to build a house here. . . . I've got my family in San Diego, and I want to get them settled as soon as I can. My wife won't feel comfortable till she's in her own house' " (254–55). The frenzied Alessandro (who knew these Americans by now — people simply of "fraud and cruelty"), his grief-stricken wife, and his baby child simply left (230).

A conceited, vicious, and revealing reversal had transpired in the Southwest at this time about family values. That the indigenous peoples of the area — be they pagans or papists — would be civilized provided important justification for Manifest Destiny, which included the taking of the Indians' ancestral lands. The curious thing, though, was that so many Mexicans — and California ex-mission and New Mexican Puebloan Indians — lived as Christian farmers while Anglo American men drank, whored, and brawled. Recall that Ramona and Alessandro had been married in a church; that when he found transgressors in his dead father's house, Alessandro "felt for his knife," thought of Ramona, and "thoughts of vengeance fled" (208); and that they obeyed "the law" when they were evicted from their lands. The footloose and seedy American Jake said to Ramona, "It is but a poor place he [Alessandro] gives you to live in" and, understanding that a "squaw wife" was "first-rate about a house, and jest's faithful's dogs," asks her to live with him: Ramona "faced him, her eyes like javelins. . . . 'Beast!' she said, and spat towards him" (298–99). Of course, it would be the Americans' promiscuous resort to guns and brutal, extra-legal violence in the cause of family and property that would bring the catastrophic end to the majestic romance of Ramona and Alessandro. It's not just love for Ramona that I have associated with Southern California but the pain and suffering of Alessandro's people that will forever and indelibly haunt the landscape. This is how history, my favorite subject in school, so confuses my sense of the putatively impassive, actually complicated, landscape: there is beauty and love there — and fire and blood. After you read *Ramona* you can feel the immensity of the ambiguity of this distress in the hills and valleys of the place.

There is one good American: she is Aunt Ri, whose deep Tennessee drawl hid "a certain gentle dignity" (273). Ramona and Alessandro transform her attitudes about Indians and Mexicans. Through her, Jackson (whose middle name was Ma*r*ia) castigates Americans and their government: " 'We're Ummerikens! 'n' we wouldn't cheat nobody, not ef we knowed it, not out er a doller. We're pore, an' I allus expect to be, but we're above cheatin'; an I tell you naow, the Ummeriken people don't want any o' this cheatin' done, naow!' cried Aunt Ri" (282). The crusty old woman rages at the lawlessness of the Americans when she hears tell of Ramona and Alessandro's displacement: " 'Why, they take folks up, 'n' penetentiarize 'em fur life, back'n Tennessee, fur things thet ain't so bad's thet!' " (281). Becoming devoted to Ramona, Aunt Ri nurses her back to health after Ramona's breakdown following Alessandro's calamitous death, and she does so with the herb she calls "old man": " 'I knowed I smelt the bitter on't somewhars along hyar'; and in a few minutes more she had a mass of the soft, shining, gray, feathery leaves in her hands. . . . 'This'll cure her, ef ennything will,' she said" (328). The one good American turns out to be a *curandera*, an Indian of sorts.

It is, upon reflection, quite remarkable how critical of American government and settlers Helen Hunt Jackson's *Ramona* actually is. The American novel in print for the longest uninterrupted time is scathingly critical of the American mission in the Southwest. I cannot resist pointing out the obvious hypocrisy Jackson reveals in the American character when she points out the greed and meanness of Anglo families who displace the Indians and the horrible consequences of Americans' ready resort to guns to settle their matters. Then, too, it is quite apparent that Jackson, through Aunt Ri, affirms those other American values of respect for equality of opportunity, compassion for those less fortunate, and equal justice under law. It is these issues that Jackson intended that her readers confront, not that they should fall in love with her main character.

"These Crosses"

Helen Hunt Jackson constructed Ramona's lineage to suit the needs of a tragic novel and not for historical credibility. She was not a real Californio like her adoptive mother, but the product of a dissolute Scottish sea captain—whose heart had been broken by an elder sister (named Ramona) of Señora Moreno—and a "squaw" of the Mission San Gabriel, already mother to several Indian children, whom he later married. When he sought a more appropriate home for their new baby he gave it to Señora Moreno's sister—his long-forsaken love—and then, as she in turn was dying, convinced Señora Moreno to agree to take care of the child: "This promise came hard from Señora Moreno. Except for Padre Salvierderra's influence, she had not given it . . . 'If the child were pure Indian, I would like it better,' she said. 'I like not these crosses. It is the worst, and not the best, that remains'" (32). "And this was the mystery of Ramona. No wonder Señora Moreno never told the story. No wonder, perhaps, that she never loved the child" (33).

Yet, "no one would have known, from Ramona's face, manner, or habitual conduct that she had ever experienced sorrow or had a care . . . and she never was seen to pass a human being without a cheerful greeting" (36). Except for her adoptive mother, everyone loved Ramona, "for a gentler, sweeter maiden never drew breath than this same Ramona, who had been all these years, save for Felipe [Señora Moreno's natural-born son], lonely in the Señora Moreno's house" (90). She is the uncomplaining woman, a rather standard fantasy figure for many men.

Ramona's beauty is a bit too racialized not to be suspect. "She had just enough of olive tint in her complexion to underlie and enrich her skin without making it too swarthy," Jackson explained. That "her hair was like her Indian mother's, heavy and black, but her eyes were like her father's, steel-blue," (40) makes one wonder about what colors and features qualify one for beauty. Would everyone have loved Ramona as much had she looked otherwise? If her father had been a Mexican or a Spaniard instead of a Scot, she would just be another mestiza, another Mexican. Would her American audience still be so enthralled with her character?

I suspect not, because Americans always construed things in nineteenth-century California as "Spanish" if positive and "Mexican" if negative. Ramona is neither, though culturally she is certainly a Californio, having been raised by the Señora Moreno. She is Europeanized, and in her case, her mysterious Indian origin only serves to exoticize her. Ramona is beautiful, strange, devoted, and uncomplaining—what more could a man want?

There is much facetiousness in my critique of Ramona here, an amusing aside that might explain something of why I love Ramona: I am just like she was. While I don't have the blue eyes of my mother, I certainly have her straight Yankee nose. Ramona and I could move in several groups and feel accepted. When we go to El Mercado in Boyle Heights or to *mariscos* restaurants around Vermont and Sunset, people speak to us in Spanish and we respond in kind. When we go to the beach or to a chic seafood restaurant at the west end of Sunset Boulevard, we become Mediterranean, apparently (and actually) prosperous enough to afford dinner and wine and the time and travel to sport a nice tan. Ramona and I could go most anywhere this way; we would enjoy together the impudent privilege of passing.

California, I would say, more than any place else in the world, is not just about ethnic and racial identity, but about mixing. Californians affirm their ethnic group and associate their politics and identity with their modern tribe. Yet, really Ramona and I are the true and increasingly typical Californians — mixes or, as Señora Moreno would call us, "these crosses." Everywhere I go I notice the various "crosses," the ones from the previous generations of immigrants to California, the ones I imagine will be most unlikely to deprecate others or fall prey to political demagoguery that exploits issues of race or country of origin. We know how much race, religion, "looks," occupation, and language and accents are matters of happenstance and irony. The critique of her is too facile; maybe Ramona really is the true, and best, Californian.

And California is about the mutable self, and about passing. People often come to the place to reinvent themselves. Ramona herself changes from Californio to Indian and then finally to Mexican. Of all things, many *americanos* have recast themselves as Spanish Californios — never Mexicans — and assume an air of nobility at the old Fiesta Days and Missions Days, carried on most famously in Santa Barbara to this very day. Mexican Americans in the 1930s insisted to the Census Bureau that they be counted as white, and the category "Mexican" indeed disappeared in the 1940 census. Now, of course, we have become "Hispanic," something that Ramona never was.

Perfect Man, Perfect Victim

Alessandro is likewise a fantasy figure for Victorian women. Much like Harriet Beecher Stowe's Uncle Tom, Alessandro is not simply the tamed Indian, but a domesticated man. "Alessandro had inherited his father's love and talent for music, and knew all the old Mission music by heart." When he sang a hymn to "Beautiful Queen, / Princess of Heaven . . . Ramona felt every note of it penetrating her consciousness with a subtle thrill almost like pain" (51–52). Again, resembling the Victorian domestic ideal in which men were to be more like women — religious, sensitive, refined, and virtuous — Alessandro "plays the violin beautifully. . . . He plays the old San Luis Rey music" (56). When Felipe faints and falls into the huge wool bag, from which Alessandro rescues him, he is forced into bed and appears incapable of recovery. Alessandro tends to him with music and builds him a bed that he places on the veranda in the sunshine. Much as a Victorian woman would do, he gave his tenderness, and that caring effected Felipe's cure, a scene reminiscent of Jane Eyre ministering to Rochester in Charlotte Bronte's great novel.

"Whenever there were troubles with the whites, or rumors of them, he went from house to house, urging, persuading, commanding his people to keep the peace," Jackson explained. "At one time when there was an insurrection of some of the Indian tribes further south, and for a few days it looked as if there would be a general Indian war, he removed the greater part of his band . . . to Los Angeles, and camped there for several days, that they might be identified with the whites in case hostilities became serious," she continued (53–54). It's not simply that Alessandro is a sell-out—taking care of the Californio Felipe or capitulating to the Americans—but rather, in her effort to make of him the perfect man and thus the perfect victim, Jackson has created the ideal domesticated Victorian man or, as Carey McWilliams put it, she "invested (him and the Mission Indians) with the sentiments of a New England school marm."[11] Alessandro's virtues are those of the female Victorian world: sensibility (understood as knowing through the senses), nurturance, self-sacrifice, and service to others. This is not to deny Jackson's and Stowe's contributions to what made for "a good Indian" and "a good Negro" in the minds of liberal whites: people who sought amelioration of their oppressed status through acceptance of the value system and leadership of enlightened Anglo-Protestants.

Oddly enough, Alessandro got to where he was not through Victorian schoolmarms, but through other Christians in robes, namely Franciscan priests who were next in line for re-creation in the Victorian female mold: "His father, Chief Pablo," Jackson related, "had been the leader of the choir at the San Luis Rey Mission in the last years of its splendor." "Father Peyri was passionately fond of music, and spared no pains in training all of the neophytes under his charge who showed any special talent in that direction," she supposed (51). Later writers would assume that "the devotion of the San Luis Rey Indians to Padre Peyri is truthfully told in Ramona. They would do anything for him . . ." Actually, Father Antonio Peyri, the true scion of the mission, wrote on Christmas Day 1828 regarding the disease and demoralization at San Luis Rey that "apathy reigns among the Indians."[12]

I tuned out, thinking "wouldn't you know it, I come here looking for everyday people's take on Ramona and I get seated next to a zealous literary critic."

"Well, you know, this IS a pageant, something different from *theater*." I find myself defending Ramona, but to little avail.

"I go to from 30 to 40 plays a year," I hear from her. "The Mark Taper Forum, Pasadena Playhouse, and . . ."

Through the second half I get more running critical review. I watch the play. It is so tragic. The americanos' avarice is portrayed, mincing no words or actions. Alessandro's end is depicted with all of its horribleness. A hundred Indians on the hillside—Soboba people—and what seemed like a similar number of other cast members receive the crowd's hearty and righteous applause. More diatribe comes as the cast takes its bows. I venture, "Now could the Pasadena Playhouse ever assemble anything like this?"

"The actors could have been more . . ." I tune back to the audience applauding the performers, knowing I should keep quiet.

I renege on my own advice as we are walking out: "Well, look at it this way. Jackson took all of these stories and wove them into the book, then came the pageant"—which my critic didn't know was written in 1923—"which is, maybe, just another version of these stories. Which really happened, for instance when. . . ."

"Yes, but it should have. . . ." I'm watching the other people now. "She just doesn't get it," I think to myself.

Afterward the Lions Club had a big fundraising dinner: coleslaw, half a canned peach, and some mighty fine beans and BBQ beef. While we ate, some of the cast members serenaded us with "Rancho Grande," "Down México Way," "Guantanamera" (it's Cuban), and "Ramona." Standing in line behind me was a woman with her mother and her son. *La vieja* spoke in Spanish, the son in English, and she in both. I asked *la abuela*, "¿Usted le gustó a Ramona?"

"Sí," she said, "pero era diferente."

"¿Del libro?" I asked.

"No, de la última vez. They strangled him before."

"Y era muy diferente en el libro," I told her and mentioned some of the ways it was, but stopped myself when I remembered I was here to watch and to listen. She was very impressed that I had read the book. "¿Pero, usted le gustó?" I repeated myself.

"Sí," she said again. "Era muy bonita." She understood it. We continued in line, and I wondered what Ramona meant to her really, this woman who returned again to the pageantry of Ramona.

At the dinner, people in the cast came around to greet the audience members. The woman who played Señora Moreno explained how everyone in the play must be from the Mt. San Jacinto College district. In years past, Ramona and Alessandro could "be professionals from Los Angeles or Hollywood but this Ramona is from here." See, I knew this wasn't the Pasadena Playhouse.

An elderly African American man asked to borrow my pen so he could ask *la señora* to autograph his program. When he gave it back I said, "I can tell you liked the play."

"Yes, it's so romantic," he said and paused briefly. "And factual about what was goin' on back then."

"Hmm, yes," I said. And thought, "He got it too." His people would know the story of Alessandro.

Surely, then, this is part of the reason that I love Ramona: I love the stories; I love the fantasy lifestyle she inhabited in the novel; I love the way Jackson constructed Mexican ways as so superior to American ones; I honor the wholeness of Jackson's telling, which includes both the beauty and the meanness; and I feel nostalgia for this place that has never really — well, yes and no, actually — existed. And I love how so many of us share this grandly encompassing story. It's probably understandable then that I yearn for a beautiful landscape, I crave generous social relations, and I desire Ramona.

Thunder and Lightning

There are so many reasons why we love. We can wonder why Ramona and Alessandro fell so completely in love. A psychologist might direct our inquiry to her relationship to her adoptive mother: "The shepherds, the herdsmen, the maids, the babies, the dogs, the poultry, all loved the sight of Ramona; all loved her except the señora." Ramona would always be searching, mostly unconsciously, for the warmth denied her by "the señora (who) loved her not; never had loved her; never could love her." Likely, the señora would always be withholding of any sort of emotion for Ramona owing to her grudging promise to her sister, Ramona's adoptive mother, to stand "in place of mother to the girl . . . and with all the inalienable staunchness of her nature she fulfilled the letter of her promise" (26–27). It is not hard to envisage the little girl's endeavors to win the affection of this reluctant mother figure, and the coldness and aloofness with which her efforts were met. Almost any reader can imagine entering into the novel to love Ramona because the señora did not. It is not hard at all then to understand the utter thrill and fulfillment Ramona would experience when Alessandro would say to her "O Señorita, then you will not be angry if I say that I love you!" And then to receive a kiss, right there, out in the open, from a man sobbing, saying "I love you!" (120–121). On the contrary, to say the least.

How could either know love except as compensation for something else lacking in their lives? Alessandro "had not thought much about women. He was a distant, cold boy, his own people of the Temecula village said. It had come, they believed, of learning to read, which was always bad" (53). Ramona did not know much of the world:

> No one would have known, from Ramona's face, manner, or habitual conduct, that she had ever experienced a sorrow or had a care . . . She had two years at school, in the Convent of the Sacred Heart at Los Angeles, where the señora had placed her at much personal sacrifice. . . . Here she had won the affection of all the Sisters, who spoke of her habitually as the "blessed child." They had taught her all the dainty arts of lace-weaving, embroidery, . . . not overmuch learning out of books, but enough to make her a passionate lover of verse and romance. (36)

Perhaps the final words of this quote would suggest that she could know of love through romance novels, but really there were very few of those in Southern California of the 1850s.

Even those of us who see maudlin, Victorian sappiness in their love can't help but be drawn—be honest, readers both female and male, at least a little bit—to how this love was so all-encompassing and passionate, so unintended and serendipitous, and so rapturous and delivering from their disappointing lives. Such a love, when one falls in love with someone they don't really know, can only derive from subconscious cravings, from frustrated yearnings. When we abruptly fall in love with Ramona, we have the opportunity to investigate the nature of our own sensual longings and emotional hunger. We can put the book down for a while and contemplate love, though such reflective devotion probably pales before that ecstatic, devouring love that has that most powerful of charges: the psychic electricity of the anxious, even neurotic, individual yearning for emotional and sensual redemption. Ramona and Alessandro's love, its thunder and lightning, is the most exciting and compelling, and the most volatile and unpredictable.

Ramona could have known of love from her faith, from her devotion to the Virgin Mary: "It is not by what happens to us here in this world that we can tell if the saints love us, or if we will see the Blessed Virgin," she informs Alessandro. Rather it is "by what we feel in our hearts . . . just as I knew all the time, when you did not come, — I knew that you loved me. I knew that in my heart." When Alessandro responds that "it is not possible to have the same thoughts about a saint as about a person," Ramona answers, "not quite, about a saint; but one can for the Blessed Virgin. . . . Her statue, in my room at the señora's, has always been my mother" (232).

We moderns often don't realize that people in the past have had many of the same emotions that we do. Love, among nineteenth-century Latin Americans, emerged from two sources: from the command to love God and thus thy parents and humankind, and love from the heart, the sort of love that was subversive because it was associated with sexual desire, exalted the self, and potentially undermined one's family of origin. Ramona and Alessandro's bond obviously exemplified the latter type in both source and consequences, but I suspect that it was in the context of the former that Ramona, at least, came to know of love. Such an interesting notion — that people in the deep past had feelings of love springing from their hearts, which may have been religious in origin, especially for the Virgin of Guadalupe for Mexicans, but that informed people about the nature of the feelings they might have had welling up in their hearts for another person. You see, when such people found themselves in situations where they might love another mortal, the love they already knew was for the Blessed Spirits. Perhaps they felt conflicted about the way those two allegedly different sorts of loves converged, but just as likely they did not. Or maybe they transformed the passion they felt for their spirit love into passion for their human love.

My own spirit love has not come from the Holy, however, but from other of the senses — from the music on the radio and from the artworks in museums. Thinking and writing about all of these matters makes me recall, makes me realize, that it was not only something of other people's devotion to God that I came to know from looking at beautiful paintings, but that I came to know, or thought I knew, something of love. No, it was not love I came to know standing before those images, but desire: Botticelli's *Venus* and Ingres's many *Odalisques*; of course, Manet's *Olympia* and Goya's *Maja*, the nude one naturally; even Parmigianino's *Madonna of the Long Neck*; and now any of Kahlo's self-portraits, especially *On the Border between Mexico and the United States*. My experience before the canvases is much like those who confront the Holy Spirits: it's more about yearning for the sublime or simply longing for a happier life. Ramona, do I ache for you because you are like those paintings? Is it that I have confused my love for you with my carnal desire for those beautiful, so apparently innocently available, women? Or is it that I simply want to share a simple and splendid kiss with you?"

Of course these sorts of passions — Ramona's, Alessandro's, and mine — would confirm everything that Señora Moreno and other elders would have said about the destructiveness of romantic love. Nothing is more important in Latin American society than marriage. Among the propertied classes the sanctified event maintained and enhanced a family's reputation and wealth, created a broader web of blood ties and alliances, and made sure that the family treasure would not be lost to undesirable outsiders. The young, those most prone to pride, passion, and concupiscence, could not be trusted to make such alliances on their own. Love could not be allowed to play itself out in often subversive and individualist ways, ones that put the self and its desires above the requirements of the family. Ideas about race and marriage were very complicated in Californio society. Some people mixed, especially in the lower classes, while others, more often in such elite families as the Vallejos, took such precautions as arranging a marriage of a daughter at her birth and acquiring a certificate of *limpieza de sangre*, or "purity of blood," which affirmed that there was no Moorish, Jewish, or Indian blood flowing in the veins of those who would carry on the family patrimony. Ramona's passion, thus, called forth an unmitigated family disaster.

Ramona's father, through his terrible emotional and financial decline, had still managed to save out a fine cache of jewels the señora was to maintain in trust for his little daughter, jewels that would fall to the Church should Ramona grievously err in life. Under Spanish and Mexican law, widows and daughters could inherit and hold property. While Señora Moreno's dislike of such mixed marriages probably precluded a significant endowment to Ramona, no doubt some dowry of land would have been hers to attract a proper husband. All this she lost when her selfish emotions for Alessandro carried Ramona away from her family bonds and obligations.

Their love proved psychically calamitous as well. It's an ironic and dangerous aspect of love, like devotion, that it contains destructive elements. Lust, passion, desire, loss of the self in one's *objet d'amour* make us humans do things that hurt ourselves and others. Indeed, Alessandro and Ramona's love brought them only abundant pain, even without the Americans' torment of Alessandro.

Deception worked its evil too. Almost everyone has a secret, something that would change one's whole social and moral stature if people knew about it. For Ramona it was her past and her genealogy, and it was a secret even she did not know. At some point, to be free of the weight, a person must release that secret. When Ramona found out that she was half-Indian, and that this secret lay behind Señora Moreno's disparagement of her, Ramona unleashed the secret and fell for the Indian Alessandro. It was either break away or let the secret condemn her to endure her pathetic life in which the señora would continue to punish her for her shameful origins.

The Good and Bad Ramonas

That we humans so consistently, across time and cultures, act in so many destructive ways is unnerving and disheartening to contemplate. Do we love within this context? Is love about creation and destruction both? When we subjugate our libidinal desires to family imperatives and to the cause of labor and the creation of civilization, does not that energy often transform itself into antisocial and aggressive acts? Indeed, does not the repression of desire damage our erotic selves and on occasion make even courting and the sex act itself something hostile? It may well be that Ramona and Alessandro prove not only Señora Moreno right, but Sigmund Freud as well. Love, like devotion, is creative and destructive both. Rethinking this, I realize that what was creative about their love was also painful, and what was destructive was also generative. There was so much anguish when Ramona had to leave her loved ones Felipe and Padre Salvierderra for Alessandro. Ramona and Alessandro lost their first child; Alessandro met a heinous death. But a consequence of their tragedy is that Felipe and Aunt Ri are transformed in their ideas about Indians; Ramona and Felipe have another child when they go to Mexico (and now I have given away the end of the story), the one that would carry her mother's name into the twentieth century; and reflective readers of *Ramona* will know the history of Southern California in new ways.

In one sense, Ramona was "good" as long as she lived up to her society's moral expectations: she was always dutiful, selfless, guileless, and uncomplaining. "This childlikeness, combined with her happy temperament," Jackson explains, "had kept her singularly contented with her monotonous life" (91). This "good Ramona" would have been rather provincial in her thoughts, wooden in her efforts to live up to her society's standards, and unimaginative in conversation. The "bad Ramona" is the one who courageously breaks free from her cultural commands, heroically challenges the racism of her adoptive mother, and bravely overcomes her fearfulness about heading into the unknown with Alessandro. Ramona's endeavors provide the best of arguments for the idea that moral judgments, especially about "good" and "bad" people and their actions, are contingent upon what one values. Do we esteem the compliant everywoman — usually a rather dull person — who does as her family and culture expect or the intrepid challenger to the status quo — often immature or impulsive — who remakes herself in some new, maybe better or maybe not, way?

Of course we proceed ahead with life and love anyway, most successfully, I think, when we acknowledge their contingencies and complexities. There is no one universal reason why we love, and my affection for Ramona reveals the truth of this to me. I fear that I love Ramona, actually, because she is the Ramona of my imagination, the one I can conjure up when I travel by book to the Southern California of the 1880s. I can make her what I want her to be when I hold her book in my hands, when I wander away from the text into this imaginary world where there is a beautiful woman whom I could be confident would never play me for a fool. "This childlikeness . . . [and] happy temperament" tells of her happy adaptation to any person, place, or situation. Part of the frustration of love, perhaps why people become destructive, is that we imagine an objet d'amour to be a particular way, and then when they don't actually correspond to how we have constructed them in our minds, we rage, and then justify actions that wind up playing our own love for the fool. I wonder and fear what would have happened had I been able to love the Ramona of my dreams, and have her love me, only to find her conversation consistently pointless, her interests sadly narrow, her religion constantly foolish, her love-making frustratingly insipid.

Could she even be such a perfect beauty? I suspect that such an exquisite woman would not have gone so unspoiled for so long. "A man must be dead not to thrill" at the sight of Ramona, Jackson exclaims (40). Yes, it's true in California then and now that the pretty women get the most attention. This means that they get the most solicitude, presents, and (usually unwanted) propositions. They may then feel the most entitled, qualified, accomplished, and deserving of more attention because of the treatment they get only because of their looks. Everything I know about men tells me that this scenario with Ramona would have been the case. Maybe it's not that my trust in Ramona is not strong enough, rather that I have good reason to think that she would be so many men's objet d'amour that they would spoil her or sour her on love.

What else does it mean to be such a perfect beauty? What man would want to love a woman who is not so beautiful as Ramona? Can he ever find her desirable if he has in his mind the image of Dolores del Río, Loretta Young, the olive-skinned enchantress on the paperback's cover, or the winner of the 1959 Ramona beauty pageant, Raquel Welch? Always yearning for, or even feeling deserving of, such a beauty makes it hard for a man to love a woman because none could ever be as perfect as Ramona. Always looking for Ramona, in whatever incarnation, means that men can't see love in front of them — a woman at once sweet and smart and strong — or even that they will go in search of a new love confident that, because their present love doesn't look like Ramona, no other man will want her. And that, of all things, he will find a woman like Ramona.

I am quite certain that more women have read *Ramona*, and cried in the movies of *Ramona*, than men. I wonder about the women who have known these Ramonas and their experiences of her. The physical beauty of this fantasy character is likely unattainable, except, in my opinion, by Dolores del Río. If they can never be as pretty and pleasing as Ramona, will they be confident in their love? If their man's standard of beauty is Dolores del Río or Raquel Welch, will women ever feel safe in their love? There is no better proof of the notion that beauty and femininity are social and historical constructs than Jackson's fabrication of Ramona. Fiction — in the pages or on the screen — too often becomes the truth of what beauty is, of how women should be, of what makes a woman desirable. I'm not sure what to say about what Jackson's ideas about these matters mean for women, but I do know that such constructions make love hard for everybody.

Books, it should be clear by now, are for me more conducive to love than movies, though not for lust and desire, which images enhance and make explicit. I couldn't love either Mary Pickford or Loretta Young, and, alas, probably not even Dolores del Río. As Ramona, Pickford swoons a lot, and there is not much that rings true when Ramona materializes as a middle-class, dedicated wife (Young) married to a convivial man (Don Ameche) who has a bounce in his step in spite of the cultural and physical debasement his people have experienced for the previous century.

The book is not only always better than the movie, but better than real life too. The book facilitates imagination in ways that the movie never can. The private world of the printed word is a special, dare I say magical, place. Rereading passages, thinking about the stories, considering oneself in relation to the characters, being transported to some place far away and long ago — or in this case, a place very near and not so long ago — all of these practices help us wonder, imagine, and engage in self-reflection. There is much more to love than songs on the radio and dramatic kisses on the screen. And there is much more to this simultaneously miraculous and bizarre landscape of Southern California than meets the eye. I guess that's one of the things I've had to learn again while writing my story of Ramona: a lover as perfect as Ramona, and a love as perfect as her and Alessandro's, exists only in a place we can explore in a book, in the imagination. Maybe, Ramona, your and Alessandro's story helps remind me that my love for Southern California must be as complicated as my love for you. Maybe, Ramona, it's not even you that I love; it's that I love imagining you, beautiful woman, who impels me to think about myself and all of us who love, in all of these good and hard ways.

Woodrow Wilson's Guns

American Liberalism and the
Dilemma of Non-Progressive Peoples

I have in a picture frame two certificates from 1926 that commend "Mrs. Lulu Gonzalez," my grandmother, for completing the intermediate and advanced programs in English at the Ninth Street Evening High School. The Los Angeles City School District provided the classes, and the little diplomas are emblazoned with the motto "Progress Is the Law of Life."

There will be more about this later.

The idea of progress has been a compelling one indeed. Not only did it promise more human happiness, but progress itself seemed inevitable. There would be not only the satisfaction of material needs through technological innovation and rational organization of society and politics but also an increase in human fulfillment as science and education swept away superstition and foolish customs regarding parents and children, love and sex, God and Man. Here's the way it was all supposed to work, the way history would unfold: individuals would be able to have dominion over their own lives, they would have the liberty to improve themselves and their station in life, and they would be able to pursue happiness, confident that reason would constrain desire. Choice (democracy) and voluntary associations (institutional complexity) would replace (respectively) deference to lord and to church as the organizing principles of society. Science and education would not only bring material comfort but would demystify the world: we humans would be as the gods and re-make the world in our own beautiful and intelligent image and with the spirit of equality and fraternity. We could do so without divine explanation and authority and decide for ourselves what to make with our hands, think in our heads, and whom to love in our hearts. This has been called modernity.

Most compelling was the inevitability of it all: humans' native curiosity and impulse to advance their societies, coupled with an innate yearning for something vaguely called "freedom," and fired by competition between humans and societies for material and military superiority, meant that change over time would always be forthcoming. We would progress through the stages of clans and tribes, slavery (Greece and Rome), the dark ages of medievalism and feudalism, and emerge, emancipated, into the fully realized world of political democracy and economic freedom. All this was, moreover, universal. All societies could go through this process, though they might need to have the way shown to them.

By 1964 it could look as if the American model of progress would triumph, and for the good of us all. Thoughtful government programs would erase poverty and gross inequality; then with less invidiousness, more education, and simple rubbing of elbows, we would get over our foolishness about race; and then science and technology would give us the leisure time to enjoy ourselves and our wonderful humanness. I have rather liked modernity, this demystified world of individual choice, material comfort, thoughtfulness, and various pleasures. I live that way, and I'm unlikely to give up my pursuit of happiness and efforts to improve and change myself.

I am like Poor Richard and Jay Gatsby: I make lists of vocabulary words (in English and Spanish) to learn and of things to do "pa' mejorarme." It's just that now I don't know if I will end up more like Ben Franklin or Jay Gatz, or F. Scott Fitzgerald himself. I only wish that the promise of modernity could have been true.

It was Vietnam that blew modernity and Liberalism all apart for me. In my very early teenage years, the War on Poverty and the war in Vietnam were both of one weave for me. People would be brought out of ignorance: they'd have education that would free them from their superstitious religious practices and from reliance on the foolishness of the so-called "wisdom" of the elders; they'd have health care that would make them physically able and enable them to avoid so many children; they'd be free, in those gross phrases of the times, "to be you and me," "to have a nice day," to "spress yo' self." Poverty, religion, Communist Party, capitalism, racism were all authorities that told people how to be, believe, and live. Liberalism, and its wars against poverty and communism, would save all these less-fortunates, these victims of superstition and exploitation.

For a lot of reasons, ones I continue to uncover and come to terms with, people don't necessarily want to be that way. Their goal is to continue as they always have. Nothing has made this clearer to me than Frances FitzGerald's description of the Vietnamese concept of the "Xa." The word refers to what the people call a "village," but it means "place where the spirits come together." The Vietnamese bury their ancestors in the rice paddies, where their spirits continue on. Later I learned about Pueblo Indian peoples who imagine that the spirits of their dead are part of the clouds, of the rain. Being something of a materialist, I acknowledge Feuerbach's notion that "you are what you eat," and yet the idea that one partakes of one's ancestors eating rice or corn is beyond my spiritual grasp. It is, though, these concepts that explain to me why these "natives" rejected modernity and Liberalism. The promise of communion with the ancestors, of doing things as they'd always been done, proved stronger than the promise of personal freedom. It was out of the incomprehensibility of this that the liberals raged, that they keep sending their guns to make people have progress.

Vietnam also demonstrated that it seemed to make little difference whether or not Democrats or Republicans, or so-called Idealists or Realists, practiced U.S. foreign policy; the outcome was the same. From 1899 to 1903, American troops brutally suppressed the Philippine independence movement. As a condition of independence, Cuba had to accept the conditions of the Platt Amendment (1903) "legalizing" American interventions in Cuba. Charles Evans Hughes's State Department chased Augusto Sandino around the mountains of Nicaragua, a pursuit that continued into Franklin Roosevelt's administration, and the efforts of the Reagan administration to destroy the Sandinistas are well-enough known; the Truman administration oversaw Fulgencio Batista's second rise to power in 1952; the Eisenhower administration was responsible for the dastardly overthrow of the democratically elected governments of Iran and Guatemala in 1954; I think of Ramona and Alessandro's people; and, well, if there ever was a non-wartime bipartisan consensus about a foreign policy issue it was agreement through the Truman, Eisenhower, Kennedy, Johnson, and Nixon administrations that the United States needed to intervene in Vietnam to contain communism. Sometimes the rhetoric turned upon natural resources and dominoes, and at others it revolved around winning people's hearts and minds, but the outcome proved the same: imposing dictators and taking the peasants' land via the expenditure of bullets and money.

I must say, though, that studying Woodrow Wilson, usually considered the quintessential Idealist in foreign policy, and his relationship to the Mexican Revolution has enabled me to discern the profound differences in the ideologies and intents of Idealists and Realists in American foreign policy, and to understand all the more why the outcome is always guns and more guns.

Different Histories

Dramatic and consequential events have transpired between the United States and Mexico. This we might expect, given the different cultures and levels of wealth, and too, perhaps we should not be surprised at how each nation's history books, and what each celebrates, tell such different stories of those events. That the United States attacked Mexico's northern territories in the War of 1846–1848 is well-enough known; it's just that the Civil War eclipsed the Mexican-American War and eventually erased it from popular memory. Because New Mexico, Arizona, and California have become part of the United States, the invasion has endured, to the extent that they are aware of it, as a rather natural unfolding of events for most Americans. It's one example of how Manifest Destiny still lives. But it is not well known on the northern side of the border that U.S. Marines attacked Mexico at Veracruz and marched to Mexico City.

What happens when people have dramatically different stories of the same events? Perhaps, then, stories, in their inaccuracies and exclusions, become dangerous.

There is remarkable omission, maybe suppression, in Americans' historical knowledge of how, on September 14, 1846, American troops and their guns easily overwhelmed what little defense Mexico could muster to defend its capital and took Mexico City. Not that Mexico had much of a chance: what meager military resources the beleaguered nation, only 25 years old, could muster had been occupied in putting down a massive revolt of Mayans in the south and numerous other peasant uprisings against those who monopolized the land and thus commanded their labor; and, upon the Yankee approach, Antonio López de Santa Anna simply took his troops and fled. What resistance there was, was as profoundly symbolic as it was pathetically and tragically futile.

Every Mexican schoolchild knows about los Niños Héroes, the military cadets who defended Chapultepec Castle in Mexico City against the onrushing Marines. Among the most potent symbols of Mexican nationalism, these boy heroes are memorialized in statues in the great Chapultepec Park; six *jóvenes*, aged 13–20, who died in vain, according to some stories wrapped in Mexican flags, trying to hold off the U.S. Marines. As with Cinco de Mayo, which celebrates a brief victory against the French invasion of 1862, los Niños Héroes are champions in gross defeat. Everyone knows about the imperious Yankee invasion and ruthless capture of the capital that forced Mexico's surrender and the cession of a third of the new nation's land with the Treaty of Guadalupe Hidalgo. Everyone in Mexico, that is.

Americans, at least those of my generation or older, have an almost freakish (non)cognizance of the invasion of Mexico City. In my fourth- and fifth-grade classrooms, as in many elementary schools across America, we sang, along with "America the Beautiful" and "The Star Spangled Banner," the "Marine Corps Hymn." This is part of how the country has achieved national unity: from "sea to shining sea" there have been many common experiences for America's children, such as these songs. It's just that while everyone knows the opening lines to the song—"From the halls of Montezuma, to the shores of Tripoli"—no one seems to comprehend the reference to the invasion of Mexico City in 1846. A stunning contrast to Mexican schoolchildren and los Niños Héroes.

Even less known in the United States are the events of April 1914. Mexican police had arrested two sailors in Tampico, a port city on the Gulf of Mexico. Indeed, they hadn't done much, and were released, but an international incident brewed. The Woodrow Wilson administration demanded not only an apology, but that a 21-gun salute be fired in atonement to the American flag in the town square at 6 p.m. Victoriano Huerta, who had briefly re-established the rule of the Church and large landowners during the revolution, issued an apology and had the Mexican officer in charge of the arrests seized, but ignored the command that the salute be fired. In order to exacerbate matters with Huerta, "President Wilson today ordered practically the entire Atlantic Fleet to Mexican waters," reported the *Los Angeles Times* of April 14, 1914, "to force a public salute to the Stars and Stripes from the Huerta government as an apology for the arrest of American bluejackets at Tampico last Thursday." We shall return to this episode later on, but suffice it to say for now that this event precipitated another American invasion at Veracruz, this time on April 21, only 67 years after the first one.

The ongoing occupation of Mexico's main port played a key role in the outcome of the Mexican Revolution. Control of arms shipments hugely benefited the Constitutionalists, the ultimately victorious faction in the revolution, at the expense of the rickety and reactionary Huertistas and the dangerously, or gloriously, revolutionary Zapatistas and Villistas. "I have only curses on my lips, rage in my heart, and blows on my fist for the blond thieves who struck at Veracruz with a cowardly naval assault," raged Deputy Músquiz Blanco in the Mexican Congress at news of the assault. Easily vanquishing the spontaneous popular defiance, which included some naval cadets, the Yankees spent little blood in the invasion, but "no matter how much was let, it would not repay a single drop of the blood of the Niños Heroes of Chapultepec . . . ," he continued. It seemed to Anglo Americans like an appropriate response to another Mexican outrage, but most Mexicans saw the invaders as Músquiz Blanco put it, "the eternal highwaymen, the eternal thieves." In Tampico, Monterey, and Mexico City, the American flag was desecrated, and in Mexico City people pulled down a statue of George Washington and dragged it through the streets.[1]

Meanwhile, in Los Angeles, Americans rousingly prepared for war. The *Times* headlined the "Thrilling Spectacle at Arcade Station Militiamen Entrain for Service Along Border — Streets Packed with Cheering Surging Crowd of Patriots." Mexicans in Los Angeles experienced the matter differently as "the police in the Mexican sections have been ordered to search all Mexicans suspected of having firearms upon their persons." It appears that under the inspiration of the Industrial Workers of the World, an anarchist organization with sizeable Mexican support, "Mexicans . . . are believed," or so the *Times* reported, "to be in a plot to dynamite the Federal building, the International Bank building, and other structures in the northern end of the business section." The *Times* could reassure its readers, though, that "every Mexican who appeared in the least suspicious was apprehended and questioned."[2]

These episodes provide examples, neither the first nor the last, of how Mexicans and Americans, these two peoples so geographically close and so historically intertwined, have such different experience, knowledge, and stories of such momentous events, indeed of one another in general.

Then, too, Mexico and America have stories about themselves that reveal them to be utterly special countries in world history. Mexico is the most unique country in the world because, in the words of José Vasconcelos, the celebrated philosopher of *La Raza Cósmica*, it has more than any other nation achieved "the ulterior goals of History to attain the fusion of peoples and cultures." Other places have experienced racial mixture, but none to the extent of Mexico, and mestizaje is part of Mexico's cultural and political ideology. The apparition of the Mestiza Goddess, the Virgin of Guadalupe, to the Aztec San Juan Diego (but really to all Mexicans) further blesses this "design of constituting the cradle of a fifth race into which all nations will fuse with each other to replace the four races that have been forging history apart from each other."[3]

America's specialness derives from its sense of itself as the end nation in human history, the one founded upon the great ideas of the Enlightenment, where notions of "life, liberty, and the pursuit of happiness" have played out without the corruptions of class warfare, a rigid caste structure, or autocracy, a place where people have come voluntarily and then joined in the national contract, a place where its wilderness outposts have brought civilization and then freely joined as states in the American union. Its political culture of electoral democracy is as natural and value free as its economic culture of free markets and individual prerogatives. Thus the expansion of this cultural, economic, and political system is value free.[4]

It is too easy to pick these national mythologies apart. Mexico's "divine mission" of mixing the old world and the new "by the triumph of fecund love" has not produced a populace any more talented than anyplace else, the Indian remains problematic and disparaged within Mexican society, and the Church has resumed its thrall over the people. America actually conquered its West and the wilderness with military might; slavery and racism belie its notions of liberty; and conformity has usually proved stronger than individualism and electoral choice. Nonetheless, these national narratives, and some would call them mythologies, have established the context in which America and Mexico tell their stories about themselves and, especially in the case of the northern republic, act in the world.

Nations may take their self-descriptions into battle, but economics and conquest typically motivate their actions. An incident precipitated each of America's invasions of Mexico, and in each case the alleged offense provided policy makers in the executive branch with the necessary rationale for military force and occupation. James K. Polk declared that "there are four great measures which are to be the measures of my administration: one, a reduction of the tariff; another, the independent treasury; a third, the settlement of the Oregon boundary question; and, lastly, the acquisition of California." When, in May 1846, after American troops had occupied the mouth of the Rio Grande, Mexican troops attacked across that river, into lands of certainly disputable title, Polk had his grounds for declaring war. The Mexican-American War was not, obviously, about retaliation for the attack, which Mexico considered a proper response to American aggression. It was about the beautiful, bounteous, and strategic prize of the Pacific Coast. He got, obviously, California.[5]

The Mexican-American War was about land, seizing it and the economic opportunity that came with it. In 1831, Abel Stearns, an expatiating Yankee who had finally settled in the little pueblo of Los Angeles, initiated a successful career in trade and married into the prominent Bandini family (a move by which he commenced magnificent land acquisition), received a letter about California from another Yankee resident in Mexico, Alex Forbes. "The opinion is heightened," Forbes said, "by the description you give of it, and confirms that if populated it would perhaps be the most delightful country in the world. How many Countrymen of mine who are jostling one another for room at home might live happily in those fertile but uncultivated plains you describe."

Richard Henry Dana, Boston Brahmin and author of the immensely popular *Two Years before the Mast*, referred to the "lazy, drawling, half-breeds" of the Mexican army, and then said of the upper class how "the men are thriftless, proud, extravagant . . ." and then concluded that "in the hands of an enterprising people, what a country this might be!"

There was more to this thing we call Manifest Destiny than simply the idea that Providence had ordained that white Americans would rule from sea to shining sea. It also included the ideas that Americans needed these lands lest the cities and farms of the East should become so crowded with people jostling one another for opportunity that, frustrated, they would turn to European-style tumultuousness, even revolution. The occupation of the Mexicans' (needless to say the Indians' too) territory would be progressive in the sense that the land would be freed up from indolent people and for enterprise. But what emerges just as forcefully from these words about the *americanos'* thinking, something frankly revealed in the words above, is that America has expected to solve its internal problems of an ever-expanding economy and population, and to maintain its specialness, through physical, external expansion.[6]

Mexicans beheld the same phenomenon but had different language for, thus different knowledge of, matters. Wrote Sub-Prefect Guerrero about the Americans to Manuel Castro in 1846: "Friend, the idea these gentlemen have formed for themselves is, that God made the world and them also, therefore what there is in the world belongs to them as sons of God." Mexicans, and much of the rest of the world where American capital and its representatives have penetrated, felt repulsion and attraction, envy and resentment, admiration and anger, and bewilderment and a desire to emulate these industrious and sermonizing people. Divined Manuel Castro before a junta at Monterey, "these Americans are so contriving that some day they will build ladders to touch the sky, and once in the heavens they will change the whole face of the universe and even the color of the stars."[7]

With historical hindsight, and even a bit of postmodern sensitivity, we can say of the americanos that, in their spirit world (uncomplicated with saints and the deification of the Virgin Mary), their One True God had made everything, but then transcended worldly existence and left management entirely up to the men who could, and usually did as in the case of the Mexican-American War, act without restraint towards His creations. The Bible "reveals every person to himself as a distinct moral agent," reflected Woodrow Wilson, "responsible not to men . . . but responsible through his own conscience to his Lord and Maker."[8] Both peoples observed this confident acquisitiveness of the Americans, and the simultaneously proud and acquiescent pastoralism of the Mexicans, but each had such different language for, thus such different understanding of, their intertwined worlds and how they were unfolding.

American actions in 1914 at Veracruz paralleled those of 1846. At the center of consideration stood American interests in Mexico. During the regime of Porfirio Díaz (1876–1911), he and his "científicos" optimistically opened the doors to foreign investors. Thus American railroad barons—the "Big Four" of E.H. Harriman, James Stillman of National City Bank, Jacob Schiff, and William Rockefeller—came to own the lion's share of the 80 percent of Mexico's railroad stock that American capitalists owned overall. Towards the end of the Porfiriato (as Diaz' regime is usually called), American capitalists accounted for the ownership of 81 percent of the capitalization of Mexico's mines. By 1910, the

Waters-Pierce Company, affiliated with Standard Oil, controlled 90 percent of the illuminating oil market and all the gasoline.[9] Land ownership is equally stunning: American corporations, consortiums, and individuals owned over one hundred million acres, some held for speculation and some actually producing. Such amounted to more than 22 per cent of Mexico's land surface. The Mexican government had sold many of these lands cheaply, some they simply conceded, and some these "investors" simply took. The Hearst family and Texaco led the list of these foreign landowners. The register of American, and British and French, holdings in Mexico could go on and on here.[10]

Mexico appeared to be not only the land of opportunity to big-time capitalists but to Americans of the more sundry sort. By 1910 more than forty thousand lived in the countryside and cities and towns of Mexico. Many of these people availed themselves of the advantageous land prices and cheap and powerless labor force that the dictatorship of the Porfiriato provided. They could own a big house, grow *guayule* for the American rubber market or graze cattle, surround themselves with apparently willing laborers and servants, and, with hard work, achieve actual wealth. They, like the Mexican *hacendados*, often bound their workers to their enterprises via the system of debt peonage. (In this situation a worker remained obligated to labor for a landowner because of the debts that he and his family had contracted with that landowner.) This has been part of the genius of North American society: not only big capitalists, but opportunistic and aggressive people of the middling sort have identified economic prospects and gone after them.

It is revealing that in 1912 and 1913 as the violence and chaos of revolution in Mexico escalated, many of the more apprehensive American small capitalists bailed out and offered their properties for sale at bargain prices. Other, more optimistic, countrymen scooped them up, confident that economic opportunity was theirs for the taking and that capital and hard work would be rewarded. It was the fearful ones who were proved right.[11]

As has been typical of all expatiating capitalists large and small, these Americans in Mexico came to feel an entitlement to their properties and privileges, a sentiment that seems to continue these days as regards Mexico's resources, laborers, and its former territories of Texas, New Mexico, and California. Curiously enough, while their friends and relatives in California fussed over the issue of whether or not Mexican immigrants would join American society, Americans in Mexico never considered becoming citizens of the southern republic. As Americans they continued to understand that it was the duty of their home country's national government to defend their rightfully acquired assets.

Woodrow Wilson and His Stories of America

There is likely no greater intellectual failing of Woodrow Wilson than his inability to understand the contradiction between his support for free trade and investment and the consequences that capital penetration had for the ability of less-capitalized countries to determine their destinies. In 1907, while president of Princeton University, Wilson could affirm that "since . . . the manufacturer insists on having the world as a market, the flag of his nation must follow him, and the doors of nations which are closed against him must be battered down." And while he acknowledged that defense of "concessions obtained by financiers must be safeguarded . . . even if the sovereignty of unwilling nations be outraged," Wilson never seems to have understood the inevitability of local outrage bursting through the thin veneer of legal protection that foreign capitalists cheerily and facilely relied upon for protection and legitimacy.[12] When he became president, the demands of those who had the concessions and properties came to bear on his administration's foreign policy and only then did he experience — but did not understand — the conflict between them and his grand prescriptions for the people of the world. There are no better examples of intimacy and strangeness than Wilson's intercourse with Mexico in 1914.

Woodrow Wilson's comments on the Mexican-American War and the predicament of Mexico in 1911 may come as a surprise to some. In his epic *A History of the American People*, Wilson wrote of "the war, with all its inexcusable aggression." Ray Stannard Baker interviewed the president on May 11, 1916, and reported that Wilson's opinion of Mexico "was based upon two of the most deeply seated convictions of his life; first his shame as an American over the first Mexican war and his resolution that while he was president there should be no such predatory war." (We shall hear of the second tenet later.) He told Congress in 1913 how "I shall follow the best practice of nations in the matter of neutrality by forbidding the exportation of arms or munitions of war of any kind from the United States to any part of the Republic of Mexico." Indeed, Wilson had consistently and publicly criticized capitalist imperialism in Mexico: "What is the underlying cause of the present troubles in Mexico?" He answered his rhetorical question in *World's Work* magazine with "Foreign interests and concessions . . ." and continued: "Who is responsible for the recurrent demand, in recent years more frequent than ever, that the United States shall take over or exercise a veiled protectorate over another of the republics south of us? Always foreign interests, bondholders or concessionaries. They are the germs of revolution and the cause of instability of government in the Latin American countries." The magazine continued that Woodrow Wilson "takes a lofty moral view of his duties and his opportunities . . . The President holds that 'the business, prosperity, and contentment of Mexico mean more, much more, to us than merely an enlarged field for our commerce and enterprise'." This only repeated what he had said to Congress earlier about how "we have the moral right in the case or that we act in the interest of a fair settlement of good government, not for the promotion of some selfish interest of our own."[13]

There is no reason to doubt the sincerity of this rhetoric either. President Wilson had adamantly rejected the "Dollar Diplomacy" of President Taft's Secretary of State Philander Knox and of Taft-appointee Ambassador to Mexico Henry Lane Wilson. Nothing more frustrated Woodrow Wilson and his plans for Mexico than the demands of American oil companies that the United States should simply use its military might again, only this time to establish a protectorate that would adamantly guarantee the property of foreign capitalists. Actually, Pancho Villa's notorious attack on Columbus, New Mexico, in March of 1916 — a move designed more to force Wilson's hand and drive a wedge between him and Mexican President Venustiano Carranza than it was to procure any arms — sparked sufficient popular clamor and support for an occupation.

The overwhelming pressure for U.S. intervention came from business interests whose spokespeople in government, such as Interior Secretary Franklin K. Lane, sought an agreement where "the government of Mexico solemnly agrees to afford full and adequate protection to the lives and property of citizens of the United States, or other foreigners . . . (to operate) industries in which they might be interested." Hoping to re-create the same sorts of protections that Americans had in Cuba, the United States would "reserve the right to re-enter Mexico and to afford such protection by military forces . . ." Taxes that were too high could be labeled "confiscatory." Carranza adamantly rejected such proposals in late 1916. Indeed, he later raised taxes on foreign capitalists and denied them the right to appeal to their home governments for protection. With tensions mounting with Germany, Wilson refused an invasion that would have restored the "rights" of American "concessionaries," especially oil companies, in Mexico.[14]

Based on a reporter's conversation with him, the *New York World* of May 19, 1914, reported that:

> President Wilson is forming a Mexican policy to which he will pledge the Government of the United States when General Huerta is finally eliminated as dictator and hostilities in Mexico have ceased. This policy has as its foundation the breaking up of the Científico or landed party, the splitting up of the great estates and their disposition so that the peons, who compose about 85 per cent of the population, may obtain them.

In other words, Wilson seems to place himself on the side of the peasantry and their leaders Francisco "Pancho" Villa and Emiliano Zapata. And, indeed, the Wilson administration had inched toward supporting Pancho Villa in late 1913, but this was only because the reactionary politics of Huerta and the nationalism of Carranza rendered them increasingly unacceptable to the Americans. With terrific bloodshed, and little or no regard for the sorts of universal rights that we associate with the Enlightenment or Liberalism, these peasant revolutionaries, these peons, fought to obtain land from those "científicos," the pretentious elites of the Porfiriato, and those "foreign interests and concessions" against whom Wilson preached.[15]

In yet other words, Woodrow Wilson, once professor of history and politics, simply didn't get it. In his worldview, there should be freedom for the individual and his capital and respect for law that protected people in their person and their property. He didn't understand how it was that freedom for some individuals to obtain property meant that others not only lost land that their ancestors had possessed but lost their livelihoods as well, a theme we saw in our discussion of NAFTA. It was law that came to protect the powerful interlopers' land and capital and law that maintained the subjugation of the landless under the system of debt peonage. Since in Mexico, law provided the means of injustice, justice required smashing the laws and the government that imposed them.

The inability to understand this grievous and deadly state of affairs arose in Wilson in part because of the narrowness of his study of history. Quite often the excitement and putative importance of grand political events like the American Revolution or Civil War, the origin of the political parties, or the evolution of the Supreme Court and constitutional law, blind people to the real stories of the epical events. There is no better way to think about this than to recall the story of Ramona and Alessandro. Instead, the fabulous story of America's specialness, with its unexamined verities regarding progress and freedom, motivated Wilson to act against Mexico in 1914.

Manifest Destiny, private property, law, and American family values took away the Indians' land and destroyed not just their beautiful love but also Alessandro and his people. You see, there is the imposing history of California — how gold was discovered there, how it became a state in 1850 with the great compromise that admitted it as a free state, and how Hiram Johnson molded the Progressive Movement there — but there are also the stories. The mixing of historical events with imagination and family sagas are what the powerless had — the stories of the lynchings of Mexicans, the annihilation of the Indians, and the exclusion of even those Americans who refused the capitalist, expansionist consensus regarding the benefits of progress.

In Mexico there were the stories of the perfidious expropriation of poor peoples' lands: In the Carlos Fuentes novel, *The Death of Artemio Cruz*, a Yaqui man "was telling about it" to Artemio Cruz, "how the government took our land away to give it to the gringos. About how we fought to defend our land and then the Federals came and cut off men's hands and chased us through the mountains. How they captured the Yaqui chiefs in a big canyon and tied weights on them and threw them into the sea . . ." The captured Yaquis were marched to Yucatán and "the women and children and old people . . . couldn't take it and started to die. Those who survived to get to the sisal plantation were sold as slaves. Men and their wives were separated. They made the women sleep with Chinese, to make them forget the language and breed more workers . . ."

Awaiting a firing squad, another man tells Artemio Cruz how the Yaqui went out at first to fight for his land. Now he fights for General Obregón, against General Villa. No, it was different in the beginning. Then it broke down into factions, but in the beginning every pueblo the revolution passed through was a pueblo where the campesinos' debts were erased, the money-lenders were put out of business, the political prisoners were released and the old bosses were eliminated. Now the men who believed the revolution's purpose was to liberate the people have been eliminated. The purpose today is to glorify leaders.[16]

Wilson could know the history of politics, but he did not, or would not, know the peoples' stories about the consequences of those politics, about what was really happening. Thus it was that the events in Mexico so confounded him.

Certain people selfishly impeded Wilson's efforts to bring progress: Mexico's own moribund reactionaries and America's and England's grasping businessmen. In Wilson's mind, however, neither Mexico's stubborn bourgeois nationalists (associated with Carranza) nor its peasantry, which seemed to be drawn to such lawless and personalist leaders as Villa and Zapata, could elevate Mexico to the sort of liberal capitalist democracy deemed necessary for progress and prosperity. Never mind, it should go without saying, those wretched anarchist radicals associated with the Casa Obrera Mundial in Mexico City and the Partido Liberal Mexicano which functioned mostly in exile in Texas and Los Angeles. All these myriad factions of the revolution proved simply too confusing for the Wilson administration.

Really, though, Wilson's cognitive deficiency had less to do with analysis and information than it did with ignorance, his sorry lack of knowledge of the stories of what were to him far distant places, his lack of compassion. He could know the history and the facts of a matter, he could know that the Mexican-American War was a "predatory" one, but it wouldn't occur to him to learn about the deep meanings of los Niños Héroes, if he knew of them at all, and what would Woodrow Wilson have known of Ramona and Alessandro? The word *compassion*, and it's virtually the same in Spanish, derives from the Latin, *compati*, "to suffer with." Wilson and the liberals could not "suffer with" the peoples whom they kept tending to with guns.

Wilson's history books show no knowledge of how the Americans had so treacherously robbed Ramona's people of their lands or of how they had so viciously separated Alessandro's people from theirs. It has been these stories that give meaning to history for most people. Such stories are based on history, but they include both the imagination and the agenda of the teller. So it was that Wilson's and the Progressives' stories told of Americans bringing peace and prosperity to the West, and the Mexicans' and Indians' stories told of death and the taking of their lands. Again, we see here how the basic matter is usually land and treasure, but people's different stories of the events — the taming of the Wild West and the Yankees' invasions full of fire and blood — are how people comprehend and interpret such matters. Whether they will have *compassion* for one another.

Ultimately, Wilson and the liberals were not about to take up the peasants' side. In large measure this had to do with Wilson's thinking about race: non-whites could not successfully undertake the project of self-control, much less that of self-government. It's hard to know exactly what Wilson thought of Mexicans. He had to have been aware of the variety of "racial types," as one would have called them back then, which prevailed in Mexico. In one utterance, in his *A History of the American People*, Wilson referred to their bravery in battle in the Mexican-American War and called Mexicans "a subtle, spirited race, tenacious to the last of all that it could hold."[17] The matter of such racial thinking aside, or that such vagueness in language could never hold muster in peer-reviewed publications in the field of history these days, this comment does elicit a "subtle," in the various dictionary definitions of that word, presentiment about Wilson's dealing with non-Anglo-Saxons.

It is not hard to imagine how Woodrow Wilson's youth, his socialization, would have influenced his dealings with people who were poor and darker than he. Ray Stannard Baker fawningly describes "the somewhat aristocratic town (Staunton, Virginia) that the little boy lived in: the heart of the Old South . . . All about were fine plantations of cotton and corn and the comfortable homes of the planters and the clustering quarters of Negro slaves." We must remember that Wilson's boyhood was spent in the slave South and, while he had had two uncles who were Northern generals, his father "sided wholeheartedly with the Southern cause" when the Presbyterian Church split over the question of slavery in 1861. Wilson's boyhood home, "The Manse," which "bore itself with the distinction and solidity befitting its position," stood across the town square from the First Presbyterian Church. "To be the minister of such a church in such a city in such a time was to be named with senators and generals: a marked man, a leader. Woodrow Wilson's father, Dr. Joseph Ruggles Wilson, was that minister."[18]

What else can we say, though, but that Wilson observed the world and saw proof of Anglo-Saxon supremacy: American, British, and German factories hummed; the United States had restored political order after the Civil War and used politics for reform in the Progressive era; and people from all over the world seemed to want to come to America's shores. As Wilson told college students in 1913, "But I claim that every race and every man is as big as the thing he takes possession of, and that the size of America is in some sense a standard of the size and capacity of the American people."[19] It also had to do with the quite apparent inability of Mexicans, and certainly other colonized peoples, to progress to

American standards of political and economic stability, something Mexican intellectuals and political leaders often acknowledged.

Wilson and the Progressives could look at Mexico and its declining, passive society, and its proclivity for violent outbursts, and conclude certain things about Mexicans, but they could also use Mexico to validate certain things about themselves, especially their position as leaders in the world historical mission of progress. In another speech of 1911, one in Denver celebrating the translation of the Bible into English, Wilson quoted Tennyson regarding "Some reverence for the laws ourselves have made, / Some patient force to change them when we will, / Some civic manhood firm against the crowd." Then he asked rhetorically, "Can you find summed up the manly self-helping spirit of Saxon liberty anywhere better than in those few lines?" Maybe it is the genius of the Americans to combine these three things here proclaimed: the ability to combine faith in God and benefit from the confidence that He ordains their actions; the Enlightenment notion that humans have created civil society and that it can be changed for the better, perhaps even perfected, through reform legislation; and that the superior moral and intellectual qualities of Anglo Saxons will guard against excess. "Men afraid of nobody, afraid of nothing but their own passions," he continued, "on guard against being caught unaware by their own sudden impulses."[20]

Simon Ortiz, the Acoma poet, explains more of Wilson to me: deeming that they "should be systematic," Wilson and the Progressives were "frightened by emotion. / The sheer joy of being men, / of being children, / was no longer theirs . . ." One can feel sad for them: "They should have seen / the thieves stealing / their most precious treasure: / their compassion, their anger."[21]

Wilson assumed, and certainly not without good reasons, that that peculiar North Atlantic way of thinking about the relation of the self and the society explained how "we shall not be poor if we love liberty, because the nation that loves liberty truly sets every man free to do his best and be his best, and that means the release of all the splendid energies of a great people who think for themselves." But there was no *compassion*.

Thus it was appropriate to extend that worldview, what we might call the emerging "American Creed," to Mexico and other less fortunate peoples, in part because it so apparently worked and in part because it was a feature of the natural progression of history. It was not "the extent of the American conquest," he continued to the students, but the "professed purpose of the conquest, which was to see to it that every foot of this land should be the home of free, self-governed people . . . I would like to believe that all this hemisphere is devoted to the same sacred purpose."[22] It was this sort of devotion that Wilson the Presbyterian had, but it was a devotion without compassion.

The powerful forces of Protestant optimism and Progressive politics distinguished Woodrow Wilson from Porfirio Díaz and his científicos. After all, Wilson's own upbringing in plantation society paralleled the landed estates of the reactionary Mexican elites who supported the Porfiriato. In each case, landed, European-American elites lorded over workers who were darker and considered inherently inferior. What differed was that Wilson, ardent segregationist that he was, still believed that such unfortunates could progress, though certainly not to the level of Anglo Protestants. Besides, Wilson did not exhibit the loathing that Latin American landed elites customarily have had for their landless, often Indian, peons.

Foreign Policy

This is how we can understand the Tampico crisis and the second attack on and occupation of Veracruz: Woodrow Wilson attempted to enforce his worldview on Mexico first by withholding guns from all sides of the revolution until some faction could be found who would affirm his Progressive ideology, and then, when no faction would exactly adhere to these notions, guns would be sold to the least evil Mexican revolutionaries. This notion historians and political scientists have often called the *Idealist* approach to American foreign policy because it has sought to extend — what the natives experienced as imposed — the peculiar, but understood to be universal, even "sacred," values of the of the European and Anglo American Enlightenment, and progress.

The so-called *Realists* have been those who have emphasized the centrality of American economic and geo-political interests to foreign policy. In their view all this idealism about trying to get people variously called "the natives," "backwards," the "colored races," or the "Third World" to adopt the right ways, flies in the face of a number of considerations: One is that these peoples' perceived racial or cultural inferiority, or their own choices, restrict their ability to become modern and progress. Two is the reality of competition from other capitalists and other nations who intend to do evil to America and its business and geopolitical interests. While Wilsonian Idealists piddle around trying to make colored villagers act with the rationality and efficiency of America's local city councils, chambers of commerce, and college faculty senates, there are, in the Realist view, other interests trying to do harm to America's prosperity and stature in the world.

In the Mexican case in 1914, these included the Germans, who most savvy people knew we would soon engage in war, and who eyed Mexican oil; British capitalists who really, really didn't have delusions about the capacities of the natives for self-government or progress; and the Mexican peasantry under the leadership of Villa and Zapata, called simple bandits, who denied the legitimate contracts guaranteeing the private property rights of foreign investors. Thus it was that American guns had to be sent to protect American interests. And, it should be noted, in the Realist view, where American interests were not so threatened the natives could be left to their senseless ways.

In the Mexican case in 1914, there was no consensus. Theodore Roosevelt (TR) railed that "there was no reason whatever for any American to uphold Huerta; but to antagonize him on moral grounds, and then to endeavor to replace him by a polygamous bandit (Villa), was not compatible with any intelligent system of international ethics." Then to "support against him Carranza, who was responsible for exactly the same kind of hideous outrages against Americans, and insults to the American flag, is an affront to all who believe in straightforward sincerity in American public life." Of course the oil concessionaries, associated with the holdover Ambassador Lane Wilson, fumed at President Wilson's parsimony. TR derided Wilson for having "interfered not enough to quell civil war, and not enough to put a stop to or punish the outrages on American citizens, but enough to incur fearful responsibilities."[23]

On other occasions there has been consensus: the Cold War and the early years of Vietnam, for example. Nightmares of Soviet expansionism could unite Idealists and Realists in the cause. The importance of European markets, and "tin, tungsten, and rubber" and the "Domino Theory" (the Eisenhower mantra) in Southeast Asia propelled Realists to military action and nuclear deterrence. Idealists (often associated with liberals and Democrats), who were concerned with winning over to liberal democracy the "hearts and minds" of the Eastern Europeans and Southeast Asians, optimistically joined the crusade.

Waning and waxing collusion over Afghanistan demonstrates this all the more. In 1979 the Soviet Union invaded to maintain in power their lackeys, first Babrak Karmal and then Mohammad Najibullah.

President Jimmy Carter, a crusading Protestant like Wilson, levied sanctions on the Soviet Union, most notably a boycott of the Moscow Olympics. At the time Afghanistan did not amount to much: its days as the crossroads between the Middle East and India had been over for a long time, and it had no natural resources. Realists howled because the United States spent much diplomatic capital on something of little or no material use. Indeed, most of the rest of the world considered this moral grandstanding and that such Idealistic efforts to enforce democratic morality were naive and foolish. But later events would change this and create consensus.

It became apparent that huge oil reserves existed in southwestern Asia in the several Islamic "istans" of the former Soviet Union, and that Afghanistan might prove pivotal in the transportation of that oil, and that the charismatic Islamic fundamentalists who had tossed the Soviets from Afghanistan would mount jihad against the political and economic influence of the West, and that this form of Islam sought to expand itself throughout the oil-rich Middle East. Now the material base existed for Realists to involve American blood and treasure in Afghanistan. As it became more and more apparent that the Taliban amounted to little more than brutal Islamic thuggery (kind of like the Porfirístas and other Latin American dictatorships) who did not "set every man free to do his best and be his best, and that means the release of all the splendid energies of a great people who think for themselves," and who simply condemned womanhood, Idealists could rally back to the interventionist side that Carter had made look so foolish. Then came the horrible catalyst of 9/11 to effect in the United States a new interventionist consensus.

Needless to say, America's recent invasion of Iraq echoes that of Mexico in 1914: grasping for petroleum resources combined with stories of elections and free markets — all assumed to be value free and natural — to produce armed attack.

It is so curious that simultaneously people feel so strongly about what constitutes right and wrong in these matters and that enlightened reflection reveals the utter ambiguity of such foreign policy efforts. It keeps being about oil: German initiatives to secure Mexican oil in 1914 and 1939, and, in the Middle East, the putative necessity of keeping gasoline steady and cheap. America won the air war over Germany in World War II because they ran out (or our bombers blew it all up) of gasoline; what a difference it would have made had in 1939 the United States not agreed to let Mexico nationalize its oil with the stipulation that none of it could go to Germany. Now we act to secure oil supplies so that Americans may command SUVs, which advertising and soccer mom and mall-shopping culture associates with family values. And then of course America acts to free up Mexicans from the thrall of the Catholic Church, what Wilson was doing when he refused to support Huerta, and, at least when they get to the United States, encourages women to disavow the rebozo, her traditional shawl which is emblematic either of her proper sheltering and protection or her subjugation and restraining.

And this is in good part why Idealists will support American efforts to smash the Taliban; it's about smashing the mullahs' viciousness toward women, about getting them to go to school and to be enlightened, and to remove their burkas. For Idealists, in 1914 and in the new century, and in the New World Border, it is above all about freedom of conscience and belief and about the idea that the people are sovereign, that they can and should rule themselves via elections. The Idealists need to ponder the naivete of the Franciscan mission when those idealistic people attached themselves to Spanish imperialism and its quest for gold.

As I said in the introduction to this piece: I wish all this could come true: that people could conduct themselves based upon their individual, but considered, prerogatives. I also wish that America could see its own utter irrationality. The production of SUVs keeps both GM and the UAW happy and feeds bucolic fantasies of family life and macho dreams of going off the road of conformity and domesticity. But really these ridiculous behemoths, some of which get only 10 miles to the gallon, make for global warming and terrible deaths when they crash. Do the math: a vehicle that gets 12 miles to the gallon costs about 14 cents per mile when gas is in the $1.70 range, but should gas cost what it does in Europe and Japan, say $4.50 and up per gallon, then that vehicle costs almost 40 cents per mile to drive. A two-hundred-mile trip would cost $80 instead of $35. Except that Americans pay billions of dollars in tax money to the U.S. military to support that cheap gas. Do some more math: divide the defense budget (about $474 billion in 2006 and about $500 billion in 2007, when we include war-related expenditures from other departments) by the population (about 300 million) and you get a family of four spending about $6,500 on the military. Of course not all that money goes to protect oil (we didn't count the secret CIA budget), but one gets the picture of how expensive it is to defend the SUV-driven American way of life, and how irrational it is. Few people make these connections: Americans, you see, are free to think in some ways but not necessarily in others.

Certainly, though, we cannot simply say that such crude economic interests solely motivate foreign policy; indeed, Woodrow Wilson resisted the concessionaries. We may say, then, that Wilson's concerns centered around ideology, not economics. Progressive change, electoral democracy, and freedom of thought comprised his goals for Mexico and the rest of the world. This is what Idealists have continually sought and what they have continually failed to achieve throughout the twentieth century. The case of Mexico helps explain this.

Profound Stories of Mexico

Mexico and the United States both experienced horrific violence — the latter commencing in 1861 and the former in 1911 — when the contradictions between Modernity and their plantation and hacienda societies could no longer be contained. It is likely true that the United States could not continue "half slave and half free" in large part because of the moral dilemma that slavery presented in the age of democratic revolutions. Perhaps more importantly, America as a society could not continue with its northern half roiling with rough-and-tumble industrialization, democracy for white men, immigration, the class struggle, and scientific change and social reform, while the southern half reflected plantation gentility, force and bondage, persecution of dissent, and retrenchment in its way of life.

Mexico entered the twentieth century with most of its population Catholic and living in rural semi-feudal conditions. Science and secular education were suppressed, and it was on its knees to European and American capital. Those who achieved independence for Mexico in 1821 were even more full of the ideas of the Enlightenment than Americans and had such great faith that liberty, property, and democracy would enable Mexico to progress like the United States and England. Then, too, masses of Mexicans, variously in touch with their Indianness, remained mystically tied to their land, their traditional lifeways, and really couldn't make much sense out of any of the great controversies of the nineteenth and twentieth centuries. In each nation's case, first in 1861 and then in 1911, the unsustainable situations exploded into terrible fratricidal war.

In the American Civil War and the Mexican Revolution, it might appear that the old had been swept away. Slavery no longer existed in the United States, and in Mexico the power of the hacendados had been broken and the Church no longer monopolized education and truth. But really, in the United States most ideas about race remained unchallenged, and in Mexico, people's bonds with the Indian and colonial past had hardly been severed. In fact, the ideology of the revolution amplified Mexico's ties to its indigenous past.

Numerous writers in Mexico have examined this condition which, while they differ in significant ways, speaks to the same penetrating rudiment of Mexico. Guillermo Bonfil Batalla in his *México profundo* (1987) proposes that there have been two Mexicos since independence. The "imaginary Mexico" is that first imposed upon Mexico when Europeans attempted to foster Christianity and to divide the world into the "civilized" and the "Indian." Then after Mexican independence (1821), Mexican elites continued the European model of development, citizenship and electoral democracy, and progress. After World War II, Mexico initiated its program of state-supported capitalist industrialization. It brought only economic chaos. In Bonfil Batalla's view, such a project could never succeed; indeed, it could only corrupt and demoralize that more weighty force of "México profundo," the powerful presence of the country's Indian peoples and legacy.

While I am skeptical of the degree to which many of those he refers to survive as Indians — that is as people whose ceremonial activities maintain their connection to their native spirit worlds — Bonfil Batalla suggests how Mexican conduct, which Americans find simultaneously frustrating and attractive, derives from its ancient and indigenous roots. People work hard and save, not to invest and have increase in their money, nor out of any notions that God might favor this remunerative discipline. Many Mexicans prefer what Bonfil Batalla declares to have "been called sumptuary expense." These include work and contributions in the *cargos*, or "community services," money for fiestas to celebrate saints or various and sundry holidays, spending money on familial or religious ephemera. What many in the United States or in "imaginary Mexico" see as backward or an impediment to progress and modernity, Bonfil Batalla understands as expressions of the weighty Indian history of Mexico.

In the context of direct European conquest, and then in the context of criollo and mestizo elites' efforts to import the Progressive, modern ideas of the European Enlightenment in the years after 1821, people in the rural villages have acted to continue in the ways they always had, or imagined they had. He argues that "these communities have an Indian culture but have lost the sense of identity that goes with it." The way they act as Indians, the way they presence themselves with such permanence and immutability, the way they stubbornly resist progress, "can be understood only within the framework of colonial domination, which limited and distorted the possibilities for growth while imposing foreign cultural elements opposed to the group's requirements for survival." In other words, as I understand Bonfil Batalla's insights, while they may not identify themselves as Indians, they still act like Indians who are actively resisting encroachments on their lands, customs, and social and political autonomy.[24] This is why the mass of Mexico will not progress in their ideas and conduct.

Fifty years previously, Manuel Ramos had argued for a similar artificiality to Mexico's soul. "Mexicans have been imitating for a long time," he stated in *Profile of Man and Culture in Mexico* (1934), "without actually realizing they were imitating." Another thing about which Americans are completely unaware is that, until recently, it was "the magical symbol of France" that Mexicans sought to copy, not the United States. "This spiritual influence reached its height in the epoch of Porfirio Díaz," he notes, "when the cultured classes dressed according to the Parisian vogue and imitated its good and bad customs." The middle class of the twentieth century mostly feels (subconsciously) insecure because of its genetic and social proximity to the lower classes, and thus is the most mimetic.[25]

His chapter on "Psychoanalysis of the Mexican" only the most faithful of Freudians will take as gospel, but I think it has much meaning nonetheless. Ramos claimed that Mexico and its people suffer an inferiority complex, "not that the Mexican *is* inferior, but rather that he *feels* inferior." Borrowing from Alfred Adler, Ramos proceeds from the view that the inferiority complex appears in a child as soon as he recognizes the insignificance of his own strength compared to the strength of his parents. Mexico at first found itself in the same relationship of filial inadequacy to the civilized world. After independence this feeling, and its sublimated expression, is encompassed in the lower classes in the concept of the *pelado*, or the "de-haired one," or the "negated one."

Such a man is "less than a proletarian in the economic hierarchy, and a primitive man in the intellectual one. Life from every quarter has been hostile to him and his reaction has been black resentment." He lashes out, often violently, against his imagined enemies in an effort to prove some sort of superiority "to renew the vigor of his downtrodden ego." Ramos continues that "the *pelado*'s terminology abounds in sexual allusions which reveal his phallic obsession." Mexicans (and Ramos means the men) have not the science, art, or industry of the Europeans or the Americans; all they have left is their manliness, their "huevos," their ability to assert physical superiority over another man. And since one supposes that all men are like this, one can only imagine that the next man who approaches him will be an enemy.[26]

There are several considerable problems with his arguments. One has to do with the validity of what is undeniably a rather crude Freudian analysis. Another is that LOTS of men are like this, everywhere in the world, and that it is not only the lower classes that engage in this compensatory virility. Actually, though, I find Freudian analyses illuminating not because of their scientific validity but because of their metaphorical power.

Ramos has given us not a paradigm of data and conclusions but one for the imagination. Yes it is the case that people in a country conquered and re-conquered, and then mimetic of the conquerors, will feel inferior. And yes it is the case that an exaggerated manliness, what is called *machismo* these days, exists as a mode of adaptation to this situation of perceived inferiority. As Carlos Monsiváis has noted, "Having been dispossessed, the never-quite-adult *macho* from the popular classes offers up the credulity of his puerile, deteriorated and sacrificial ego for commercialization." (This might explain why Mexicans in Mexico so love the Dallas Cowboys and perhaps even more the Dallas Cowgirls.) Amongst the dominant classes "*machismo* becomes a technique of concealment . . . *machismo* comes from repression." To affirm oneself as the macho is to concede subconsciously that one IS a pelado, controls little of his life, and lacks the emotional depth to negotiate his troubles and fears.[27]

No one has spoken to these matters with power and eloquence, and stunning intellectual depth, greater than that of Octavio Paz. His *The Labyrinth of Solitude: Life and Thought in Mexico* (1950, 1959) is now commonly reviled for its notions about women, yet its profundity remains. To Paz it's not just that Mexicans feel inferior and have attempted a delusional imposition of the values and conduct of Western Civilization. It's more: Catholicism, in Paz's view, may have destroyed the plurality of gods and languages that prevailed in the pre-Columbian world, but it did replace them with a God that maintained people's spiritual ties with the cosmos. Liberalism, with its emphasis on equality and the individual, severed Mexicans' relationship to the spirit world. The liberal reform movements were "attacking a very concrete and particular affirmation: that all men are the sons of God, a creed permitting a genuinely filial relationship between the individual and the cosmos." No longer children of God, Mexicans became orphans. "Our solitude has the same roots as the religious feelings," Paz claims. "It is a form of orphanhood, an obscure awareness that we have been torn from the All, and an ardent search: a flight and a return, an effort to re-establish the bonds that unite us with the universe."[28]

There are so many passages in *Labyrinth of Solitude* where one will have to stop, re-read, and then re-think what one knows. Too often his apparently incautious abstractions will give pause to a reader, like when he generalizes about Mexicans and Americans. "The Mexican tells lies because he delights in fantasy, or because he is desperate, or because he wants to rise above the sordid facts of his life; the North American does not tell lies, but he substitutes social truth for the real truth . . . They are optimists and we are nihilists . . ." I read these passages and I think that he has read Woodrow Wilson: "They are activists and we are quietists; we enjoy our wounds, and they enjoy their inventions." I think of my grappling with the Enlightenment when Paz says how the "North Americans consider the world to be something that can be perfected, and that we consider it to be something that can be redeemed."

I read Paz and I know what is preternaturally disturbing about Woodrow Wilson when he affirms "men . . . afraid of nothing but their own passions." Paz could be describing the American president, that son of a Presbyterian minister, when he says, "They believe in hygiene, health, work and contentment, but perhaps they have never experienced true joy, which is an intoxication, a whirlwind. In the hubbub of a fiesta night, our voices explode into brilliant lights, and life and death mingle together, while their vitality becomes a fixed smile that denies old age and death but that changes life to motionless stone."

He could be describing the liberal Protestant man in general.[29]

What Time It Is

I am sure that we all wonder about the validity of each of these far-reaching, venturesome, and highly interpretive views. I will only affirm their erudition, compassion, and bravery. And ask my readers to think of these efforts metaphorically. Surely there is some profound enlightenment, some presumptuous and even pompous conclusions, and certainly audacious and penetrating insight in what each has to say.

It would be easy to disregard what must be seen as gross essentializations of Mexican and American cultures and of understanding them to be immutable. Mexico and Mexicans and America and Americans are very different countries and peoples now, and in the middle decades of the twentieth century and in the 1860s, from the way they were at the time of their colonization and wars for independence. What may have been apt characterizations of people in the nineteenth century likely do not apply in the era of the New World Border.

There are other explanations for the traits that we might call those of *México profundo*. Especially the Indians of Mexico, but the lower classes in general, have experienced a profound domination at the hands of reactionary elites and foreign capitalists, one based on caste and class and one that cannot help but have had depressing psychological effects. The evolution of underdevelopment, in other words, has had consequences beyond the simply economic. The Indians since the reign of the Spanish are not likely to have an optimistic attitude toward the future. The question here, though, is the degree to which this has to do with their tragic historical experience or with their relationship to time. The answer is some of both, but I am veering in the direction of matters of orientation to time as the primary answer.

What Woodrow Wilson, the liberals, reformers, and just rather generally what Euro-Americans have expected from Mexicans, and other people deemed unenlightened, heathen, or primitive, is that they adopt a new way of being. It's not much different than what the Spanish demanded from the Indians of the Americas, namely, that they put aside customs of the ages and an orientation to time and the cosmos that made the world understandable and survivable. It is not simply part of the Protestant and Progressive ideologies to think that people, especially poor ones, could do much better than putting their genius and financial and labor resources to something more useful than big churches, and this is a sentiment I know well.

I remember how angry I was when I first went to Italy, back when it was the Third World — the Mexico even — of Europe. So many poor people and so much wealth in the churches. Or when I went to Mexico for the first time as a teenager and saw poor people bloodying their knees as they proceeded to the Basilica of the Virgin of Guadalupe. I didn't understand then that these people were living in the mythic present. For them the supreme miracle of the appearance of the Virgin of Guadalupe is not mere fable or even sacred story. It's that the spirit of Her very self exists in the now, and palpably in the glorious church. They are expressing their devotion to the immanent beliefs that have been unchanging. They spend their genius and their treasure, princely or trifling, on maintaining the institutions that reflect the great faith, not on making themselves or their environment different. For days before December 12, the Day of the Virgin of Guadalupe, people prepare for pilgrimage. Literally millions converge at the Basilica on Her Day. Everything else comes to a stop while they draw their blood both in pilgrimage to the Majestic Mother and to commune with their Savior in His hour of passion.[30]

To the Aztecs only a thin membrane separated this physical world from the parallel world of the spirits. We might say that "hierophanous" places are the ones where this membrane can be transversed, where humans can enter into the spirit world. The Virgin of Guadalupe appeared in 1531 to Juan Diego, an Aztec and now a saint, at Tepeyac, the hill that was home to the important goddess Tlazolteotl. The basilica which houses the sacred image of the Virgin is there now; Tepeyac is a hierophanous place. We moderns, steeped in science and materialism, cannot know these places or the experience of entering into the other side, or how complex this life truly is.

Mexicans bring their *ofrendas*, their offerings, to the Virgin here and to other places. Offerings, not supplications, have been the essence of Indian spirituality whether it be of sage smoke in the sacred directions, of pollen on a hunted deer's nose, or of hearts to the angry Aztec sun and war god Huitzilopochtli. In México profundo the holy provides the authority on how to think, be, and conduct themselves. People are connected, in other words, not to history, which brings progress, but rather to the cosmos and its cycles.[31] These matters of time, and devotion, again.

Liberals, on the other hand, perceive themselves and their society as being attached to history, which is rather like a highway and which is taking them someplace new and presumably better. They cannot understand why so many Mexicans, and so many other peoples of what is revealingly declared to be the "developing countries," have a different relationship to the future, indeed to time in general. Maybe this is because Mexico's profound Indianness still persists in the form of a cyclical sense of time; maybe because mimicry — of Liberalism and progress and consumerism or anything else — can never genuinely work; or maybe imperialism has made them pessimistic; or maybe because Mexicans, in their souls, act not to progress but to commune with the supernatural.

I think about time again, like when I think about the California missions. I know now that linear time is only one kind of time. Mythic and cylindrical time are other kinds of real time too. Thinking in mythic time people know two eras: the sacred time, usually when people and the rest of the natural world were created, and profane time, or when everything else happened. In that former era, the First People governed matters and they were the ones who made the world — in its physical, mystical, and social structures — and whose potent and sublime spirits still circulate and affect matters in the present. In the second era, human beings have been responsible for history, but most certainly, the characters of the myths still circulate; those from what we might call long ago or "mythical figures" are still present in the world. Their presence and interventions in this world — what we moderns call superstition or magic — are taken for granted.

It should be easy to see how for traditional Indians and many Mexicans that sacred time has been the one most worthy of reverence, the one most exemplary and deserving of praise, and mimicry. For that was an era in which there were no missionaries, no corrupt and warring generals and politicians, no foreign imperialists, and women and children respected sagacious male elders. But it is not simply a past time; elements of mythic time still present themselves as people engage in the ancient ceremonies — songs, dances, rituals — that invoke spirits and allow participants to commune with the personages of the great and true myths. The personages and ceremonies of mythic time continue to exist in present time, making "the now" what has been called "the mythic present."[32]

Thus it is that people act in time not to get to some new place, but in a way that is more cylindrical. Imagine a line that moves around and along such a cylinder: it does go someplace but not very fast — actually what is most important are the repeatable events around the cylinder, the ones arrived at in an almost circular fashion. It's about doing things as they have always been done, or at least as the stories of sacred time have told that they were done. Imagine, now, going along time on the cylinder: there is some change over time, but the important moments are the repeatable ones, the ones that have always been done, at least in the mythic imagination.

The ethnographer priest Padre Gerónimo Boscana, whom we will meet again in the next chapter, illustrates this sense of time when he says of the Juaneño (actually Acjachemem people) that "these Indians lacked in the first place a chronology and starting point whereby they could reckon the dates of past years . . . and therefore their calendar was confined to the months of the year from tropic to tropic, or to the return of the sun . . . and for this reason they did not know . . . how much time had elapsed since this or that thing had happened."

Likely the most startling outcome of these reflections is that different people have different conceptions of what time it is. In the modern conception of time, one based upon Newtonian physics, time exists independently of peoples' origin stories. What time it is derives from the rotation of the earth (every 24 hours) and its orbit around the sun (365 days, plus a bit). Actually, physicists now affirm "atomic time," a calculation of time based upon the oscillation of electrons in a cesium atom. Everyone in the world is living right now in the same number of years (measured even in billions) after the creation of the universe, after the appearance of particular comets and eclipses, in the same geological age, and before the next (predictable) astronomical event. This may be true in some ways, but these are not the ways everyone has measured time. Europeans and Americans even judge people by their conception of time. "They did not know anything more than the present time," said Boscana of the Juaneño, "putting their reason to use (only) with natural instinct, as it were, like so many animals."[33]

The ancient Mayans understood celestial bodies in spiritual ways, as living entities with a spirit. These spirits interacted with the cycles and beings of this world; their actions, celestial events, did not happen independently of people's lives and cycles. Humans had 10 fingers and 10 toes, thus they measured time in 20-year cycles (*katuns*) and then 400-year cycles (*baktuns*). Since 13 was a holy number, multiplying it by 20 gave 260, or the number of days in a holy cycle. The calendar had 360 days, or 18 months of 20 days each. While such events as planting and harvesting were cyclical, different Mayan groups measured time based on births and deaths of their own kings, but they all measured time from the era of the Olmecs.[34] Christians measure time from the birth of the Holy Savior, Moslems from the *hejira* of Mohammed, and Jews from the *creation*. Pueblo Indians of the American Southwest mark time from the *emergence* and acknowledge that different peoples emerged at different times.

There is irony here that emerging during Wilson's administrations were "pre-millennial dispensationalists," people who believe that we are in "End Times." Like medieval Christians and nineteenth-century millennialists, those associated with evangelical and fundamentalist Christianity believe that the end of the world will happen in their lifetimes. Religious fundamentalism was gathering force in Wilson's era, seemed to be discredited with the Scopes Trial of 1925, but now at least 20 percent of Americans have this political orientation. In their view it is time to prepare for the end. It is not time to reform society in the ways that Woodrow Wilson imagined and certainly not in the ways associated with liberal tolerance. Part of the reason for the demise of Liberalism in America, that which seemed to be a natural progression from Wilson's New Freedom to Roosevelt's New Deal to Kennedy's New Frontier to Johnson's Great Society, lies in the reality that so many see themselves positioned in time not at the edge of a brighter future but at the ledge of the end of the world.

Modern natural and social science, on the other hand, expects and even demands that everyone agree on what time it is and that movement through time is linear and associated with progress. The level of technological and social complexity a society has achieved has become the measure of the progression through linear time. Woodrow Wilson and the Progressives assumed that they had progressed the furthest, and this notion — cultivated in the late nineteenth century with America's Indians — has continued to influence powerfully American foreign policy for a century.

Modern Times

What has become clear to me, this man afflicted with a confused love of fickle, deceitful modernity, is that the way people *are* has to do with history and how they have adapted to its slings and arrows. There is no natural state of existence, no authentic self, no predictable development, no one true way of relating to the supernatural. There are only adaptations — with usually remarkable variety in human agency — to nature, history, and the ancestral commands of culture.

These *archaic* peoples endeavor always to return to first things, to the ways matters went in sacred time, to engage in life as it has always been done. We moderns seek almost always new things, novelty and invention, and making things *better* than they were, usually with technological innovation. I've come to understand that modernity is not something that I chose after reading books about the Enlightenment; modern is something that I am. I quickly learned the bell schedule in junior high, to save some of my allowance so that I would have more later, to calculate my projected expenses for going out on dates relative to my-then-meager income, to not simply imagine going to graduate school but to delay gratification so that I could go and then succeed.

I learned the history of those who went out and changed things: I learned about those who created the fruited plains from the old Indian lands or those who capitalized and organized the great factories, or maybe about those who changed American political thinking like Thomas Jefferson, Abraham Lincoln, and Franklin D. Roosevelt, or maybe those who changed the way diverse Americans interrelated like Jackie Robinson and Martin Luther King Jr. In college I learned to take different sides in these matters and to be critical of the relations of power; I sided with the Indians, the workers, reformers, and those who struggled for civil rights, but I never challenged the idea of progress. By internalizing the virtues of the dominant American culture and its history, I have become equipped to prosper in this individualist, market-oriented society. I've come to understand that by claiming that I'm "modern," I'm not so much free to make choices as I am well prepared, well adapted — effectively socialized in other words — for success in this peculiar culture of modern America.

All of us make up stories to affirm our virtue. Either formal mythologies that enhance the quality of life in the sacred times or epic histories that celebrate progress and transformation, these inventive and ontologically useful creations confirm that how each of our societies has acted in history is virtuous and appropriate.

Once this notion is taken to heart, it makes moralistic suppositions and directives about progress and religion, and by extension materialism and family, regardless of conviction, not only foolish but dangerous. This is why Woodrow Wilson and Victoriano Huerta, Porfirio Díaz and James K. Polk, can seem like such preposterous figures in this postmodern day and age: each knew himself to be right based upon eternal verities. Indeed, we have unveiled something of the dictatorialism of Wilsonian Progressivism: the Progressives were *administrators*, people who whether by reform (especially in education) or imperialism would make people *progress*, whether they wanted to or not. It's just that now we know that the way Americans *are*, and the way Mexicans *are*, regardless of what we may think of the peculiarities of the arguments of Bonfil

Batalla, Ramos, or Paz, are different adaptations to the exigencies of history and culture, not indicators of progress along some historical timeline.

I suspect that I am not alone when I say that the hardest thing to stomach about Woodrow Wilson has been his stubborn self-righteousness and his imperialist hypocrisy. Reading through some of his collected papers, I think I understand him a bit more now, though I don't like him any better. It really didn't occur to Wilson, or to William Jennings Bryan, his secretary of state during the Mexican crisis, that they pursued a shabby and contemptible imperialist policy. Even Wilson's most ardent sycophant among historians explains that "they were both fundamentally missionaries, evangelists, confident that they comprehended the peace and well-being of other countries better than the leaders of those countries themselves," and that "missionary diplomacy found its apogee in Wilson's efforts to shape the Mexican Revolution into a constitutional and moralistic pattern of his own making."[35] It's the priests and Indians all over again, and the devoted and the avaricious.

Wilson and the Idealists, and the Spanish friars and the Church, really did think that they were doing well for the natives when they blustered into their lives. Those who would make of the Indians peons, or even slaves, on their haciendas (then), and those (now) who would make of the natives workers on their corporate farms (on either side of the border) or in their maquiladoras, understand that their actions were about commanding labor and making money, their feverish hosannas about improving the natives' lives notwithstanding. The thing of it is, though, the consequences are so much the same: guns.

The natives really can't tell whether or not it is Woodrow Wilson and Lyndon Johnson sending the Marines to their shores in the cause of progress and democracy, or Theodore Roosevelt and Ronald Reagan in the cause of American interests. The outcome is consistent. When the mission friars found that the Indians wouldn't instantly convert to Catholicism, or that they constantly apostatized, they sent the troops and their guns to enforce Christian faithfulness; when the Wilsonians found that the American Indians, the Mexicans in 1914, or the Vietnamese wouldn't accept the True Faith of Liberal Democracy, they sent the troops and their guns. These outcomes really didn't differ much from when — in the cause of holding or getting land — Spanish troops reconquered New Mexico in 1693 or Polk took California in 1846 or when Nixon undid Allende in Chile or Reagan the Sandinistas in Nicaragua.

Brave New Worlds

Of course people on both sides of the border have resorted to racialized explanations for most all of their differences. "Así son los americanos," say the Mexicans about the northerners' ambition, acquisitiveness, and imperiousness. "You know how it is with these Mexicans," say the Americans about how those south of the border (and the ones in the north) are so lethargic, profligate, and passionate. And they speak with some repulsion and attraction in the tone of their voices. The idea that these traits derive from anything "in the blood" is a notion from the nineteenth century and no longer to be taken seriously: that so many Anglo-Saxon Americans and mestizo Mexicans act like the other one is supposed to, not to mention genetic science, quite disproves racial explanations. As far as I can tell, literally millions of industrious Mexicans do so much of the physical labor and service labor in California, the Southwest, and even Las Vegas and Chicago, and ride buses to work, and millions of putatively industrious Anglo Americans work long, air-conditioned hours before computer screens and drive nice cars. Obviously, yet these explanations survive. And that the way Mexican culture affirms spending money on a saint's fiesta and American culture affirms joining a church for business contacts, and that Americans have one sense of time discipline and Mexicans are ready to do something when it's time to do it, provides more proof of the idea that conduct and sensibility are constructs and adaptations and that they have not much to do with correct behavior or morality. And that anyway, really, there exist huge overlaps of the population who do things like each other, or, if not, like the other one is supposed to be doing.

Yet, I think, and here I will take courage from the Mexican authors cited above to make gross claims, Mexicans and their particularism have an easier time accepting difference than the Americans and their universalism. In the Mexican view, one which the imperfectability of humankind and the unruliness of nature so informs, the idea that everything will conform to some divine or Enlightenment plan is an impossible one. Only unruly passion and the inevitability of sin are givens. In the pietistic Protestant mind and the liberal reformer plan, like those of Woodrow Wilson and Jimmy Carter, there can be, if not perfection, then at least improvement in the human condition and enhancement of human happiness. I am inclined to see this in a combination of the ways people on both sides of the border do: the modern American side of me wants to believe in progress; the Mexican side knows that the project of modernity is really about adherence to certain culturally specific norms. Or maybe it's the reluctant postmodern side of me — that understands progress and freedom as a snare and delusion — that accords with the Mexican side.

Then, too, Mexicans, as I read about them and function with them as a *pocho* tourist in Yucatán, Mexico City, and Baja California, find attractive the shiny products that putatively emanate from America. TVs, VCRs, boom boxes, CDs, videos, and fashion are the things that people want to have and which will give them feelings of status and worth. (I own all this stuff and much more.) These are mostly the products of Japanese corporations and are all made in Asia, but they are associated with the United States, its consumer culture, and the prowess of America which enables it to project its ways around the world. Manuel Ramos would likely speculate that Mexicans like these things so much because it is how they continue to mimic those cultures perceived as superior, first the French and now the Americans.

I find it hard to believe that most Mexicans really understand what profound changes it would take, what it has taken the United States, to achieve such a consumer society. In the Mexican view, things *happen to* families, villages, and the nation. This is part of the famous *fatalismo* of Mexico and Latin America. It does not mean that things will ensue in some pre-ordained way, but rather that sin and happenstance are inevitable, indeed more potent forces than planning, intention, and reason. Their history of conquest, colonization (from Spain to European and American corporations to NAFTA), and political and economic chaos gives Mexicans plenty of reason to have this orientation to history and present-day dilemmas.

Not very many people in the world understand that this consumer culture has come at the expense of family and tradition, of faith and eternal verities, of doing things as they had always been done and being attached to place. We are starting to understand here why Mexico has both sought to become modern, but has floundered so dreadfully, and, at the same time, to maintain its traditions, but has been so powerless to do so.

Land, labor, family, worship, and consumption have always been tied together in the traditional village. What the patriarchal family put together on the land was what they consumed, and these productive activities are what held together kith and kin. For people to buy the products of world capitalism, they must put aside this old-fashioned conduct in favor of leaving the farm and engaging in individual wage labor and then taking the money from there to the marketplace for things to affect their individual preferences. What people don't understand is that the inevitable consequence is to replace the father both with the employer as the director of production and with the salesman as the arbiter of taste.

Yet, liberals on both sides of the border have insisted that it is part of the natural progression of human history and development for people to cut loose from the ties of place, kin, and spirits and then to "progress" into a new world of liberty, equality, fraternity, and the individualist pursuit of happiness. They believe that reason can not only provide the body discipline that mission priests sought to bring the Indians, but that it can demystify the natural world and make it understandable and amenable to human control and manipulation. This is the sort of worldview that politicians from both the PRI and the PAN (Mexican political parties) have sought to bring to the Indians to modernize Mexico. Most recently Chiapas has exploded into rebellion against these efforts, notably commencing on the day NAFTA took effect, in order to restore the old Indian-based land-tenure system and to be free of federal orders and control in favor of the local conventions, the ones associated with México profundo. Don't let their use of the magic of the Internet to propagandize their cause and cell phones for communication mislead you. Recall that they are Indians and that in México profundo magic is an accepted part of life.

For Woodrow Wilson, the Bible, in contrast to the Catholic clergy, "reveals men unto themselves, not as creatures in bondage, not as men under human authority, not as those bidden to take counsel and command of any human source."[36] And while God exists for most Americans, for only about 20 percent is He the arbitrary figure of the Old Testament who holds our fate in his omnipotent hands. Americans exalt freedom of conscience: while consumerism certainly colonizes people's tastes, and politicians adroitly exploit moral anxieties, Americans do not kowtow to explicit commands from priest or lord, and in no place is this more affirmed than in American Catholics' cavalier use of birth control. Education, science, and, ideally, the people (democracy and individual conscience) have become the new authorities. Self-improvement, technology (and not just in transportation and communication, but in medical science, especially in contraception and the control of childhood diseases), and the depreciation of deference have brought forth the affluence and personal prerogatives that large numbers of Europeans and Americans experience, and which is understood as the natural progression of history. This matter of devotion again.

It's difficult to say these days which style of life is better. "Freedom" is a good thing, no doubt, though American politicians' inane and irresponsible use of the word usually renders it meaningless. But it is true that because we moderns are much less beholden to family, community, and place, we can strive, innovate, and produce more, and think and make moral judgments for ourselves. I will always celebrate the U.S. Constitution that established, to my thinking, two (among other, of course) stunning notions when seen from a historical perspective: namely, habeas corpus (no one shall be taken from their home or detained without due process) and popular sovereignty (political power resides with "We the people"), and I celebrate how the unfolding of American history has, however unevenly, come to include, however incompletely, women and non–Anglo-Saxons in this Progressive project of democratic politics. Then, too, with all this freedom, the autonomous individual is often lonely, and the norms and images that consumer culture, capitalist media, and fundamentalist religion purvey make contemporary Americans and Mexicans look, think, and act very much alike, no doubt, too.

This is why I think of modernity now as a dilemma rather than as a goal or a place in history. This has required me to come unstuck from the Progressive view of time and history, the one that Woodrow Wilson and Benito Juárez, and lots of other people like Thomas Jefferson, Karl Marx, and Martin Luther King Jr., assumed to be true and inevitable. Pancho Villa himself, while he reviled Woodrow Wilson, spoke of "the real people of the United States of North America, whom I respect and admire for their glorious traditions, for their example of order and economy, and for their progress."[37] You must bear with me, dear readers, as I try to fathom these matters. All I really know now is that neither the Wilsonian Progressives, nor the Mexican liberals, have understood the requirements for everyday Mexicans to move into the modern world. And that, while controversial in their densely literary and transcendent views, Bonfil Batalla, Manuel Ramos, and Octavio Paz have penetrated for me something of the depths not only of Mexico but of modernity and its constrictions and insolvencies.

What is clear is that missions, moral example, and guns never succeed in making whole cultures "modern." Woodrow Wilson's supporters affirm that the president's "broad objective — the establishment of a constitutional government in Mexico, responsive to the social and economic needs of the people and amenable to his direction efforts" — was "commendable." The only problem was that "he used the wrong tactics." "Missionary diplomacy," states Arthur S. Link, biographer and compiler of the 69 volumes of Wilson's papers, correspondence, and speeches, "reached its apogee in Wilson's efforts to shape the Mexican Revolution into a constitutional and moralistic pattern of his own making."[38]

Maybe, but readers, as you and I have been wrestling with these matters of the motivations of U.S. relations with countries we sometimes call "Third World," sometimes "developing," and used to call "backward," doesn't it seem that policy makers are mostly concerned with the ability of those countries to maintain order within their borders and to not destabilize regions the United States considers within its interests? In other words, as long as a country will play along with transnational capitalism, which the United States leads, then they will be seen as virtuous. In the case of Woodrow Wilson, though, we must add that for a country to be virtuous it must accede to being remade in "a constitutional and moralistic pattern of his (Wilson's) own making." Mexico was failing on all counts in 1914.

Thus it was that Woodrow Wilson's guns would come into play. Such an invasion had been planned for several months. The several Texans in Wilson's cabinet, under the leadership of Wilson's closest political confidant and political strategist, Col. Edward House, prevailed upon the administration to ready the U.S. military to invade and protect American corporations' oil, rubber, copper, and zinc interests, ones of significance both for profits and military preparedness for the European theater. While the arrest of the sailors and the refusal of the Mexicans to atone with the 21-gun salute galvanized popular opinion, the pending arrival of the *Ypiranga*, a ship owned by the Hamburg American Packet Line and carrying arms for Huerta, convinced Wilson to act. He had already given permission for the guns to be shipped. On April 21, instead of simply seizing the ship and its contents, the American fleet attacked Veracruz.[39]

The Mexican federal army — in disarray, of course, given that it was in the middle of a revolution — removed itself, and then armed civilians and naval cadets resisted the invaders, a replay of 1847 in Mexico City. "The American warships bombarded the city for hours," John Mason Hart writes, "and their upgraded guns took a terrible toll on the populace." Hundreds, maybe thousands, were killed. The Marines then occupied the city, and the action briefly united Mexicans as riots broke out across the country.[40]

More and more devotion to "the manly self-helping spirit of Saxon liberty." Less and less compassion. More and more guns. More and more violent intimacy between America and Mexico.

There are too many inconsistencies in Wilson's actions to make a coherent story or to explain his immediate political motivations, though I think the mostly unwittingly ideological ones are apparent. For a while, while the reactionary Huerta briefly established power, Wilson seemed to lean toward Villa. Both Huerta and Carranza railed vehemently against Wilson's bellicosity over the arrest of the sailors and even more so over the occupation, while Villa seems not to have voiced objection. Yet Wilson would soon throw his support to Carranza who, the administration decided, would more reliably defend foreign interests and maintain order than the much more volatile Pancho Villa. The U.S. military simply confiscated all arms coming into Veracruz and warehoused them, but released some to Tampico, which the Constitutionalists controlled, and none to areas under Villista control.

At least two things are clear, though. Constitutionalist General Álvaro Obregón, now well armed in contrast to the previously ascendant Villistas and Zapatistas who could not get arms through Veracruz, triumphantly marched into Mexico City in August 1914 and soon consolidated power. (Obregón later had Carranza assassinated.) And the Wilson administration used the sale of arms to one side, and refused it to the other, to influence the outcome of the situation. This was not the first or last time American policy makers would use this strategy. In the Russian Revolution, in Nicaragua in 1909 and the 1980s, in Vietnam before formal engagement, in Guatemala and Iran in 1954, in Chile during the regime of Allende, in Angola and South Africa in the 1980s and 1990s, and one could go on and on, American foreign policy could profoundly influence the outcome in favor of political leaders friendly to U.S. interests by selling them crucial arms and withholding them from others. At the same time America can feign neutrality and non-intervention.[41]

So maybe this episode at Tampico and Veracruz was more than "missionary diplomacy" and a failure of tactics. Maybe this rather brief chapter in American foreign policy — one that took place with that most intimate of strangers, Mexico — reveals the essence of U.S. foreign policy, more so than, say, entry into World War I. (The fateful assassination of

Archduke Ferdinand came two months after the occupation of Veracruz.) The deployment of Woodrow Wilson's guns, and his administration marshaled armaments in several different ways in Mexico in 1914, reveals something of the authoritarianism of the liberal, Progressive state. It is easy to attribute Wilson's actions to the exhortations of the Texans, people who were more frankly imperialist. But let's think about that word: "imperialism" comes from the Latin *imperare* which means "to command." To liberal Progressives this effort "to command" might well seem value free. When we take to heart what we've learned from Octavio Paz, Manuel Ramos, and Guillermo Bonfil Batalla, we see how Wilson's effort can only be understood as *imperial* because, indeed, it attempted to command people whom he saw as inferior to reorient themselves to the cosmos. This episode at Tampico and Veracruz reveals as well how distasteful and dangerous such unconsciously imperial endeavors have been and forever will be.

∴ 5 ∴
Death and Birth
The Missions of California

Up and down the coast of California stand the magnificent missions. Imaginatively restored, they stand as monuments to the Franciscan fathers from Spain and the Indian peoples of the place. They eulogize the great Padre Junípero Serra; they intimate that not all that happened with Indians proved good. Frozen in time, the missions, as presented to the tourists and the schoolchildren who visit them in the yellow busses, seem to be part of "the distant past," a place in time when people lived, worked, worshiped, and thought in very different ways from the ones we know now. This is and isn't true that the missions belong simply to a time irrevocably long ago.

I think of my ancestor, Felipe Sotomayor, who saw the missions, though certainly not at their pinnacle. It is easy to imagine what he would have thought of the Indians around the towns and the missions. He would have seen them in terrible physical and spiritual decay and chaos. Those he would have encountered "in the wild" would have terrified him. In either posture they would have seemed irredeemable. "Horrible" is a word that is the same in Spanish and English and is likely one he would have used to describe them.

His grandson, my grandfather, believed that Indians and all "backwards" people could be elevated through education to civilization and the values of the Enlightenment but, emphatically, not by *conquista espiritual*. In 1964 he published in Mexico a short book titled, of all things, *Cristianizando*.[1] In it *mi Tata* Jesús contrasted *religión espontánea* and *religión dogmática*. The former he defined as "an inborn impulse that moves us to wish the best for our fellow beings, as much as our own well being." "This true religion is humble, discrete, austere, and its actions conform to its words," he explained and then cited "Tomás Jefferson, Abraham Lincoln, Miguel Hidalgo, and Benito Juárez . . . que fueron religiosos de verdad."

"Nevertheless, in these four cases," he maintained, "we are dealing with four illustrious heretics." "None of these were 'believers' of the category of those who would strike you in the chest and half close their eyes before predetermined images," but rather "were great believers in humanity."

Surely, Padre Serra and the mission fathers of California would have fallen into the category of "dogmáticos," not the "librepensadores" whom my grandfather celebrated and encouraged others to emulate. He believed in enhancing "la libertad" and "libre albedrío." Don Jesús, too, was a man of the Enlightenment, one who believed in liberty and free will, very much the opposite of Serra, who loathed the Enlightenment and for whom these notions simply translated into sin. As has been becoming apparent in these pages, I have been following in my grandfather's freethinker footsteps, not Serra's.

In that critical spirit, I will say that it seems to me that what Tata is describing is not religion, but the transcendent human heart, the very one that I bring to my considerations of the missions.

There is always this astonishing awe I feel — an Old Testament sort of awe — gazing upon a California mission: there are sensations of wonder, fear, reverence, dread. A sojourn to a California mission is a journey to a place in the deep past when the word "awe" had those sorts of indications. Knowing life, labor, sadness, belief, evil, and desire in that place requires a relationship with the distant past: that is, a period in time when people understood these matters in rather wholly different ways. When, indeed, human beings were human in ways most difficult for us in the present to understand or know.

Virtually all of the missions of Alta California emerged in the eighteenth century, when it was the far northwestern territory of Nueva Espana. They don't look these days much like they did when the Spanish Crown included California in its realm, but even more awe will be inspired when we think of them as part of colonial Mexico. America did not free the Indians from the thrall of the missions; Mexico did in 1834. California's most fabled landmarks, its most poignant monuments to faith, are Spanish and Mexican.

On several occasions I have tried to see the missions through a camera's lens. This is the modern person's way. Simultaneously the viewer captures the mission and imprints it, and detaches oneself from the experience of it. Standing before Mission San Luis Rey just north of San Diego, I become aware that there are several ways in which I can photograph the beautiful building. I can try and get one that is just like the picture postcard for sale in the gift shop: the gleaming white edifice built to the glory of God and to bring civilization to the Indians, with exquisite flowers and a palm tree, set off against the stereotypical California blue sky. I take another one which I frame with the signs off to the side selling burial plots: far from a relic of the past, this photograph shows how the mission serves the tangible needs of its present parishioners, and the financial needs of the Church. I stand back 50 yards from the spot of the first photo and contrive another shot, this time including the bare ruins of the soldiers' quarters and the sign explaining that their reconstruction awaits funds.

This is the story not told there either in the little guide brochures or in the docent tours in any of the missions: only force could hold the Indians in the missions where they labored for the Crown and the Franciscan hierarchy. A more complete reconstruction of these architectural monuments would show how their design emphasized surveillance and domination as much as the Faith. The camera cannot render my sadness and anger at the missions, which, as usual on these perpetual visits, waxes profound.

There are only two sure notions about the missions of Alta California. First is that the Indians died there, but there is much argument about why. Second, beyond that, is that they mean very different things to different people. Think of how diverse people will position themselves to view the missions either through their own cameras' lens, or simply in their minds' eyes. Proponents of Western Civilization, of indigenous peoples, of Catholicism, or of liberal diversity, are all scripted to understand the missions in different ways, as do students of architecture, mythologies, theology, or social history. These, actually, accord almost facile, even indulgent, discussions. The wonder of the places most compels me.

There is this mystery there, something that always beckons my return, something that speaks to me, even from that deep past. These are alive places, not objects that can be faithfully captured in a photograph. I wonder why I want to buy the dinner plates for sale in the gift shops, some souvenir I can take home to remind me on a daily basis of these awful places. And I wonder why, when I'm alone in those places, my eyes always tear up; I bite my lower lip; and then like so many of the Indians, I too must flee.

Yet, along with my sadness and anger, I have great reverence for the missions, this knowledge that they are much bigger than I, and that they have something to say to us in the present. I have studied them in some depth. I have read in the padres' own hands their accounts, some few remaining Indians' descriptions too, and the observations of outsiders. I know that what I learned in third grade in the Los Angeles city schools was at best foolish, at worst pathetically racist. But that curriculum reflected the way most everyone, even in Indian communities, understood the missions.

The best book, back then in the 1950s, was E.B. Webb's famous *Indian Life at the Old Missions* (1952). She told how "the bells rang merrily calling neophytes . . . From the choir loft came the clear, melodious voices of the Indians, their singing mingling with sweet, haunting music of flutes, violins, bass-viols, and trumpets rendering the old hymns and chants taught them by the padres." My investigations in old mission documents revealed few, if any, such instances. There is much more about the soldiers and commerce, the running away and the punishments, and about the death, than the singing.

My enigmatic reverence remains, though. There is something more haunting for me than any music I might imagine coming from the mission church loft — perhaps even more than all the death I feel in one of those incredible buildings. People of Mexican descent are the ones most in awe, most responsive to the mysteries of the missions: besides my scholarly investigations, beyond my childhood school field trips and family vacation visits and my frequent returns as an adult, through my tears of rage and grief, I realize that I was born there.

This may be the hardest realization for me, one that my competent camera cannot capture. My privileged existence, one so full of blessings, cannot obscure the fact that I emerged actually from this process where in military conquests and in the hothouses of the missions throughout Spanish America, but most cosmically in Mexico, the Spaniard met the Indian in profoundly unbalanced ways, and created the mestizo. All this happened (though it continually reoccurs) in that deep past, the historical time so difficult to comprehend.

I suspect that this is why I so love Ramona, the creation of Helen Hunt Jackson's famous novel, and why her figure still reverberates in the imaginations of so many Southwestern residents of Mexican descent. (In the novel her mother is Indian, but her father is Scottish — not exactly a classic Mexican, but then neither am I.) She is my, our, connection to that distant, otherwise impenetrable, past.

I will continue to contradict myself about how distant is this mission past. While it is always risky to generalize about such matters, part of what has helped me envision the missions (and history in general) as "living" are Indian concepts of time, ones that contrast with universalized European constructions of linear time. For example, sometime in my 40s I learned that in the Tewa language the words for "yesterday" and "today" end in *geh*, which means "place." And at the Tewa-speaking Pueblos along the Rio Grande, neither geh is very far away. Thus these "time places," like the ones where the Spanish priests brought the Indians the faith and the diseases and when there was so much blood and death, are not very far away either, if one thinks more in Indian ways about time.

It was a birth conceived amongst so much death, so much ignominious death, though it was not what the Franciscan priests intended. They had simply sought to slay the pagan culture of the Indians, not kill their mortal beings. Some of them dreamed of a communal heaven on earth, some of them schemed about temporal power on a faraway frontier, most all of them were devoted to the Word of God, and all of them were fooled by the power of the Indian spirits. The Franciscan fathers, under the leadership of Padre Junípero Serra, intended and anticipated so much Glory when they founded and named San Diego Alcalá, that first of the missions of Alta California, in 1769. They would bring glory to God as they brought more vassals into His earthly kingdom, more who by knowing His only begotten Son would have everlasting life, and more who would create a blessed communion of souls on this earth when they shared in the transcending power of the holy sacraments.

While "to God alone be given all the honor and glory," as Serra stated, personal glory for the mission fathers could come in several ways. Serving God's mission would earn them favor in heaven and power in the True Church. It must be understood, too, that this was a great warrior church, one whose Christian soldiers — of both the cloth and the uniform — had fought and defeated infidel Moors, pagan Incas and Aztecs, and now sought to extend His realm to New Spain's far northern frontier. They revered not the Virgin of Guadalupe but la Conquistadora, a version of Our Lady of Bethlehem, still on display at Mission San Carlos Borroméo (Carmel). Padre Serra placed the regal statue of Mary with baby Jesus in her arms, both with crowns, in the mission in 1770. The archbishop of Mexico, Francisco de Lorenzaña, had given la Conquistadora to bless the expedition to Monterey. Virtue and honor derived from triumph and conversion, by one means or another, of non-believers. Martyrdom meant for a padre instant communion with Christ.[2]

"The kindly, old Spanish padres" is a phrase that comes to mind when many think of the missions. Only a very few can be thought of as simply "kind"; most were young and only a few got old in California; and many were Catalan rather than Spanish. In terms of personality they comprised a diverse bunch of spiritual fishermen. Padre Antonio Ripoll came from Mallorca, the same Catalan-speaking Mediterranean island from which came Padre Serra, at the age of 25 to Mexico and then arriving in San Diego at age 27. He almost grew old at Santa Barbara, but he secretly fled back to Palma in 1828 fearing banishment of all Spaniards after Mexican independence. Padre Ripoll, who "loved his neophytes as a devoted mother," cried and cried when the Chumash revolted in 1824, killed soldiers, and exchanged their Christian spouses for their previous ones. The Río Ripoll runs through Catalunya, and the landscape there looks much like coastal California.

Another, José María Zalvidea, arguably the most successful priest in terms of baptisms and accumulating material wealth for San Gabriel and San Luis Rey, came to California at age 26 from Bilbao in the Basque region. Over his long career he became noted for his outstanding viti-culture and learning the Gabrieleno language. He scourged himself and engaged in verbal battles with the Devil whom he often told aloud, "Vete, Santanas." He spent the last weeks of his life with nails in his feet to atone for his sins.

Another Mallorcan, Gerónimo Boscana, had been a professor of arts at Palma before arriving in Mexico for mission work at age 27. He arrived in California in 1806 and served 12 years at San Juan Capistrano beginning in 1814, two years after the terrible earthquake of 1812 had knocked the mission down. His enduring legacy remains *Chinigchinich*, his ethnography of the Indians around San Juan Capistrano.

Poor Andrés Quintana. He arrived at age 28 to Mission Santa Cruz and before his 35th birthday the neophytes killed him in retribution for his brutal whippings. They crushed his testicles, smothered him, and resumed sexual licentiousness.

That most famous California missionary, Padre Junípero Serra, had been professor of philosophy in his native Palma. Along with another Mallorcan, Francisco Palóu, who would later write an extensive biography of Serra's epic life, Serra departed from Cadiz for the 99-day voyage to Veracruz, Mexico. For eight years, Serra evangelized in the Sierra

Gorda region around Jalpan and served as commissioner of the Holy Office of the Inquisition there. In September 1752, he wrote back to the Inquisition in Mexico City about "several persons of the class known as *gente de razón*, that is to say they are not Indians, who are addicted to the most detestable and horrible crimes of sorcery, witchcraft and devil worship." According to Serra, "these persons" were "flying through the air at night [and] are in the habit of meeting in a cave . . . where they worship and make sacrifice to the demons who appear visibly there in the guise of young goats and various other things of that nature." The seventeenth-century nun and visionary, María de Agreda, inspired Serra profoundly. She mystically traveled from her convent in Spain to Texas and New Mexico where she encouraged the Indians to accept Christ and the Franciscans. Palóu carried her four volumes, *The Mystical City of God*, to California to give inspiration to the Franciscans.[3]

These were largely earnest men, ones with enough devotion to God and the Church to journey from the Iberian Peninsula across the Atlantic to Mexico and then all the way up to California, which is a lot of devotion. They were great believers in the supernatural, whether it be the Divine Grace that carried María de Agreda to the New World or the Devil who enabled flight in Jalpan. Later, others would follow in the footsteps of Padre Serra to California, but for different reasons like work, safety, and commerce. Journey from Mexico to California, perilous travel at that, is hardly new; it's our discussion of it, and especially the meanings we find in it, that changes.

Protestant Americans can readily comprehend and then debate the legitimacy of this Spanish effort to conquer and transform the Indians in the cause of civilization. That effort reverberates with their own experience with Indians, slavery, the failure of Wilsonian Idealism, and the Cold War crusade and Vietnam. They have a much harder time understanding this Catholic communitarian impulse. The missions sought not simply to create an expansion of the Castilian realm through conversion, but to create a new society of people joined together through communion with the Holy Spirit: a utopia, actually, one not only engendered in Christ but a spectacle of moral perfection to contrast with the evil and corruption of the rest of the world.[4] As empty as the ritual of the wine and the wafer might have been to the neophyte Christian Indians, it symbolized the union of the Church, the Holy Trinity, and the believers. These were bonds that would transcend economics and politics, ones that would foster human relations based upon something more than the material, profane world.

The labor the Indians did needs to be understood in a similar vein. The notion that the missions were a "forced-labor system," indeed something akin to "slavery," emerges most surely from the historical record.[5] Certainly, the assumptions about who should do the work in California, which we have traced from our discussion of the New World Border back to the time of Ramona and Alessandro and then back to the Californios, had their origins in the mission labor system. Yet we must also understand that in the priests' minds disciplined, communal labor produced a crucial mark of civilization. Work, in other words, had importance and dignity beyond the merely instrumental: it was associated with being civilized, and it sought to provide these fledgling communities of believers with a physical sense of cohesion, even solidarity, that would parallel and fortify their holy communion. Of course the forced nature of these labors only resulted in the Indians' persistent disdain for these new disciplines that sought to supersede their own work rhythms and spirits.

One would think that as the priests grew more frustrated with, even vengeful toward, the Indians, and then as the Indians died, that this communitarian vision would have died too. Yet, this impulse has reoccurred in Latin American history in efforts often associated with Liberation Theology, and even in the forms of the Cuban and Nicaraguan revolutions, to create societies in which the pursuit of individual prerogatives and wealth have been rejected in favor of devotion to purposes considered more eminent than personal liberty and accumulation. Belief in such higher ideals, be they based on Marx or Jesus, seems mysterious or foolish at best to Protestant America, and at worst, anti-American or the product of subversion. They are, though, quite real, quite compelling, and ring, if not merrily, sonorously through the California missions and the Latin American egalitarian and communitarian imagination.

These different reconstructions of the missions derive just as meaningfully from how we think about and use history. If we find in the study of history a storehouse of the great traditions, leaders, and ideas, usually of Western Civilization, then we are likely to see Junípero Serra and the other mission fathers in a particular way.

Other groups have insisted that their traditions and ideas should be included in the storehouse, and that the great ideas — monotheism and body discipline as regards work and sexuality are two that come to mind when we think of the missions — are to be understood in relation to different groups in different time periods. When these great impulses are seen to be destructive of peoples, as many have seen the missions as catastrophic for the native peoples, then we have the often-rancorous, but often-creative, debates about the big ideas of the world and its histories. Usually this is called the "canon" and its "challengers," and it is played out everywhere from our classrooms to the media to discussions of the possible canonization of Padre Serra.

The outcome may be intense partisanship — and I will confess to being a partisan. It can also be sweeping relativism — an acceptance of the notion that people in the present construct historical narratives with their own values and agendas. Thus no one fabrication of a historical episode corresponds to reality any better than another. Here I would say both that no one story can be the true one, but certainly, though, some stories of the missions are truer than others.

It seemed like a good idea at the time, the effort to bring to the Indians the true Word of God and everlasting salvation. The priest Juan Diaz chanted a mass for Juan Bautista de Anza as he set out for Mission San Gabriel in 1774: "An act of thanksgiving to the Infinite Majesty, who deigns to reward with full hands the Catholic zeal, constant piety, and religion of our invincible and most amiable monarch, enlarging his dominions so easily, exalting his arms, and trusting to his fervent charity the task of converting so vast a heathendom to the fold of our sacred religion." The viceroy in Mexico City, Antonio María Bucareli y Ursúa, echoed the same sentiment when he entertained "strong hopes of extending, among the many heathen tribes . . . , the dominion of the king and the knowledge of our true religion (which is the principal purpose of his Majesty . . .) by means of the missions." We have, then, missionization as a righteous act. Or in Spanish something that was "justo." Interesting words — *justo* comes from Latin for "lawful, rightful, proper." Righteous is actually a more engaging word — it derives from the old English for "right" plus "wise." At the time, all boded well, for, as Padre Fermín Lasuén, successor to Padre Serra, put it, "The country is most beautiful, the heathen very numerous and very docile, and by planting crops we may be able to replant our voices, with all assurance that with the favor of God the most abundant harvests for things both eternal and temporal may be reaped."

While Padre Lasuén lumped together all of the "heathens," we can be sure that more diversity prevailed among them than among their would-be spiritual conquerors. The Ohlone people of the San Francisco and Monterey Bay areas traced their ancestry back to the sacred figure of the complex and sly Coyote. The men hunted deer, and nearly all of the women made intricate baskets from reeds and, with their children, gathered huge quantities of shellfish from the bays. Around Monterey you can stand upon a few of the remaining middens, the piles of shells and other refuse that mark where numerous Ohlone once lived.[6]

The sea provided Chumash people with much of their food, too, but it was the men and their finely hewed *tomols*, wooden boats 12 to 30 feet in length, that brought in fish from the Santa Barbara Channel. This highly complex society valued the beauty of the women's baskets and the men's tools and their tomols. The Chumash held sacred wondrous swordfish that helped the people, who were indeed people themselves, by driving whales ashore for them to eat.[7]

To the south of the Chumash lived various Shoshonean-speaking peoples such as the Tongva, and such Yuman-speaking peoples as the Kumeyaay, from what would become the San Gabriel and San Diego missions areas respectively. They would become Gabrielino and Die-gueño peoples once they experienced the spiritual conquerors. They held sacred the eagle of the sky and the dolphin of the sea. The Kumeyaay, like their neighbors the Tipai, ranged into what is now Mexico. Their neighbors in the interior, the Cahuilla, avoided missionization. The creators, Chinigchinich for the Gabrielinos and Mukat for the Cahuilla, were much like the people — often unpredictable, unstable, and susceptible to moral lapses. Cahuilla people harvested a stunning variety of foods from their local flora as well as deer, rabbits, and most every other form of animal life of their desert region. Many animals were sacred to the Cahuilla, especially the eagle. Their stories tell of the remarkable days when Lake Cahuilla (which archeologists confirm to have dated from around 700 to 1400 CE) provided them a rich harvest of fish and fresh-water clams.[8]

From San Francisco to the south the plentiful acorn provided remarkable nutrition. Harvested in October and November, it had to be pounded and pounded to be rid of its bitter tannin. With the possible exception of Dieguenos who may have sown grass seed, California Indians did not engage in agriculture. Instead, most California Indians developed a sophisticated system of burning the landscape to enhance the growth of desirable edible plants and of forage for hunt animals and to flush game from their hideouts. With more plants and animals to eat, peoples such as the Chumash, the Ohlone, and Pomo could give more attention to their artistic and ritual activities.[9]

Mostly they lived in roundhouses made of thatch or reeds: "The Indians say," according to the great French explorer Jean-François de Galaup de La Pérouse, "that they love the open air, that it is convenient to set fire to their house when the fleas become troublesome, and that they can build another in less than two hours."[10]

Over time the approximately three hundred thousand Indians and the land had achieved a fragile adaptation to one another in the place that would become California. Confinement—"reduction" was the word the Spanish used—to the missions would require new, very difficult, adaptations for those coastal peoples whom the priests secured for evangelizing.

Neophyte Indians would have to work by the clock, not the seasons; raise cattle, corn, and wheat and eat the strange foods that derived from them; the young men would be immured in the *obraje*, the workshop where they would learn new occupations; and the young women would be confined to the *monjerio*, the women's dormitory where they would be forced to adhere to Catholic notions of female sexual purity. Their bodies would be disciplined for work and to refrain from sex. Governor Borica stated of the monjerio that it was "so poorly ventilated and so pestilent . . . I was not able to stand even a minute in them."[11]

Above all else in matters of outward deportment, the Indians would have to be clothed. The priests rarely commented on the Indians' phenotype, their skin color or nose shape, but instead on their nudity. "I say something I could not believe when I had read of it, or had been told about it," said Padre Serra when he first encountered Indians in Alta California. "It was this: they were entirely naked, as Adam in paradise before sin . . . and not for one moment, while they saw us clothed, could you notice the least sign of bashfulness in them for being in such a state." From Monterey in 1775, Serra pleaded with the viceroy to send clothing "to cover in some fashion the nakedness of so many girls and boys, men and women . . . for the sake of decency and modesty, especially for the frail sex." Of course the *partes vergonzosas*, the "shameful parts," were most in need of covering.[12]

As myriad and dramatic as these changes were—and we should not forget the infestation of the missions and clothing with fleas—matters of the spiritual realm proved most profound.

After all, it was really only these matters of religion that the Europeans had to offer the rest of the people of the world. Here and there, European technology has helped those called "the natives." I think of metal pots that made women's food preparation much easier, but the Indians of the Americas had enough food and had evolved lifeways that maintained a sometimes vigorous and dynamic, sometimes fragile and precarious, balance with their environment. It is, though, certainly true that many more people can live in the Americas because of advances in agricultural technology. But at the time of missions the Spanish priests had only God to offer the Indians: obviously, then, one's evaluation of their efforts will have to do with whether one believes that the imposition of the One True Faith helped the Indians in either this world or the next.

Many of the expressions of Spanish secular and religious authorities of the eighteenth century use the phrase "conquista espiritual" when referring to the task of securing California for the Crown and the Faith. Indeed, for the Gabrielino and Juaneño people their great creator/prophet Chinigchinich, whose prescriptions and rages caused the people terrible fear, had already told them of the correct ways to be and about the proper relationships between humans, animals, plants, and the spirits. Knowing, then, that this would be a war between Jesus Christ and Chinigchinich — both demanding and wrathful gods — helps us understand the missionization of the Southern California coast.

Such would be of necessity a very deep conquest. For Indians a spirit of some sort animated everything — trees, human bodies, mountains, and animals were all alive not simply mechanically, but spiritually. In the Christian view only humans had souls or spirits. It is hard for non-Indians to grasp how two-leggeds and four-leggeds and winged creatures all existed in the spirit world, but they did. One could enter there via dreams, a shaman, or a brew of the hallucinogenic, but wicked, jimson-weed. Cahuilla people tell how they would sing over the body of a hunted deer both "to enlist the aid of the guardian animal spirit so that the animals would cooperate with the hunter," as John Lowell Bean explains, and so that the hunters could explain "to the spirit of the animal what they were doing and acknowledge their appreciation to the animal for allowing themselves to be killed." On the practical side, such ritual would "carry a good report of the hunter's activities" back to the spirit world so that the deer spirits would continue to allow their corporeal manifestations to be hunted.[13]

Human sexuality, these mysterious desires for carnal pleasure and release, were understood to be expressions of some spirit that animated the body. Erotic passion derived not from our sinful flesh or our body mechanics, depending on which Euro-Christian point of view you might favor, but the spirit or spirits that enliven us humans' bodies.

These spirits, like more generally rain, the sun's heat, witchery, female and male procreative power, or any other life forces, could never be simply good or evil; they just *were* in pre-contact California, and their ethical value was quite situational. It was not the Indians but rather this spirit world that the padres set about, quite frankly, to kill.

Padre Lasuén understood all this, in a way simultaneously dim and profound, when he said in 1804 how "here then we have the greatest problem of the missionary: how to transform a savage race such as these into a society that is human, Christian, civil, and industrious. This can be accomplished only by 'denaturalizing' them. It is easy to see what an arduous task this is, for it requires them to act against nature." The native peoples, then, would have to be despiritualized as they understood it. Here is one of those things that I know is more true than others: the goal of the Spanish Crown and the Franciscans was the cultural death of the Native Peoples. This was the general European-minded design — "to kill the Indian and save the man" in the words of the founder of the Pennsylvania Carlisle School.

The contrast between the dance and the word has made this most clear to me. Christian religion tells us that "in the beginning there was the word. The word dwelt with god, and what god was, the word was." (John 1:1-4) The Word of God is the center of the Christian religion which the Spanish priests would bring to the Indians of California, indeed all of the New World. But for these people, not the word, but the body, the dancing body, connected them to the spirit world.

At solstices, the people danced; before and after the hunt the people danced; so that the acorns would grow, the people danced; to mourn the death of an elder, or to welcome a new child, or for a young woman's first menstruation, the people danced; so that their enemies would be vanquished in war, California Indians danced. Padre Boscana, in his ethnography *Chinigchinich*, describes how Juaneños (Acjachemem) danced to celebrate "Pames" or "bird feast." In sacred times White-headed Eagle Maiden had run away. When Chinigchinich found her he transformed her into a bird. Boscana described how the men danced in imitation of Chinigchinich with a "feather ornament made like a crown from various feathers of birds, placed on the head."[14] With their bodies, then, the dancers intertwine with the great cycles, and they join with the animals and the great and sacred beings in the spirit world. With the heart, not the head, the dancing bodies literally, for Indians do not abstract in these matters, join in the great mysteries of life. The dancing body is for Indians what the word is for Christians, the center of their spirit life.

It should be apparent, but rarely does it enter into the discussion, that it was this fundamental difference that caused so much of the trouble when the Franciscan fathers, who condemned the body, encountered dancing Indians who celebrated this world of fecundity, who connected their often-naked bodies to its cycles, who acknowledged the bodies' desires. Boscana described another dance "called *Aputs*, which signifies naked or in one's bare skin." In this dance "just one woman stripped herself naked (although she had very little to take off) . . . , and the other people all around in a circle, men and women, big and little, and she in the middle, her hands placed underneath her breasts as if holding them up, dancing in the middle of that circle, and all watching her dance and observing her movements and actions. She herself sang, but her song was confined to naming her private parts and those of the men."*

These priests, these usually celibate fathers, represented the ultimate of the Europeans' mastery over the body, of how the head, reason, would discipline the body and its urges for gratification and connection with those cycles that brought the body into being in the first place. To Boscana and the priests, and later the Americans, such dance was "an infamous thing and a diabolical invention," something not much different from "the natural instinct of brutes," from which the people had to be saved. Certainly, "Aputs" is a dance of creation, a connection to the time place when the people first came to be and to women's remarkable procreative ability. Perhaps the dancer mimicked Tamáayawut, the woman associated with earth when "there was nothing," but who, when impregnated four times by her brother, who was associated with sky, gave birth first to earth and sand, then the rocks, then the trees and shrubs, and then finally to the mysterious chief Qüiot (or Wuyóot).[15] In this way the dancer's body could be connected physically and spiritually

---

* Such statements present us with a creative dilemma: can we believe the Padre's account? Of course he is bent on showing the Indians to be "savages" and would thus exaggerate or fabricate. On the other hand, we have reason to believe that people who watched porpoises and dolphins cavort off the coast (and I have), and who held them sacred, would mimic these beautiful animals in their frolicking and then consider such dancing very *natural*.

(for these would not be separated) with the Creation in sacred times and Procreation in the present.

Now this embracing of life is why we are drawn to Indians dancing: we moderns lost something when we subjugated our bodies to our reason; when we created oppositions between the spirit and the flesh, between reason and passion; when we separated ourselves from the other animals and made of them strangers; when our naked bodies became *vergonzoza* and when desire became something to fear or condemn as sin.

"Es pues la cuestión: si sus habitantes están adictos a la independencia" were words that accompanied the discovery of the original inhabitants of California. "Discovery." Did it mean, as the Latin origin of the word suggests, the negation of a state of being hidden, thus opening it up to view, or does it have to do with getting to possess, control, and use as one wishes the resources and people of what's being discovered? The Franciscans would bring civilization — encapsulated in the phrase "gente de razón" — to the Indians. They would be "people of reason," ones who mastered their dancing bodies like the priests mastered their bodies' desire for sex. The body would not exhibit independence from the discipline of the mind, and it would be clothed. The mission fathers would bring Indians the ability to subjugate the body for European-style work, and so that their Christian word would tell them how to be. Thus, discovery of the Californian coast translated into the possession, not the opening to view, of Indian peoples, but something else too, something very different, something very unintended, something very much a consequence of the Church's decision to attach itself to Europe's imperial conquests.

Three years after that first founding of a mission in Alta California, Padre Luis Jayme (sometimes known by the Catalan spelling of his name — Jaume) gave to Padre Serra a letter to be delivered to the viceroy in Mexico enumerating the outrages that the Crown's soldiers were delivering to them, to the Indians, and to God. "There is not a single mission," he told, "where all of the gentiles have not been scandalized." More explicitly the soldiers are "seizing and raping the women." These are the stories of imperial conquest: "Soldier Casteló carried a gentile woman into a corral . . . and the said soldier had intercourse with the woman and sinned with her. When he had raped her, the said soldier came out of the corral, and the soldier Juan María Ruiz entered the same corral and sinned with the said woman." They released her and then "the soldier whose name is not to be known seized another woman violently and carried her into the same corral and sinned with her there. He came out, and the soldier Bravo entered and sinned with her." Such episodes, when contrasted with Padre Boscana's statement of how dancing Indian women were "an infamous thing," challenge us to question even more the "conquista espiritual": After Bravo left, "the soldier Juan María Ruiz entered and did the same. He came out and the soldier Casteló did the same." Casteló and Ruiz "gave this woman some red ribbons." Padre Jayme feared that "the gentiles therein many times have been on the point of coming here to kill us all."[16]

This was not news to Padre Serra. Only two years previously, at the founding of Mission San Gabriel in 1771, "the soldiers," Serra simultaneously fumed and grieved, "clever as they are at lassoing cows and mules, would catch an Indian woman with their lassos to become prey for their unbridled lust. At times some Indian men would try to defend their wives, only to be shot down with bullets." "Even the boys," Serra continued in a letter to the viceroy with loathing and bewilderment about the soldiers, "who came to the mission were not safe from their baseness."[17]

No wonder then how on the night of November 4, 1775, Kumeyaay peoples of the vicinity of the first of the missions, San Diego Alcalá, attacked and burned the mission and created the first martyr of the Franciscans' cause in Alta California. Awaking a little after midnight, finding the buildings in flames and the heathen vociferous, and no doubt in a rage about the soldiers, Padre Luis Jayme confronted the marauders with the command "Love God, children." For him this moment portended immediate communion with his Savior, but they also marked a turning point in Spaniards' attitudes toward, and hopes for, the Indians. It is not thoroughly agreed that both heathens and neophytes participated in the ruin of the mission and the brutal killing of Padre Jayme. Most likely, neophytes did participate because, as Captain Rivera y Moncada testified, "they wanted to live as they did before."

In 1785 a young Indian woman named Toypurina led the Indians surrounding Mission San Gabriel in revolt against Spanish authority. The attack failed because Toypurina's special powers failed to kill the padres as planned. At the inquest after her capture, Toypurina, alleged to be a sorceress, stated that she commanded a chief to attack "for I hate the padres and all of you, for living here on my native soil . . . , for trespassing on the land of my forefathers and despoiling our tribal domains . . ."

Those inside the mission expressed different reasons for wanting the death of the padres and soldiers. The inquest said that Nicolas José, the neophyte who convinced Toypurina of the necessity of terminating the interlopers, desired the extinction of the padres and Corporal Verdugo because they disallowed him his "heathen dances and abuses."[18]

These were the first and only major attempts on the part of the Indians to rub out the missions before they had much actual experience with Hispanicization. (Once Indians were missionized, their revolts would aim to expropriate the missions and their produce.) Now, though, neither religious nor military authorities echoed their initial optimism about their prospects. "I have had such anguish," said Serra of the event at San Diego, "in my desires to see advanced the spiritual conquests in which we have been engaged . . . that so much greater now is my pain." To Anza, "the event has filled everybody with terror and caused them to realize what the natives of this region are capable of attempting, which formerly they did not believe." Only a few months before the debacle, Palóu waxed poetic: the two San Diego friars "were both very happy, seeing that they were gathering in abundance the spiritual fruit of that vineyard of the lord, for on the 3rd of October in the same year . . . they had baptized sixty heathen." No longer does one read the optimism of, for example, Padre Francisco Garcés on his journey with Anza from Tubac to San Gabriel in 1774: "Oh! what lands so suitable for missions! Oh! what a heathendom so docile!" The Indians now existed as fearful creatures in the minds of the Spanish.[19]

The revolt at San Diego only emphasized the increasingly apparent failure of the Indians to flock to their priestly shepherds. In his "Report on the Californias" of November 30, 1775, Lieutenant Pedro Fages wrote that "the compliance and meekness of the Indians" in the missions "is the effect of a just fear ("un justo temor," he called it) rather than affability and goodness." Any accomplishments on their part toward civilization proved "in truth very rare." On the other hand, he described the rivers and lands of the area that would eventually be the pueblo of Los Angeles (1781) and how it would be easy to grow fruit, beans, corn, and wheat.

Disaster even accompanied the founding of Los Angeles. Captain Rivera y Moncada had brought the Sonorans who would found the little pueblo as far as the Colorado River. He dispatched them toward San Gabriel, then crossed back over the river and camped with his men and stock animals at Purísima Concepción, a mission presidio outpost. Their mesquite plants trampled, their lands invaded, their lifeways under threat, Quechan people attacked and killed over one hundred Spanish men, women, and children, including Captain Rivera y Moncada. Padre Garcés and three other friars achieved martyrdom at the hands of Indians who clubbed them to death. This event, along with rise of the Apaches, effectively closed the border between Sonora and the *provincias* of New Mexico and California until the American military, with fire and blood exceeding that of the Spanish and the Quechans, could reopen it nearly a hundred years later.[20]

There is terrible irony here: the soldiers' activities proved central to the "conquista espiritual." Obviously, as in the history of the world as a whole, the rape of the indigenous women of California was part of conquest as much as the men's guns. Less initially apparent, though, was how these barbaric acts introduced certain microbes into the Indian population. Syphilis and gonorrhea raced through the Indian villages. Then, after their social and spiritual structures increasingly unraveled, simple prostitution and concubinage in and around the presidios and Spanish towns further disseminated terrible sicknesses, ones the shamans could not heal.[21]

Gonorrhea dramatically inhibits contraception, and syphilis, the more fatal of the two, can be transferred to the young. But the diseases have meant more than the morbid statistics about the decline of the indigenous populations. Defenders of the Franciscans' efforts attribute the calamities at the missions not to imperialism or Christianization but to the "immorality of the soldiers." Actually, the priests blamed for what they called the *gálico* not only the soldiers, but the Indians themselves: "They shamelessly pursue without restraint whatever their brutal appetites suggest to them," claimed Padre President Lasuén: "Their inclination to lewdness and theft is on a par with their love for the mountains."[22]

We need to imagine how the Indians would have understood the terrible afflictions. Indians of coastal California where the Spanish went suffered arthritis: they did not build houses that kept out the cold and damp of winter, it being warm enough most of the year. Perhaps because they left bacteria and viruses behind when they came across the Bering Straits (or across the oceans, too), or because they did not domesticate hoofed animals which passed diseases to humans, American Indians did not experience such rampaging diseases as influenza, smallpox, syphilis, or cholera until the white people came, and then with devastating results. The wreckage, though, happened as much in the Indians' spirit worlds as on their bodies.

Indians have understood that illness derives from an individual's incorrect relationships to other humans, animals, or spirits, or from other people bewitching them or thinking bad thoughts about them. These the shamans or medicine men could correct or counter via entry into the spirit world. It was the case, though, that these microbes proved immune to such doctoring. Not only, then, did the germs ravage Indian bodies in California, and the rest of the Americas, but so too did they lay waste to the spirit world. The calamitous entry of the diseases manifested that the spirit world had been thrown completely out of whack, and that the Indians' holy men could not right it.

Death could happen fast, as when 471 out of a neophyte population of 1,136 died of measles in the outbreak of 1806 at Mission San Francisco. Or it could be more gradual as at Mission San Carlos Borromeo, which saw its numbers of neophytes and converts drop from a high of 876 in 1785, to 550 in 1808, to 165 in 1834.[23]

Only thus, then, did the Spanish succeed in killing the spirit world of the Indians. Only then could the Christian God make His way.

Writing about the first baptisms at Mission Santa Clara (1777), Padre Palóu declared that "for as there had come upon the people a great epidemic, the fathers were able to perform a great many baptisms by simply going through the villages. In this way they succeeded in sending a great many children to heaven."[24] It was the triumph and the tragedy of attaching the Christianizing mission to imperialism.

As Randal Millikan has put it, this was "a time of little choice" for California Indians who had been experiencing the Christian onslaught. Their villages and spirit world were unraveling, and "the Spanish missions continued to beckon, offering them access to a European vision of a meaningful life in exchange for cultural and political obliteration." Knowing that their lives in the missions would not be happy, they nonetheless, sometimes as whole villages, would move into a mission. Their infants were dying, their forage areas encroached upon, their shamans powerless, the spirit world amok, and Chinigchinich prostrate before Jesus Christ. By 1820 all the lands on the southern coast were empty of villages; by 1830 the same was true of the San Francisco Bay area.[25]

Indigenous peoples would always resist such a forceful conquest, the soldiers would be necessary — "the presidio needs more people to contain the uneasy and pernicious disposition of these natural Christians and heathens," confessed Serra; and then those soldiers would proceed as usual.

Optimism continually waned: "Their characteristics are stupidity and insensibility," declared Padre Venegas in the early 1830s; "want of knowledge and reflection; inconstancy, impetuosity and blindness of appetite; an excessive sloth and abhorrence of fatigue; an incessant love of pleasure, and amusement of every kind, however trifling or brutal; in fine, a most wretched want of everything that constitutes the real man, and renders him rational, inventive, tractable, and useful to himself and society." In some of these charges he's actually accurate; he simply condemns the manner in which the missionized Indians remained true to their old ways in which their bodies remained in sync with nature, not the priests' clocks.

The outcome of this frustration was rage, and tortured logic to defend the priests' actions: "I do not doubt," stated Padre Serra to Governor Neve, "that in the punishments we have been discussing there has been disorder and excesses on the part of some fathers, and that we are all exposed to err in that regard." "Let me tell you, Sir," Serra wrote to Commandant General Teodoro de Croix, "they are our children; for none except us has engendered them in Christ." Forgiveness combined with violence: "We shower all our love and care upon them. And great was our joy when we secured a general amnesty for those who had set fire to the Mission at San Diego and had most cruelly murdered its principal minister, the Reverend Father Professor Luis Jayme." "Nevertheless, when it seemed to us that they deserved it," Serra informed Neve, "punishment with whippings or confinement to the stocks, according to the gravity of the offense, was carried out." Such *castigos* sought to "put a stop to the many offenses which they commit against the law of God," especially such as leaving the mission for a "gentile woman and leaving their Christian wives behind."[26]

Eulalia Pérez, the Hispanicized Indian woman who accompanied the priests from Baja to Alta California and served as *llavera*, or key keeper of the monjerio, or women's dormitory, recalled "the punishments that were imposed":

> stocks and confinement—and when the misdeed was serious the delinquent was taken to the guard house, and there he was fastened to a cane or a post, and given 25 lashes and upwards, according to the offence.
>
> Sometimes they were put in the head stocks—other times they put a bayonet through the scalp and fastened him this way—this

punishment was known as the law of Bayonne, and was very painful.

Indian bodies were maimed, but the wound went far deeper.

Modern people, and the Catholic hierarchy in particular, cannot understand what it meant to disallow the Indians' "heathen dances and abuses," and then to unleash punishment on Indian bodies that engaged in the rituals, or that fled the missions to return to their home villages for those dances. The body connected Indian people to the spirit world, to the rest of the cosmos, the part that is non-material. To sever that bond was to sever the Indian relationship to the world as they understood it. Maintaining and enhancing those connections was part of how they were human in that distant past. To prohibit their gentile dances — indeed to flog or imprison neophytes for escaping so that they could engage in them — was to kill them as human beings.

With only their physical selves continuing, "reina la apatía en las misiones," declared the 30-year veteran of San Luis Rey, Padre Antonio Peyri. Indeed, "apathy reigned," and there was little spirit left in the mission Indians. A few mission Indians had been petitioning for their release previously, but in 1834, out of some combination of the ideologies of Liberalism and private property, lust for the vast mission lands, and frustration with Indian progress toward Christianity, the Mexican government "secularized" — terminated that is — the mission effort and gave Indians their independence. Mostly, Indians fled the fleas and the confinement and this unfathomable labor system and its hurtful regimen. And they fled the intolerant God who despised their spirits and religious conduct. Some went to the towns, others attached themselves to ranchos, others distanced themselves by joining distant *rancherías* in the interior, and some few remained at the missions.[27]

The priests and some later students of the missions equated baptisms with *cristianizando*. This is dubious at best. Indeed, some Indians born and raised in the missions could be considered good Catholics, but what in creation could characterize the religiosity of those missionized in those times of little choice? Recall that they were hearing a Latin mass, being evangelized in Spanish, and trying to make sense of it all in their own language. What did the words they were saying to themselves and to each other about God, Christ, baptism, the Holy Eucharist — all of which they could not possibly have understood — create and convey? Responses, I would think, would vary from confusion, to more apathy, to occasionally rich syncretization of the Spanish and Indian spirit worlds.

I can't genuinely feel or comprehend this separation from, or confusion in, the spirit world, not knowing of it in the first place. Awareness of the death, though, is impossible for me to avoid. At most missions, monuments have been erected to the priests, or they are buried conspicuously on the grounds, or even in the nave of the church. The names of the Indians never appear. Actually the courtyards at Mission Santa Barbara and others cover the bodies of the Indians buried there.

When I saw Chumash activist Ernestine de Soto speak, she pointed out how "you'll walk over hundreds of bodies, maybe thousands, under the pathway." A wooden cross usually commemorates the thousands of Indians buried in the graveyards of the missions, the presence of their remains otherwise unmarked. "They don't even have our names," she declared. I tried to photograph the cross at San Luis Rey once; it didn't come out because I got the exposure wrong, or maybe it was because of something else. After that I came to stand simply in dread before the crosses. "I don't think we're resting peacefully," she stated. Indeed.[28]

We are confronted with the reality that at the creation of what we might call historical California, that is when its European settlement, Christianization, and mixing of bloods and cultures commenced, there was much ruin and tragedy. I want a more praiseworthy origin story for my California, a genesis to esteem. This is another reason why the old story of the missions, the one that celebrated the padres and their mission of bringing civilization to the Indians, was so appealing; we expect something glorious at our beginning, something transcendent. But, and here my Catholic readers may well agree, that conception has often been fraught with sin.

It was a bizarre, but in many ways logical, unfolding of events. But as with many ideological "isms," once one makes the first declarative step, a remarkable series of conclusions can follow, ones that can become twisted and tortured over time. Recall the priests' initial basis for missionizing the Indians of California, indeed in all of the Americas: "Extending . . . the dominion of the king and the knowledge of our true religion," and of making "la conquista espiritual." Nowadays, in fact for at least the past several decades, the rhetoric of anti-imperialism, self-determination, and ecumenicalism has replaced such frankly imperial, anti-democratic, and intolerant ideology. In other words, the Spanish missions, while they can be understood in their eighteenth-century historical context, cannot be justified on their original grounds in the twenty-first century.

This means that recent defenders of the missions, such as Father

Francis F. Guest and Monsignor Francis Weber, cannot use the dogmas of the eighteenth century to affirm their cause. They must avow new foundations for the Franciscans' efforts, ones that involve defenders of the missions in unsound, dishonest argument. An often-repeated one is that "aboriginal peoples have a right both to their culture and to the Gospel." Now, in the first place, the Church of those centuries — ones that saw numerous Liberal revolutions — placed itself in implacable opposition to any notions of natural rights or religious liberty. One thinks here of Pius IX's *Syllabus of Errors*, the first draft of which appeared in 1869: it resoundingly condemned such false notions as "every man is free to embrace and profess that religion he shall consider true," or that "it is lawful to refuse obedience to legitimate princes, and even to rebel against them."[29] This is the way the Church thought about evangelizing and fleeing back then.

Now that the credibility of these notions has been swept away in favor of democracy and religious tolerance, defenders of the missions must concoct new defenses of the missions. Indeed, if the California Indians had a "right" to the Gospel, then more tortured logic ensues. You see, the Catholic dogma of the time maintained that those who accepted the Word and knew their Savior through the rituals and teachings of the Church would have everlasting life. Those who heard the Word but either rejected it, apostatized, or committed heresies were condemned to the horrors of Hell. The departed souls of those such as the California Indians before 1769 who had never heard the Word merely floated in limbo for eternity. We see here the magnitude of the priests' obligation to the Indians. Once having exercised for them their right to hear the Gospel, the padres had to keep the Indians faithful, or be responsible for their eternal damnation. It is crucial to understand the consequences of allowing an Indian to return to "the wild" after hearing the Word. It meant Hell, forever.

As Father Guest put it in his defense of the missions, the "discipline" that the fathers used on the Indians was necessary because "as legal guardians, the friars were looked upon as responsible before God for the religious education of their neophytes." Anyway, whipping was part of Spanish culture, and if it was done to those considered children, it was actually rather light. Confinement — necessary for conversion — meant fatal diseases, but the Europeans suffered frequent and devastating plagues. In an article published in 1983, Guest can still speak of "the great contrast that existed between their native aboriginal way of life and the civilized life of living at the missions" to explain Indian flight from the mission and then to justify the force necessary to keep them there. He's right, except that the brutality that the soldiers exercised in recapturing *huidos* shatters any such distinctions between the "civilized" and the "uncivilized." Nonetheless, all this follows from the notion of the "right" of the Indians to the Gospel and that "the Indians . . . entered them (the missions) voluntarily." The Church would *never* have made such arguments in the centuries past.[30]

If one wonders about Indian involvement in establishing this "right," or believes that different peoples' different relationships to the spirit world and the body's desires are equally valid, or questions whether or not Spaniards' physical abuse of themselves or their own people legitimized whipping Indians when they fled earthly princes, Faith, and the fleas, then these long justifications for the events at the California missions will seem, at best, pedantic. Indeed, Guest, for very understandable reasons, gives no legitimacy to Indian belief systems. Nor does he ever question, or acknowledge, the ongoing consequences of his Church's unthinking decision to attach itself to Spanish imperialism. Guest acknowledges that "the Spanish . . . were engaged in what we now see to have been a largely quixotic venture, a titanic enterprise that called forth their noblest efforts but was destined, almost of necessity, to fall short of success," but never questions the legitimacy of the mission effort. Monsignor Weber goes so far as to say that "the mission system as it unfolded in California needs no apologies."[31] Ultimately, I am convinced, these disputes over the California missions derive not from malice, but from differing values over whether or not people should be left to worship the gods to which they are accustomed.

The task of religious tolerance is much easier for tribal peoples. Their gods are local and unique to them and their place. It is reasonable and expected, then, that distinct peoples in separate places will have different gods. The Christian and Moslem god, on the other hand, is the god of all humanity. The Christian God's first commandment, "given to Moses in the midst of fire and smoke, thunder and lightning," ordered that "thou shall not have strange gods before me." (Catechism 254–55) I take this as a frank acknowledgment that there are other gods, but that they are not to be tolerated. The priests were fulfilling their Old Testament charge to rid the Indians of the strange gods. And, we must recall, the priests lived in that deep past in which one needful and indispensable truth — God as expressed in the Holy Trinity and represented on earth by the One True Church — instructed and ordered all life everywhere.

One of the great questions for the twenty-first century, if we are to have peace, is how can people hold something like religion or values as true for themselves and their culture, but acknowledge that they may not be true for others. It's a difficult task now, and one that would have been impossible for the Catholic missionaries then.

So much death. Of the Indian gods and of the Indians. But there was something else that died in those missions. The idea that we can create from people deemed either culturally destitute or vacant an ideal community, in this case Christian, one in which the ideals of love and compassion will guide people's lives, perished there too. This is a compelling vision, one that actually lives in very different form with modern communitarians, even to celebrants of us humans' seedy passions. Its ruination in the missions is associated, in some elusive way, with the reverence, sadness, and anger I always feel in those places. Such a utopia was the priests' goal — to release the Indians from their thrall in the Devil and then make of the then–tabula rasa beings a purely theological society in which the transcendent values revealed in the Bible would operate. Spiritual communion with Christ would bond such an ideal society, one that would be free from the evils of the material world and the desires of the flesh. But it was not actually the Devil that held the Indians, but rather the strange gods that they held sacred. And the priests were, their protestations notwithstanding, grievously and inextricably part of avaricious and covetous Spanish imperialism.

It is hard to find heroes in this story of dystopia, of disease and apathy. The martyred Padre Jayme or the grieving Padre Ripoll who wailed at the Chumash Revolt of 1824 were the only tragic figures. Perhaps we could elevate the mysterious Toypurina or some other Indian leaders to heroic status, but they failed and died sometimes miserably or anonymously. Toypurina, though, was banished to Monterey where she married a soldier and had three children with him.[*32] The Indians who simply endured would be hapless heroes at best. Surely it is the figure of the founder, Padre President Junípero Serra, who is mostly associated with eminence. Just as surely his status is hugely controversial.

* Her son, Cesarino, became a soldier and seems not to have had children. The daughters of Toypurina, María Clementina, and Juana, both married soldiers at excruciatingly young ages. Their descendants (each were widowed and remarried) eventually merged into Californio society. In turn, their descendants blended into Anglo American society.

Many Californians are well aware of how Serra is alternately constructed as saintly benefactor of the heathen and woeful Indians and heroic defender of their interests against the avaricious civil authorities of New Spain on the one hand and as intolerant, imperialist enslaver of indigenous people who brought them only soldiers, disease, and death on the other hand. People are less aware of how this dispute doesn't have that much to do with whether or not he should be made a saint. (Anyway, both sides are correct in their views; they simply differ over the righteousness of imposing gods and technology.) A person becomes a saint only after her or his grand virtue and consummate devotion to the Faith has been exhaustively established, and when her or his ability to effect miracles has undoubtedly manifested itself.

These matters can only be considered within the context of Catholicism. After all, no one pretends to make of Serra a *California saint* or even some kind of an Indian shaman; he would only be a *Catholic saint*. The first part of the requirements have been proved beyond a doubt, as the ten thousand pages of documents that the Franciscan order has sent to the Sacred Congregation for the Causes of Saints in Rome will attest. There can be no repudiating that Serra served the Faith and defended it against its enemies, and it cannot be denied that the treacherous journey to the New World, followed by excruciating (he suffered an agonizing inflammation of the foot) travel to the Californias exhibits extraordinary devotion to the Faith, its propagation, and the Church. The criterion of treating people with sympathetic respect for their cultural beliefs, lifeways, sexual moralities, and gods has simply not been one for Catholic sainthood.

Padre Serra has had one miracle attributed to him, and this begat his beatification. Unlike Protestantism, for whom the phrase "communion of saints" refers only to those on earth whose belief in the Savior unites them in future salvation, Catholic doctrine affirms a communion of saints uniting "the faithful on earth, the souls in purgatory, and the saints in heaven in the organic unity of the same mystical body under Christ its head, and in a constant interchange of supernatural offices." Rituals such as those done around the Virgin Mary or the other saints can activate that relationship, as can prayer, and bring about the intercession of the saints either with God or with events on earth. This is why there have been miracles, the most inspiring events for the formation and increase of religious feeling. To have the idea that some people or icons are sacred is one thing. But to believe that the holy actually have power to intervene in the operation of the profane world — phenomena that have been witnessed and testified to — manifests what some would call True Belief.[33]

These tenets must be understood in order to evaluate Padre Serra for sainthood. Will he have the spirit power to intervene in this world at least one more time? Will his stature be considered sufficiently holy, in spite of the physical destruction of the Indians and the acknowledged excesses in the discipline necessary to keep them on the path to salvation, to warrant canonization? These are questions for true believers to answer.

The figures of Junípero Serra and the more dedicated mission priests still hold much for the rest of us to contemplate. Perhaps one can grasp his dedication to the salvation of the Indians in spite of his travails with the civil authorities, the soldiers, the tenacity of Indians' spirits, and his own tormented body, only if we understand devotion. Those who celebrate Serra and the priests find in the depth and breadth of their hardship, suffering, and sacrifice testimony to the depth and breadth of their devotion to God. Taking one's devotion and then serving God in such a profound and self-sacrificing way as suffering with the heathens in the cause of their salvation is the highest and most sublime of human callings. Exactly the same actions others will take as fanatical, intolerant, or quixotic. They don't understand devotion. If God doesn't exist, or if She is actually tolerant and not jealous, or if there truly are other legitimate gods, then the zealous actions of the priests, indeed all missionaries, will appear foolish, bigoted, unfair, imperialist, or self-serving.

Only recently have I come to comprehend "devotion." Since I was a teenager I have always been attracted to medieval and Renaissance art. I had always figured that it was the allure of the deep past which these visual images helped re-create for me on museum walls. The beauty and grandeur of Giotto's *Christ Entering Jerusalem*, Fra Angelico's several *Annunciations*, Piero della Francesca's *The Discovery and Proving of the True Cross*, Michelangelo's Sistine Chapel, are only a few of the paintings for which I see not only beauty of conception and rendering, but feel Old Testament awe.

These creations are the fruit of devotion to a Great Spirit, to something greater and more magnificent than mere human beings. I stand in awe before Fra Angelico's *Annunciation* in the Prado, or Michelangelo's *Pietà* in St. Peter's, or Raphael's *Madonna and Child* in the Vatican Museum, and I begin to comprehend this affection that I actually don't have or experience: devotion. It is akin to the faith and devotion that Padre Serra and the Franciscans had for God and his representative on earth, the Holy Church, only they had much more of it. Their devotion led them to the New World to destroy the Indian spirits, and all too often Indian lives. Gazing at the works of art, I realized that devotion is best considered like the Indians do with rain and fire and sex: they are part of the world and the human condition, neither inherently good nor bad, sometimes generative and sometimes destructive. It depends on the time and place, the situation and the consequences.

These art forms do more than simply expand my imagination about such ethereal concepts as faith and devotion. They represent for me what is the most excellent in human invention, a reassuring sensation when I contemplate the destructiveness of the missions. It also reminds me why I'm a humanist and not a theist; I celebrate the creations of humans, not God. And I attribute pain and suffering not to God's will or any fall from His grace, but to the actions of humans. For me the missions will always be about the people who have worshiped and been punished there, who worked and sickened there, who were born and died there. And about the people who have continued from there.

I spoke to some people at a symposium on the missions and asked them why they were interested. "We're descendants," they said. Imagine that: their tribal identity in doubt and the language and ceremonies long gone, they have left a sense of having ancestors who experienced the missions. I think of Ernestine de Soto's mother, the last Chumash-speaking person. Though a Christian "Mission Indian," when she died in 1965 the language died. Forever. With the death of the ceremonies and the language — the dances and motions and words sung that connected people's spirits and bodies with the cosmos — people could never again be Chumash, in the full sense of that expression. Was it everlasting life that the Spanish brought to the Chumash, or everlasting death?

Actually, one thing I've learned from listening to these people's stories is that this is likely the wrong question. Strange happenings have visited the Indian peoples of California, and they have had to adapt to new ways of being Indian. This occurred with the Cahuilla people when the Colorado River altered course and created Lake Cahuilla, and then when it changed again and dried up the lake. After the missionaries, the disease, and the violence so mercilessly reduced the languages, ceremonies and populations, Indian peoples — as Catholics, as descendants, on the reservations and rancherías, as apparently everyday folks obscured in various neighborhoods and isolated locales — have continued in new ways.

If they bothered to inquire, most non-Indians in California would be amazed at the re-vitalization of ceremonials in Indian communities, sometimes funded with casino money. Kumeyaay people, the decendants of those who dispatched Padre Jayme and for a while were known as Diegueño, meet with their relatives from Baja California (Kumiai) for feasting, bird songs, dancing, and discussions about pollution and water. A Chumash tomol is afloat in Santa Barbara harbor. The Konkow Valley Band of Maidu near Oroville people continue the Salmon Celebration in September. I've watched Soboba people dance at the Ramona Pageant.[34] No doubt these dances have different meanings then and now, but that's the point about continuing in new ways.

There have been the legal and institutional struggles with the state and federal governments over acknowledging tribal status. Some peoples, especially those whose language and ceremonies have disappeared, are not recognized by one or the other government. Descendants of the missions often can't be sure who their pre-Spanish ancestors were. Others have been simply designated as "bands." Unrecognized, many of them cannot receive the educational or other benefits due them as Indian peoples.[35]

What is "in the blood," as we shall see in our next chapter, is very complicated, and likely even more so for people who have endured nearly two and a half centuries of colonialism. Most California Indians are of mixed blood and thus carry the heritage not only of indigenous peoples but of the various conquerors.[36]

What happened to Ramona and Alessandro happened over and over again. Deborah Miranda (Esselen) tells how "My father opens a map of California — / traces mountain ranges, rivers, county borders / like family bloodlines. Tuolomne, / Salinas, Los Angeles, Paso Robles, / Ventura, Santa Barbara, Saticoy, / Tehachapi. Places he was happy, / or where tragedy greeted him / like an old unpleasant relative . . . The government paid those Indians to move away, / he says, I don't know where they went."[37]

I think of the weight of history as I peruse my back issues of *News from Native California*. The magazine carries articles about efforts to retrieve language and traditional skills, about battling environmental racism, about famous California Indians, and an increasingly rich calendar of events. My confidence in the human spirit is revived.

Theists and humanists will always discuss the missions with contrary presumptions about their nature, ones that remain thinly veiled beneath the surface. Differences over the narratives at the missions — whether we should memorialize the devotion of the fathers or the destruction of the Indians — revolve not simply around partisanship, but from adverse epistemologies. Then, too, even within each worldview there will be differences. Polytheists who celebrate the diverse Indian spiritualities will take umbrage at the glorification of the monotheists' God's victory over the pagan spirits. Humanists will differ over whether or not the missions represent the destructiveness of human religious zealotry or the creativity of humans in the matter of their architectural beauty and the accuracy of their speculative restorations.

The presentation of a mission will always irritate someone; people will always hear very different messages from them. Missions San Gabriel, San Buenaventura, San Diego, and San Luis Rey are functioning parishes wherein reigns the Word of God without dissent. ("We witness here," says a sign at San Gabriel, "the beginning of a new civilization wherein Christianity was introduced to a pagan sphere," and even refers to "the daring redskin, the blithe spirited Mexican, the valiant Spanish soldier and the venturesome 'Americano.'") La Purísima and San Juan Capistrano emphasize the handicrafts developed there, though the gift shops maintain the Holy line. Located in wealthy communities, Santa Barbara and San Carlos Borroméo (Carmel) are beautifully maintained tourist destinations, though at the former there is an effort at including the Indian peoples' contributions. Emerging from the 16th Street Mission station from the BART, one asks in vain, in Spanish and English, for directions to the Mission Dolores (San Francisco de Asís). Neither the recent immigrants nor the hip denizens of the Mission District know where it is. The curator of the mission is a deeply Catholic Ohlone. At San Francisco de Solano one can see inscribed in granite the names of nine hundred Indians, two hundred of them children. Visiting schoolchildren touch them.

This is the only place, though, that the Indians are meaningfully memorialized. The arguments between humanists and theists, multiculturists and True Believers, and indigenous peoples and the advocates of Western European civilization are too profound to make for much agreement over the narratives at the missions. It's what people believe so powerfully in their hearts that will make arguments over the presentations of the missions forever irrational and belligerent.

To center the narrative on the intended destruction of the Indians and their cultures would be, obviously, to nullify the devoted efforts of the padres to bring them everlasting salvation. To negate, in other words, the whole purpose of the Catholic Church and the Christian Faith.

To affirm Indian ways of treating the land and its spirits would challenge the benefits of the technology the Spanish brought to those who lived in awe of the natural world. To negate, in other words, science and technology which has enabled over thirty-five million people to live in California, many of them in some degree of comfort and abundance.

How to present the obraje, the monjerio, and the soldiers' quarters? As the places where Indian bodies were disciplined, where the venerable spirits that animated them were cast out, where sexual desire was mutilated? To negate, in other words, what Euro-Americans understand to be civilized — monotheism and body discipline in the service of methodical labor and monogamous marriage.

The teacher in me, of course, sees the missions as a superb place to present these sorts of dilemmas of the human condition, to enable people to conceptualize the body, belief, labor, desire, and technology in new ways, to make people aware of the varieties of human experience and diverse knowledges of these matters. As with the Smithsonian's troubled Enola Gay exhibit that attempted to contextualize the dropping of the bomb on Hiroshima, people are not ready for views that challenge what they know to be true about matters of righteousness of cause, on whose side God seems to be, and Euro-American supremacy. As suggesting that the bomb was not dropped simply to save American lives, proposing that there was more to the story of the missions than simply devoted priests bringing civilization to pagan, licentious Indians, or more to the story than intolerant religious bigots destroying simple, natural Indians, dares people to reject certainty in favor of ambiguity and subtlety, which are never as pleasing or gratifying as Truth.

We have, then, competing truths, the handling of which our modern sensibilities may better equip us for than those of the distant past. In times or places when there has been only one Truth, then a purge, an inquisition, even genocide has been the response to difference. To repeat three things central to my views of the Indians and the Franciscans: I remain wedded to the notion that some stories are indeed truer than others; that, via my adoration of Christian art, I have come to know something of the "truth" of people's devotion to the One True God; and that like other elements of life, devotion can be destructive or creative. I have learned from the missions, then, one of the great tactics for living successfully in our age — the ability to hold two, or more, opposing ideas in the mind, and then be able to care, and to function, and to find some peace.

And, really, the competing Truths are probably necessary: no one person, no one story, is big enough to include everything that must be considered about the missions. As in all these matters of the calamities that humans inflict on one another, some people will forever be angry and want to fight, or revel in their wounds, or exalt their status as victims. Others will be willing to forgive, and yet others may even acknowledge their vanquishers' superiority or blame themselves. If we could admit the contingencies of our own stories, of our own truths, when we can concede that other peoples' stories could be true too, then, I think and hope that we will be less likely to inflict harm on them. We need all of the people, all of the stories, all of the Truths, for completion and for the ability to continue on this landscape in good ways.

When, though, will we allow the competing narratives to be heard? How then to achieve some reality in the way the missions are presented, how to make them live as monuments on the landscape, how to make California history live for young people, how to allow the Indian peoples buried in the courtyards to finally rest in peace? For me, as should be apparent to readers already, it is the secular humanist notions of appreciation and respect for people's authentic stories, and some faith that we humans actually can apply compassion and reason to resolve what bedevils us, that will make peace in the missions.

I know that this won't work for everyone. Perhaps another, grander, answer can come from the people in the middle of all this controversy, those who were born there. At a few of the missions is an image of the Virgin of Guadalupe. She is mestiza, the "goddess of the Americas," and she is the One who forgives. And forgiveness should now be the nature of the matter of the missions of California, because, may I remind the Church of Paul's admonition about those who carry the Word of God to others, "For we are made a spectacle unto the world, and to Angels, and to men." (Corinthians 4:9)

She is not just any Virgin Mary. She is not Nuestra Señora de los Remedios, a 13-inch figurine carried in the saddlebags of one of the original conquistadores. While she is associated with many miracles, she also represents the Spanish conquest. (During Mexico's war for independence, followers of Hidalgo carried the Virgin of Guadalupe into battle, those loyal to Spain carried Remedios.) She is certainly not la Conquistadora, a rosy skinned and blond saddlebag virgin, this one at the

Church of San Francisco at the Plaza in Santa Fe, who represents the Reconquest of New Mexico after the Great Pueblo Revolt of 1680. And she is not la Conquistadora of Mission San Carlos Borroméo (Carmel). No, She is *la Virgen Morena*, the dark virgin, the one not carried from Spain but who appeared in Mexico to the Indian Juan Diego, now the first indigenous saint, on the hill that had been home to the popular Tonantzín, the vanquished Aztec mother goddess of the earth, fertility, and corn. She holds her hands in the Indian position of offering rather than the Christian one of supplication; she protects and forgives, brings health and happiness, and offers solace and comfort in times of fear and tragedy.

Conceivably, it could be in Her name that the Church could ask for forgiveness; in Her name that Indians could be memorialized at the missions; in Her name that an example could be set for people transcending tribal loyalties. The missions spoke to their devotees in one way when most Euro-Americans believed that everyone should be Christian and that it was appropriate and to their benefit that indigenous people adopt the ways of what they called "civilization." The missions speak to us now in a very different way when it is apparent that presumption of religious or cultural superiority results in genocide. The twentieth century, for all of its various and splendid advances in science and material abundance for some, was also the century of the Holocaust, of vile racist conquests, of unconscionable slaughter of civilians in its world wars, of unspeakably horrible tribal warfare among people of all colors and religions.

This proves both that we moderns are not so superior to those of the distant past whom we so often smugly condemn for their inquisitions, imperialism, and intolerance of other belief systems, and that we, armed with utterly lethal technological warfare, must fashion new ways to relate to other human beings who are different from ourselves, whoever "we" (and "they") may be. Perhaps I am too much a man of the Enlightenment, but I still believe that thoughtful people of good will can make the world a better place, can make peace.

Such an endeavor requires reconciliation, a word of poignant meaning. It means conciliation (a word that derives from the Latin for "to combine or unite") between persons, or people and ideas or conditions, most commonly. Its theological meaning has to do with people reconciling with God, of correcting their relationship to Him. I think here of how pertinent and seemly would it be for the Church and the Indians to achieve such a reconciliation after the Church's "conquista espiritual." It might not only recondition the Church's relationship to the peoples it conquered, but it might rectify the conquering Franciscans' relationship to God in whose name, and to whom they were so devoted, they initiated the ruination of the Indians of California.

And reconciliation has another meaning too: it refers also to "the cleansing, purification, or reconsecration of a desecrated church . . ." As long as the Indian peoples in the missions are not resting in peace, as long as their suffering goes unatoned for, as long as the errors made in the name of God are not righted, then the missions will be places of sadness and anger.

Reconciliation, then, has several prospects. Most simply and imme-diately it can make peace between the descendants and the conquer-ors. This is only good and just. Most importantly and profoundly it can demonstrate to the world that peoples can replace conquest and holy war with compassion and grace. This would please all the gods — Yahweh's admonition about the others notwithstanding — too, I'm sure. And I wonder what it would be like to go to the missions of California where there had been reconciliation, a reconsecration of places made blasphemous and obscene by disease and rape and death and war be-tween the peoples and their great spirits. No more tears of rage and grief, but some sense of the possibility that people can treat one another with compassion and charity, and hope for humanity and the future.

There are, though, prerequisites. Acknowledgment that to try and destroy another peoples' ways is the wrong thing to do. The padres brought clocks and constructed sundials so that the Indians would know what "time" it was, something the natives never understood. Now it is time for the Church to know what "time" it is: as when the Church acknowledged that it erred for condemning Galileo's conclusions about how the earth revolved around the sun, it is time now to acknowledge that missionization was the wrong thing to do. It's not that the Church should, or even could, have known that in 1769. It's that we all know it now: after the events of the twentieth century there is no other conclu-sion. And there must be an appeal for forgiveness; something that can best be done in Her name, the mestiza goddess Guadalupe/Tonantzín.

It would be hard to imagine another figure so appropriate for such a task. I will not say that I literally believe in the divinity of any saint, but I do believe in the power of la Virgen as a unifying force. She even speaks to secular people like me: I recall my grandparents' back yard where Tata had a beautiful tile picture of Her. Beneath he had written "Whether you are fact or fiction, we love you. Our independence owes you a lot." This is another example of how She can speak to people like my grandfather, a skeptic in matters of the Church and a veteran of the Revolution, at the same time She can speak to True Believers who know in their hearts that She is responsible for miracles.

The missionization of the Indians in the Americas can be understood in several ways. One of them is that evangelizers waged war against local spirits in the name of God. It is, thus, a spiritual matter, one that can find "conciliation," a "combining and a uniting," only in spiritual ways. Appeals to tolerance, learned discourse about the missions, the passage of time, cannot have the conciliatory power of the mestiza goddess Guadalupe/Tonantzín.

The missions will always be telling us things. We will never have mastery over them. The religious iconography, the restless souls of the Indians buried there, knowledge of people's anguished lives there in the distant past, the epic travels that brought the two peoples together in tragedy and calamity, the speculative architectural restorations, and the tourist and gift shop versions continually and autonomously tell conflicting stories of the missions of California, ones not amenable to conciliation.

To genuinely hear what the missions tell us, it should be apparent now, we must acknowledge and hear the Indian, Spanish, Mexican, and American stories of the places. There is no other way unless we are to reduce the missions to merely architecture or monologue. In those missions of California, these four peoples' histories and destinies are thoroughly interwoven. Not faith alone, not even in the venerable Guadalupe/Tonantzín, will combine and unite these narratives, though perhaps the effort would best be made in Her name. I have come to understand how, at least for me, it has been language and history that have calmed the dread I feel at the missions. A dread that is mysterious is scarier than one that is named; it has been for me language that has thus identified that foreboding at the missions.

And it has been history, but only good, hard history—the kind where you study the documents, read philosophy and theory, and then apply grand compassion, consummate care, and difficult honesty when you speak and write—that has given me understanding of those awful places. And it has been the awe of these places that has taught me about the nature of metaphysical knowledge, what mi Tata called "religión espontánea," but what I still call the human spirit. Know then, dear reader, how and why I *need* this language and history: there is some comfort in the words and the good, sometimes enduring, sometimes concealed stories which, even if they do not give complete meaning and understanding to the missions and to the other stories here, at least give some expression to the awe, and safety from the dread.

How the New World Border Changes
Who We Are and Where We Are

In the same picture frame that holds my grandmother's night school certificates commending her acquisition of English is a photograph of her and a ribbon that declares her an Honor Student. In the snapshot she and the other largely Mexican immigrants sit dressed in their nice clothes and looking rather languid. It is hard to tell from what the estranged look derives. Perhaps it is from the photographic technology that required that people remain still; perhaps it is from being an adult in a school for children, and my grandmother never went to school in Mexico; perhaps she simply didn't want to become American.

She had four children at the time. These are some of the stories they would tell as adults: as a young mother, and it is always hard to imagine one's grandmother, *mi Noni*, as a young woman, she would bring home the songs she learned at night school. The whole family would sing "Just a Song of Twilight" and "Keep the Home Fires Burning." Lulu went on foot from the eastside to look at schools for her children, which would help decide where the family would live. She found and liked what she called La Politécnica, or Polytechnic High School, which was then located on the near south side of downtown LA.

One day my grandfather, *mi Tata*, came home from labor in the furniture factory and found a note on the door from his wife informing him that she had sold the house and giving him the address of the new house to which she had already had everything moved.

My grandfather believed in a prosperous, modern Mexico, the opposite of *México profundo*. He fought in the Mexican Revolution and, according to family lore, was one of those pistoleros who rode around on a horse and expropriated the lands of the rich and the Church and then gave them to the landless poor. For this the Church (and Woodrow Wilson) condemned him. His name was Jesús.

Then he took his visions of justice, prosperity, and education for the children with him when he represented the state of Sonora in the Mexican Senate. It's hard to know if he came up against greed, or the forces of reaction and the Church, or México profundo. The newly powerful ones told him that he would have to leave Mexico or they would kill him. In the footsteps of Padre Serra, he came north to the America from which had come Woodrow Wilson's guns. In Los Angeles Jesús González-Monroy was simply a Mexican who worked in a factory, and he was safe and his children went to La Politécnica.

Tata, with his job, and Noni, with her shrewdness, kept the family out of the agricultural fields. This was a great and meaningful accomplishment for Mexican immigrants of the era.

My grandparents never became American citizens. They always thought that they would go home to live again in Mexico. They are buried in the Evergreen Cemetery in East Los Angeles.

My father, Jaime González-Monroy, was a busboy at the Trocadero on Sunset Boulevard in 1932. Before the customers arrived, his job was to de-vein the shrimp. That means to clean out that little brown line along the top, that little bit of shrimp caca that the crustacean did not get to excrete. The chefs were all French, and the sauce chef, in particular, befriended him. He wanted this energetic, smart Mexican teenager to apprentice with him. For some reason Jaime opted for industrial labor downtown, which would lead him to unions and politics. Imagine if I had been the son of a Frenchified Mexican-American sauce chef, or a farm worker.

When I was in high school, which was also on Sunset Boulevard, I took Spanish and did quite well. In class we would sing songs in Spanish. Outside of school I only sang them to myself. My musical tastes were limited to the songs on the AM radio — American music and the British Invasion, only songs in English, with Rhythm and Blues and Motown high on my list. These are all signs of my family's journey to being American — my songs were all in English whether it be the Stones, Dylan, or the Temptations. Spanish was a "foreign language." My high school diploma lists that as my major.

In the summer of 2003 I went to Southern France, including St. Tropez. There at an outdoor restaurant — I had an exquisite fish soup and a coq au vin with a pretty good sauce — a group of singers played songs in Spanish, ones I remembered from high school Spanish class. They played "La Bamba," "Guantanamera," as at the

Ramona Pageant too, but without Castilian accents. I assumed they were Mexicans, though they didn't exactly look like Mexicans and they did not quite sound like Michoacán. When one came around for tips I asked him, "¿De dónde son ustedes?" He shook his head a bit and said "No, Romani." He confided, "Gitane."

I put a euro or two in his basket and gave a fake French look, like when you purse your lips and thrust your chin forward. These Gypsies are from nowhere, but they are everywhere. A long, long time ago they came from India — why they look a bit Mexican — and settled first in Romania — why they speak Romany, a Romance language like Spanish. Globalization and migration are not new.

After them came a *banda* who sang in good Castilian Spanish and with theatrical cultural garb. When the tip-getter came around, I asked him in my very best Spanish, "¿De dónde son ustedes?"

"De Saragoza," he said proudly and with a perfect Castilian lisp. "¿Y usted habla español? ¿De dónde es usted?" he asked.

"De los Estados Unidos, de una familia mexicana."

Without much pause he exclaimed, smiling and confidently, "¡Sómos todos Hispanos!" and nodded when I put the euro in his basket.

What would Noni and Tata think? Their gringo-ized grandson was now "Hispano."

Any reader of this essay will find some things to disagree with, and this is good. I'm sure we can agree that Los Angeles has lots of people in it, but we will disagree about whether or not that is good. I'm not sure about the matter myself.

I had a relative hiatus from visiting Los Angeles between 1984 and 1994. The summer of '84 I had a research fellowship and far more tickets to the Olympics than I could use. Apparently people living in Colorado Springs, home of the Olympic Training Center, got most of what they requested on their ticket order forms. I was popular with my friends and relatives in LA, needless to say, what with my fistfuls of tickets. Going to the different venues — the Coliseum, Long Beach Arena, Pauly Pavilion, and the Olympic Auditorium — I surveyed the city anew. It seemed much the same, except for Hollywood where the specter of AIDS had begun to cast its morbid pallor.

Ten years after that I took my children, then 8 and 13, to see the city of my birth and upbringing, the same one to which my monolingual, Spanish-speaking father came in 1922 when he was about my little son's age. I wanted to show them the schools I went to. Two full-time police officers guarded Hollywood High, my old school. Two boys had recently been shot in a drive-by on the front lawn where I had strolled by a thousand times. The principal told me how two more had been shot after getting off work as busboys at the Old Spaghetti Factory; one was killed and the other had been busy in the quad showing off to his friends the bullet wound in his butt. I had been a waiter there when I was writing my dissertation.

In the *Poinsettia*, the Hollywood High School annual, from my years the "N.E.S." (non-English-speaking) kids had two pages at the end for their pictures, which were smaller than the rest. Their names were Spanish, Chinese, and Armenian. In 1994, according to the principal, there were 56 mother tongues and the school was 80 percent English as a Second Language. I was taken aback; my children were not impressed. They had Wendy's on their minds.

Gone were the old independent stands whose distinctive burgers clogged my arteries three decades previously, but their favorite fast-food chain awaited us only three blocks from "dear old Hollywood High." What a scene, one quite different from the old days driving around with "When a Man Loves a Woman" on the Volkswagen AM radio. Like virtually all fast-food outlets in Los Angeles, there was now someone with a paper cup begging for change at the end of the drive-thru. Sitting in line in our renta-Chevy, I discerned that apparently there had been a fight over the cup position between at least two of the half-dozen African Americans hanging together on the sidewalk at Wendy's. One helped the loser with his bruised face while the rest hassled an Indian man, nearly passed out, with peed-up pants.

The disturbance certainly advertised poorly for business: two Mexican or Central American employees from inside, both wearing their Wendy's-issued, impeccable shirts and paper hats, had come out to diffuse the commotion. But they didn't speak English, the blacks towered over them, and the Indian was now prostrate on the pavement. We got our order; I dropped a little change in the cup; we drove away, doors locked, windows up, no "Whenna" on the radio.

We cruise by a Home Depot where you can buy anything and everything, even a Mexican day laborer. Now there are signs at the Home Depot warning "Jornaleros, Busca Empleo en el Centro de Trabajo." The single men used to lounge on the parkways in front of the colossal stores waiting for work. When a contractor's pickup truck, or a suburban SUV, would stop to get day labor, the guys would leap into action and beg for work. Few sights indicate social dissolution more forcefully and poignantly than the beggar. "The spirit of community," Raymond Williams tells us, "has been dispossessed and isolated to a wandering, challenging if passive, embodiment in the beggar." He continues, quoting Wordsworth, "It is no longer from the practice of community, or from the spirit of protest at its inadequacy, but from 'this solitary being, / This helpless wanderer' that the instinct of fellow-feeling is derived."

I didn't understand the feelings within me about these men begging at the Wendy's and the Home Depot, or what to tell my children about who they were and what they were doing. I only knew that I harbored an uneasy irritation. Yet, somehow I maintain with them some sense of "community against the rigours, the cold abstinence, the selfish ease of ordinary society," some sense that they are worthy of moral consideration.[1]

I yearned for things to have not changed. This is a common sentiment. People like their places and people to remain familiar. Trips like these, though, have convinced me of the impossibility of immutability as regards the urban landscape and those who inhabit it.

The New World Border has accelerated the devolution of my familiar. Really, then, that's what this chapter will be about. How things as apparently unchanging as environment and people are transforming so rapidly and unalterably. And, central to our premises in this book, this is yet another vexation that Mexico and America share: both countries, ones so steeped in their imagined pasts, are encountering metamorphoses they often did not intend but that are certainly consequences of decisions elites have made about their politics and economics. The streets of cities and towns on both sides of the border witness changes associated with the new world border that are palpable and inescapable, and will continue to unfold in ways that will often be uncomfortable and disquieting.

As we toured around the city, the floor of the back seat of the renta-Chevy filled to calf-length with fast-food wrappers. I quickly gave up on English and ordered in Spanglish: "Un Quarter Pound Single con lechuga, tomate, mayonesa, no cebolla; un Kid's Meal con chicken nuggets . . ." Even I was taken aback at how food industry workers were all Mexican or Central American.

When I had been a waiter in 1976, about half the busboys, and all the dishwashers and the unskilled kitchen staff, were Spanish-speaking.

At my tables I always wanted the Mexican-born busboys because they cleaned off the tables much faster than the local high school kids who, like me at that age, had better things to do. When there was trouble in the kitchen, it was usually I who was summoned from the front to translate and negotiate. After awhile, several of the illegals asked me to stand with them at the cash register as they were paid lest there be any "questions." This seemed like no big deal at the time; indeed, I was a bit honored.

By 1994 there was no way that I would send my children to "dear old Hollywood High" and there was no way that my son could get a job (not that he would take one doing "Mexican work") as a busboy in a Hollywood restaurant.[2] I was surrounded by Spanish. Mexicans filled up the parks, even my beloved Fern Dell where car lovers used to wax their vehicles in the shade of the trees, gays would lounge on the grass, and I would kiss girls while "Whenna" played on the AM radio. I wondered who these people were who, along with hundreds of thousands of Asians, had changed dramatically my old home into something unfamiliar to me, something even—dare I say—distasteful. Really, all along I knew the answer to my disturbing question: they were my ancestors.

And this answer is much more conflicted, controversial, and complicated these days. It's made even more messy and nasty by the way most people comprehend it. It seems to be about nationality and race. I understand this: all one has to do is LOOK and one sees that it is brown, Indian-looking Mexicans taking over the public schools and parks and monopolizing the jobs that teenagers and even African Americans used to get; that so many blacks, especially the young males, are idle and menacing; that it is Asians who run so many of the remaining small businesses. I stop at a mini-mart for gas for the renta-Chevy and snacks to quiet the kids and ask the Indian man (the South Central Asian kind) for the best way to get to such-and-so a place that I used to be able to get to with my eyes closed. He's never heard of it. This is more infuriating than Zorro in an orange *chaleco*.

My response so far is the classic one: my familiar is disintegrating and my inclination is to condemn it, fear it, and want to arrest whatever is causing it to disappear. I look at the people whom I associate with these changes; they look alien. My impulse is to blame these people—the different ones—for the contamination they bring, for what aggravates me. This is how we come to construct ideas about people who appear to be of a different "type." Maybe that "type" we understand in terms of appearance, and that appearance might have to do with their demeanor, conduct, or even something we might call "race." It is about "spectacle," or how people display themselves, especially in ritualized manner having to do with dress, swagger, and their style of personal association, that makes us think in terms of certain people being "other," of being different and troubling.

But it's NOT about nationality and race, at least not mostly, and not as much as it used to be. It's about history and politics, and economics and globalization, and creative destruction. To say that it is about nationality and race is to grievously misunderstand and to live in dismay, bewilderment, and anger. And fear of contamination and corruption. The reality of any matter — the scene at the Wendy's, the overcrowded and troubled schools, and whatever else — lies not in simply what one sees, but in how one describes it and discusses it. Any "truth," and I use that word with stern reservations, derives from the human intellect and imagination that one uses to explain and name a situation or people. I will also say that there is nothing like history and hard social analysis to bring a modicum of peace to someone, and there are many such people besides me who have watched these changes, found them distressing and entertaining at the same time, felt such sorrow (usually a sentiment with connotations of superiority), and genuinely feared for the future of California, Mexico, and America.

Academic liberals, and I need not remind my readers that I am a liberal arts college professor and (if we had such a moniker) a card-carrying liberal humanist, are often accused of being out of touch with mainstream America. This is true and in no place is it more so than in the matter of race. Most people in America, and an even greater majority in the rest of the world, have come to think that what race you are is what you are, or what you should be, and that phenotype or lineage have much to do with intellectual and moral capacity, or at least character. Let me present our case, one that represents the lived history of Mexicans on both sides of the border, even though most of those Mexicans would not side with the liberal humanists in this matter.

Let's get some things straight right away. Science, genetic science in particular, has made it clear that there is no difference between the so-called "races." In fact there is only ONE human race. People around the world, and in California, have different "phenotypes." That word refers to the apparent differences in "looks" — skin color, hair texture, the shape of facial features. Genetics, and specifically the Human Genome

Project, has demonstrated that these different phenotypes are simply adaptations to different environments and that these evolutionary acclimations have actually happened only recently in human history. Humankind emerged from Africa and then those who lived in places with intense sun evolved dark skin while those in cloudy places evolved light skin which better absorbs vitamin D. People who have lived at high altitudes evolved barrel chests to hold big lungs and people who have lived in areas with malaria evolved the sickle blood cell to defend against it. In terms of our genetic makeup, however, we are 99.99 percent the same regardless of our phenotypical differences.

To understand this in more depth it is useful to understand what is meant by the parallel notion that "race" is a "construct." Certainly, Africans, Caucasians, and Asians (and then those more inexplicit ones— "Indians" we might call them—from the Americas and South Central Asia) all act and believe differently, but it has nothing to do with their "race" because, as genetic science has shown, there is no such thing as "race," only phenotypical differences that have no bearing whatsoever on moral or intellectual capacity.

"Race," then, is something that people make up about other people for all manner of reasons. Maybe to take their land (think of Alessandro's people), maybe to put them on boats and make them work in the heat under the whip (think slavery), maybe simply to explain why they are so stubbornly odd (think about the inscrutability of the Chinese), or maybe to explain why the once-familiar landscape has changed, people ascribe qualities to other people with different phenotypes and then assume that somehow those phenotypes are an indication of "race" and then that "race" is what explains how and why those other people are different. They may be different all right, but much as phenotypes are evolutionary adaptations to environment, distinctive social and personal characteristics derive from how diverse peoples have undergone dissimilar social evolutions based upon their unique relationships to time, physical environment, and their gods.

Having said this, that there is really no such thing as different "races," I will now say that nevertheless "race matters," and does so quite significantly. You see, once these ideas about race, especially as a category that can explain behavior, have taken hold of people's minds, then "race," this artificial construct, becomes a powerful and enduring force in human societies. "Race" becomes how people think about and evaluate and treat with others who appear different.

That people of African, Mexican, Asian, and Native descent have been treated as slaves and niggers, as dirty and servile workers and spics, as coolies and slants, as naked savages and redskins, means that their historical experiences have been materially different from Euro-Americans, and intensely so. It means that their labor and/or their land have been unfairly expropriated, their persons pained and humiliated, and that their capacities to affect their material and social lives is much less than those with privilege and power. Race may be something humans have constructed for various reasons and rationalizations, but we can't simply declare race something we need to get over with like the flu: it's why some people have real estate and some don't; why some have capital and some have only their labor; why some have higher education and some only their muscle and patience; why some have access to political power and others only their bodies in streets.

There are few better illustrations of these concepts, that "race" is constructed and mutable and that it is a meaningful social category, than the ways in which various Mexicans — the mixed people who often defy categorization as one way or another — have been specified, how they have been treated, and how they have labeled themselves.

The story of Mexican *mestizaje*, the process by which the Indian and the Spanish blended their cultures and bloods, has been told many times and in many ways. The legend of the first mestizo, and thus the first Mexican, is part of the creation myth of modern Mexico. His name was Martín and he was the child of Hernando Cortés and Doña Marina. Bidding his wife *adiós* from Havana in February 1519, Cortés went to conquer the Aztec empire. While exploring the coast the people of Tabasco made him a gift of a woman, the sublime La Malinche, herself of royal lineage and mistress extraordinaire to several important caciques. Cortés and the Spanish conquistadores called her Doña Marina. Much is important about her — she became the translator for Cortés and the Aztecs and very much the "woman in between" who facilitated, depending on point of view, either the conquest or accommodation of the natives and the Spanish.[3]

Their romance, which lasted as long as Cortés had use for her, produced this first mestizo who, regardless of how one shades the historical conquest, is all bound up with conquest, adultery, and the violation of indigenous women by European men. Octavio Paz has most poignantly and famously addressed the dilemmas of this mestizaje, of how Doña

Marina became la Chingada, the violated (but literally "fucked"*) one. Paz expounds that when Mexicans shout "'¡*Viva México, hijos de la chingada!*' we express our desire to live closed off from the outside world and, above all, from the past. In this shout we condemn our origins and deny our hybridism."[4]

Nueva España, what everything in the Spanish Empire from California to New Mexico to Texas down to Chiapas and Yucatán was before Mexican Independence succeeded in 1821, wrestled with this matter of mixture in creative, if not by our standards, utterly archaic, ways.

There was this *casta* system there, the program by which colonial Spain sought to codify the races. The bringing together of Spaniards, Indians, and Africans proved to be one of the more complex consequences of empire especially once they all started having sex, be it coerced, felicitous, sacralized, or scandalous. Obviously a Spaniard and an Indian woman begat a mestizo and a Spaniard and an African a mulatto, but what if a mestizo got together with a mulatto? In eighteenth-century New Spain, the product might be something like a "morisco" or a "lobo." At different times and places in the New World, there were in the area of 15 such categories. Curiously enough, if the parents were not of the same category, then their children would be something different from them.

This was the great idea that, out of the wreckage of Spanish imperialism to which the Catholic Church had attached itself, came from the variously sanctified and base mixings of the Americas: the stunning idea that people were not one thing or the other, nor even some cross between two civilizations, but some new mestizaje, some new way of being altogether.

I recall Ramona and me: Alessandro and Ramona's child would be some sort of mestizo while, because he could claim to be Spanish, Felipe and Ramona's children would be *castizo*. But if I were to beget children with one of Ramona and Felipe's children, or maybe even

---

* This is a matter of hugely revealing importance. Inasmuch as we shall be dealing with the ways in which Mexicans and Americans are different, we have here in the use of "chingar" and "to fuck" a stunning, perhaps binding, similarity. Americans say "don't fuck with me" while Mexicans say "no me chingas." Mexicans say "ay, chingos de carros" while Americans say "a fuck of a lot of cars." Americans say "I've been fucked" while Mexicans say "me ha chingado."

Ramona herself, we would begin the process of becoming more *torna atras*, or "turning back" towards the category of pure Spanish. (Interestingly enough in Peru at the same time, a mestizo and an Indian woman begat a *cholo*, which indeed seems to be the origin of that word, and which now describes the rebellious youths of present-day Mexican American neighborhoods.)[5]

My point is not that this is a "good" system of racial classification; there is no such thing, and obviously, it was utterly hierarchical and has bequeathed Latin America a fairly rigid caste system, which Enlightenment ideas about equality have only barely punctured. Rather that such taxonomy, such a way of categorizing, is much more fluid and ambiguous than what most Americans are accustomed to. One is not either/or — black or white — as in the United States and inheritor of the categorization of whichever parent has the lowest status. This difference is most remarkable when we consider that in the United States a black woman who conceives a child with a white man gives birth to someone who will be designated "black" and that a white woman who conceives a child with a black man will also have a "black" child. The "half-breed" emerged as the exception to such racial either/or thinking. But surely such a product of a white man and his "squaw wife" found herself or himself cast out from both societies. A "breed" had neither the Anglo-Saxon robustness associated with civilization and progress nor the pure and uncorrupted relationship to nature associated with primeval Indians. This is the sort of mindset that Anglo Americans took into their dealings with Mexicans, at least before the New World Border.

It could almost be funny. One Boston Brahmin in the 1830s, Richard Henry Dana, anticipated the conquest of California and proclaimed Anglo-Saxon superiority when he claimed that "forty Kentucky hunters, with their rifles, and a dozen of Yankees and Englishmen, were a match for a whole regiment of hungry, drawling, lazy half-breeds." There seemed to be something in the Mexicans' mixed blood that made them deficient: "In their domestic relations these people are not better than in their public," he declared, and then continued that "the men are thriftless, proud, extravagant, and very much given to gaming; and the women have but little education, and a good deal of beauty, and their morality, of course, is none of the best."[6] Dana wrote these things in his famous and often-reprinted *Two Years before the Mast*, which was about his travels from Boston around Cape Horn and up to California in the 1830s. "A matchless tale of adventure," as the back cover says, which was high on the list of adventure stories for boys in my junior high school.

I could include countless statements likes these. One of my favorites comes from Dr. George Clements, who was the LA Chamber of Commerce's semi-official "Mexican expert" and manager of its agricultural department: "The Mexican is an Indian and must be considered so," the medical doctor noted in 1939. "He is undergoing active evolution and we must always take this thought into consideration in dealing with him. His wants are few and his habits, while docile, are not in harmony with western civilization."[7]

In the minds of Mexicans this very same hybridity translates in completely different ways. Most famously, when José Vasconcelos discussed "the ulterior goals of History to attain the fusion of peoples and cultures," he affirmed that Latin America's "predestination obeys the design of constituting the cradle of a fifth race into which all nations will fuse with each other to replace the four races that have been forging History apart from each other." In his fabled *La Raza Cósmica*, the quixotic Vasconcelos, Mexico's minister of education from 1921 to 1924, presidential candidate in 1928, and frequent exile, said of the Americas that "unity will be consummated there by the triumph of fecund love and the improvement of the human races." Vasconcelos, himself of European ancestry, celebrated mestizo people, "the synthetic race that shall gather all the treasures of History."[8]

I'm not sure what predisposes the two different peoples to their opposite ideas about mixture. Perhaps it is the food. An American plate tenders victuals with the servings separate; meat, potatoes, and vegetable do not touch on the plate, or, if they do, only barely. On a Mexican plate, a mestizo plate, the offerings mix together; cheese enchiladas (and it was the French who introduced Mexico to *enchiladas suizas*, with cheese that is), beans, rice, a tamal come nearly mixed up together, always on the verge of combining. Poking the food around with a tortilla and mixing it with salsa or *mole*, all ancient Mexican Indian staples, completes the gathering of all the food treasures of history.

Or we can rely on the vagaries of history and culture to explain why a descendant of Puritans "identifies Purity with health" and, as Octavio Paz further puts it, senses that in "every contact is a contamination." Thus it is that "foreign races, ideas, customs, and bodies carry within themselves the germs of perdition and impurity." Mestizo culture is different: "Mexicans, however, both ancient and modern, believe in communion and fiestas: there is no health without contact," Paz asserts. He tells how "Tlatzoteotl, the Aztec goddess of filth and fecundity, of earthly and human moods, was also the goddess of steam baths, sexual love and confession." "And," echoing the ideas of México profundo, "we have not changed very much, for Catholicism is also communion."[9]

Another Boston Brahmin, echoing his forerunner Richard Henry Dana, fears the mixture that Mexicans bring. Citing statistics on the numbers of Mexican-descent people who continue to speak Spanish, Samuel P. Huntington, in his notoriously inflammatory *Foreign Policy* article of March 2004, claims that "if this trend continues, the cultural division between Hispanics and Anglos could replace the racial division between blacks and whites as the most serious cleavage in U.S. society." Citing dubious sources, he specifies "Hispanic traits": "Mistrust of people outside the family; lack of initiative, self-reliance, and ambition; little use for education; and acceptance of poverty as a virtue necessary for entrance into heaven."[10]

I don't know which is the bigger threat to him — that the people on his plate of America stay separate like his steak and potatoes, or that they smush all together like some enchiladas and beans.

What does one say to this? He's right that, in many areas of the country, enclaves of Mexican immigrants likely will not assimilate any time soon. It's not about race to this modern critic; it's about comportment. We have another Woodrow Wilson in Samuel P. Huntington, one who does not understand the sources of different peoples' unfamiliar conduct. Mexicans are not pre-disposed culturally or racially to be one way or another; it's because this sort of bi-nationalism is part of the New World Order, the new system whereby labor and capital flow back and forth across borders, or, more accurately, erases borders. And, as we know from our reading of Guillermo Bonfil Batalla and Octavio Paz, Mexicans may indeed honor the family more than the individual (and I hate to be the one to remind Huntington and his ilk that this is Christian "family values") and that Mexican history predisposes people to believe that chance and circumstance and sin and human foible, and not reason and orderly progress, are factors in personal and national history.

In his classic response to the corruption and contamination that immigrants allegedly bring, Huntington has stumbled upon what may be America's most disconcerting problem in the New World Order, one that has its roots in the contradictory display of the immigrant as both threat to, and confirmation of, America. This country has been, of course, "a nation of immigrants," one that has absorbed millions of people from various (mostly) European cultures. The foundations of assimilation—work structures, urban political machines, the military, popular culture, and especially public schools—were designed to revolutionize the individual and to make of her or him an "American." When actually successful, or at least solidified in the national mythology, this process of rejecting the old in favor of America bears out the view of the nation as the culmination of world civilization. When, however, they and the exigencies of transnationalism insist on maintaining national subcultures, the immigrant comes to threaten America and its creed.

Of course, during the great era of European immigration, say from the arrival of the Irish in the 1840s to the dawn of World War I, America always had plenty of foreigners who lived in their ethnic enclaves and who bothered Anglo Protestants and their sensibilities. Maybe from the movies or service in war or on the shop floor, people who were once Italian, German, or Irish came to adopt what Huntington calls the "American Creed," which is actually a phrase the British literary giant G. K. Chesterton coined early in the twentieth century. For Huntington this includes the rule of law, individualism, the work ethic, "and the belief that humans have the ability and the duty to try to create a heaven on earth, a 'city on a hill.' "[11] In public schools from New York to Chicago to Los Angeles and every city in between, schoolchildren learned to respond to bells and the clock, to go to school (and then, of course, to work in the factory) even if it was one's or the old village saint's day, to delay gratification for future reward (homework), to read about the Westward Movement, to elect the class president, to sing the same songs, and to play baseball and four square. By the time of the Cold War, the children and grandchildren of immigrants who had successfully internalized the Creed even intermarried; they dutifully affirmed the quality of life in America; and they earnestly bonded over the threats that communism and the entry of Negroes into their neighborhoods allegedly posed to their lifeways.

Indeed, it was not the Declaration of Independence, the Constitution, or the rhetoric of Lincoln that united white Americans, but what the New Deal delivered them. As D.J. Waldie puts it about the LA suburb of Lakewood, "The small houses would be affordable, so that even a machinist could buy one." But he adds the caveat, the one about conforming to the Protestant work ethic, "Living in them would, however, require orderly lives." The advertising for places like Lakewood earnestly promised "restrictions of an all-inclusive nature." Written into deed covenants, these restrictions prevented the sale of lots to Negroes, Mexicans, and Jews.[12]

Go figure on the Jews being excluded—I guess that in many Christians' minds they will forever be those who have most explicitly rejected Jesus Christ as their lord and savior. But with the blacks and Mexicans, the threat has been clear: disorderly behavior, chaotic (read also "extended") families, revelry, and work rhythms based not upon the clock. These were all things associated with the peasant cultures of Europe, exactly what these relatively new Americans had given up in favor of the disciplined, Protestant creed, the one that had enabled, along with federal government programs, their modest prosperity.

Never mind that, at least in those times before globalization and de-industrialization dried up job opportunities for African Americans, Mexicans and blacks did so much of the hard work. If these groups appear "thriftless," perhaps it is because such exclusions barred them from owning homes, the primary method by which the white middle- and blue-collar classes have accumulated a little bit of capital.

One part of the Creed—the prerogatives of the individual—has meant that people have been free to have such restrictive covenants, to act in such exclusionary, anti-social ways.

It seems, too, that Woodrow Wilson's ideas about liberty, progress, and democracy being the natural endpoints of social evolution have fallen by the wayside of history. The implosion of the Soviet Empire at first signaled the end of the only significant obstacle to capitalism and elections becoming universal, but religious fundamentalism and tribalism have replaced the Evil Empire as challengers to the Enlightenment. Americans like Huntington have come to acknowledge that this Creed is not the natural outcome of the unfolding of history but is specific to the United States and, maybe, Great Britain. Because of the way America has evolved, most citizens of the Republic, regardless of family origin, "see the creed as the crucial element of their national identity."[13]

Is it that Mexicans so distance themselves from "the Creed," or is it that they present some other aggravation? Recall the photograph of my grandmother in her English class. It is only one of many such images in America's conception of itself as an immigrant nation; the most important and compelling one, though, is certainly those visions of immigrants taking the oath of allegiance as they are sworn into citizenship. In this iconography, the immigrant bolsters what Bonnie Honig calls America's "fictive foundation in individual acts of uncoerced consent." The remarkable rhetoric in the Constitution about government authority deriving from "the consent of the governed" finds its validation in the immigrant who conclusively concurs in citizenship. The naturalized citizen — the one who has learned English and can name presidents and important dates in U.S. history — emerges "as living proof of the would-be universality of America's liberal democratic principles." Only the ideas about democracy and the experience of wilderness can vie with this notion of voluntary consent about what has made for American "exceptionalism," or the idea that America really is God's favored nation or the culmination of Western Civilization, or both.[14]

In February 1998, the national soccer teams of Mexico and the United States squared off in a big match in the Los Angeles Coliseum, centerpiece for the 1932 and 1984 Olympics. But unlike those Olympics, the United States was not the home team. Virtually all of the 91,255 spectators, and the nearly 7,000 who watched next door on closed circuit at the Sports Arena, were from Mexico. They spat and threw beer bottles at the American players who were more than shocked at their treatment where they had naturally assumed home-crowd advantage. The throngs were thrilled at Mexico's victory.[15]

On Saturday evenings and Sundays, the Mexican soccer fans' less-rowdy compatriots can be seen worshiping at such missions as San Gabriel and San Luis Rey. At mass the old missions cease being landmarks of California's fabled Spanish past and become places where the Mexicans can be with their gods. And maybe the soccer episode and the worshipers at the mission churches reveal what so hankers so many Americans. The Mexicans are not immigrants in the process of giving their uncoerced consent, but rather people who understand themselves to be HOME. It is at home that people can conduct themselves in their familiar ways, proclaim their familiar allegiances, and affirm their familiar gods. This is what Mexican immigrants understand themselves to be doing; Americans see their refusal to consent.

To clarify my thinking about these opposite perspectives, I attended in June 2006 a presentation by the Minutemen and Friends of the Border Patrol. Typical of the New World Border, I got not clarity but more complexity. I imagined that the Minutemen, those who have gone to the border to help patrol, would be a bunch of right-wing rednecks, as would Friends of the Border Patrol. Both are multi-ethnic organizations and both despise George Bush and his Republicans; Andy Ramirez

of Friends stated simply that "it's the political elites and the corporations" who are behind all these troubles. Aside from some wild numeri-
cal claims about the number of illegals in the United States and their
cost to taxpayers, each of the half-dozen panelists had their stories to
tell about being outraged by immigrants and fairly reasoned arguments
about how multi-national corporations are concerned only with their
bottom lines and are intent on "abolishing the United States of America." Latinos and African Americans in the Minutemen are pissed at how
immigrants are taking up what little cheap housing stock exists in Southern California, crowding into the schools, and not playing by the assimilationist rules to which they had adhered. Ultimately, they simply expect
corporations' and immigrants' "complete adherence to the rule of law,"
that America shall remain the land of opportunity for "Americans," and
that the old paradigm of voluntary assimilation shall prevail. I can't be
too angry at them.

This argument over what shall provide national adhesion in America is not an easy one.

Shall it be fidelity to this creed or tolerance for diversity? This is in
large part what the so-called "culture wars" are about. Shall we cohere
based on common faith in individualism, progress, the nuclear family,
and Christianity and its values? Or shall we cohere based on tolerance
for differences in matters of familism, doing things as they have always
been done, and for a variety of relationships both to the spirit world and
to sexuality? It has been the Hollywood film industry (including the porn
industry in that once-square San Fernando Valley), the feminist and gay
rights movements, and the immigration of Mexicans (but other Latinos
and Moslems too) that have pressed America to exchange the Creed for
tolerance of diversity regarding faith, family, sex, and progress. A curious combination of conservative, liberal, and postmodern challengers —
ones that often share little, especially as regards family and sexuality,
and ones that are not going away.

I will venture to say that I have some understanding about why
"diversity" is so difficult. In my view, there exist two kinds of diversity.
One type is very much the ideology of the New World Order and corporate capitalism, both of which need "diversity" in order to sell goods and
services. Presumably, Latin America, China, India, Iraq will more will-
ingly open their trade doors to American multi-nationals if the corporations' representatives are the descendants of people who emigrated from
those countries, or at least to people who have learned in school how to

be "culturally sensitive." Indeed, to be Latino (not Mexican), Southeast Asian (not Middle Eastern since 9/11), is to be "special," maybe even to have some celebrity status. One who represents diversity can expect to have representation in most every aspect of American institutional life, from the TV to the military to high school and college English departments. That they no longer have this sort of celebrity status is one of the things that irks many Anglo Americans. Really, though, this sort of "diversity" has more to do with capitalism in the twenty-first century than an assault on the American Creed.

Actually, diversity's most successful progeny understand the mutability of the self and are really multi-cultural practitioners of the Creed. Ultimately this sort of diversity is functional and ultimately not problematic: it does not threaten property relations or the capitalist appropriation of resources and wealth, only Protestant sensibilities about what represents, and is, America. I can think of few people more firmly positioned in the "diversity thing" than myself.

The other kind of diversity affirms that cultural change usually happens because of the influence of the more powerful, usually the Euro-Americans. Thus it is that cultural retrenchment in the face of what is really Euro-American economic and cultural imperialism emerges as the goal of these multi-culturists. For this group there is no "public square," "great or canonical lists of literary texts" (even ones "corrected" with a significant dose of Third World, minority, and women's literature), or "common values" that don't actually reinforce the hegemony of the powerful Euro-American-minded people. Affirmation of commonalities that might emerge from such liberal diversity projects only suppresses difference, which has been the goal of Euro-American imperial assimilationists all along. These more radical multi-culturists resist cultural change in the cause of defending the powerless against globalization and Euro-American cultural centricity. Usually certain people have set themselves up as the authorities for how a culture *is* and how it should *stay*. They have a hard time answering questions about corrupt and vicious Third World elites, or how it is that individuals and cultures seem to be so mutable.

These people are often very challenging to talk to. Likely harder than liberals who are satisfied that their mildly integrated reading lists and appeals for tolerance will call forth justice and peace, and certainly as difficult as conservatives who believe that the values of Christianity and Western Civilization are universal.

For those of us who have either experienced or studied (and some of us have done both) the history of Mexican people in the United States, this is all something of a re-run. In the 1920s, the decade when my father's family arrived and settled into Los Angeles, the "problem" of the Mexican wasn't much different. They were alien, "hacienda-minded" (as one sociologist put it), and unwilling or unable to change their ways. Then came World War II to further prove the mutability of the self.

It is something of a truism that *gente* went into the war as Mexicans and came out as Mexican Americans. Whether in the military in this war against racism and fascism, or on the home front making steel, harvesting crops, maintaining railroads, and grieving the loss of loved ones in battle, it was a quick and natural leap to assume that one deserved all of the rights and privileges of American citizens. In this great war in the cause of democracy, gente became imbued with the notion that discrimination in schools, theaters, and public swimming pools no longer need be tolerated. Especially under the leadership of the returning GIs, people who had been Mexicans in 1940 began affirming their rights as Americans by 1950. Many even became citizens and voted. They adopted much of the American immigrant paradigm: over time, though affirming origin and faith, the children of Mexican immigrants would begin the process of assimilation into the hyphenated American melting-pot just like the Italians, Irish, Poles, and Germans. They were truly Mexican-Americans; they even adopted much of the Creed. Their political activities were no longer concerned with Mexico but with America — ending segregation in schools and discrimination in hiring, breaking down stereotypes, and participating in local politics.

The old-style Mexicans, who had been so leery about the intrusions of americano ways into their traditional culture, didn't seem to mind that this new generation took action to oppose bigotry against la gente. *La Opinión*, the Mexican newspaper of Los Angeles, wrote affectionately of these new "*mexicoamericanos*," usually in the labor movement, who opposed discrimination. In early June 1945 the paper reported proudly that there had been formed "el Sub-Comité Mexico-Americano Pro-FEPC" to pressure the California State Legislature to establish a fair employment practices commission. That the article referred to "líderes de la colonia local," and listed my father's name among them, is revealing about this matter of identity.[16] Born in Mexico in 1915 and arriving at Adams Street Elementary at age seven and monolingual in Spanish, my father had by 1945 adopted English as his public language, married and divorced an Anglo wife, and become active in an American labor organization, the CIO. Yet, *La Opinión* still referred to him as part of "la colonia local": in their view he simply lived in a Mexican colony that happened to be in Los Angeles, which had been a Mexican town to start with anyway. Sometimes he was Mexican and sometimes American.

Meanwhile, in New Mexico descendants of those who settled when the place was part of the Spanish Empire (before 1821 that is) ceased calling themselves *nuevo mexicanos*, a legacy of the regionalism of New Spain and then the disunited Republic of Mexico, in favor of "Spanish American." This was in part because of the fact that, though their origins were certainly in Mexico, nuevo mexicano lineages had lived longer under Spain than Mexico: the Americans conquered them in 1846 only 25 years after Mexican independence. But becoming Spanish American also had much to do with distinguishing themselves from those more recent arrivals from Mexico who seemed to bring with them discrimination and opprobrium from Anglo Americans who didn't care to distinguish old settlers (*pobladores*) from the ill-bred peasantry fleeing the Mexican Revolution and poverty.

Perhaps the single most legendary event in twentieth-century New Mexico happened in Bataan. After the fall of Manila to the Japanese in January 1942, soldiers from the 200th Coastal Regiment gallantly held Bataan until April. With no choice but to surrender, there ensued that singularly heinous event in the annals of the American military, the Bataan Death March, in which Japanese troops starved and summarily executed many of the captives in a forced march to a prisoner-of-war camp. Most of them were Hispanic and Indian New Mexicans, now American martyrs and heroes. Across from the state capitol in Santa Fe stands the Bataan Memorial Building, which houses the New Mexico State Department of Education. Of course there is also a Bataan Memorial Museum, which is next to the Children's Museum on Old Pecos Trail. This heroic, sometimes tragic, service in war made Mexicans in America worthy of moral consideration. "Mexican" in New Mexico has been the most complicated of all.

It should be apparent now that the definition of "Mexican" is something that is "constructed," and that it is constructed over time and in the different contexts of conquest, labor, war, nativism, and so on. To Dr. Clements it meant one thing, to the advocates of the assimilationist paradigm — who always remembered Bataan — another, to Samuel Huntington it carries yet another set of implications. The meaning of the word has not much to do with "race" and everything to do with what people choose to make of it. But it gets even more complicated and revealing.

Despite the best efforts of the "GI Generation" to assimilate and break through the barriers that Anglo America had contrived to keep them, and especially blacks, out of mainstream society, a combination of americano exclusiveness, Mexican stubbornness (Bonfil Batalla would note the Indian legacy of "Mexico profundo"), the example of the Negro civil rights movement, and the Vietnam War all contrived to turn many of those of Mexican descent from the classic American model of assimilation of immigrants. César Chávez brought the plight of farm workers to national attention with the poignant and colorful[17] grape and lettuce boycotts beginning in 1963, and students in 1968 in Los Angeles and Denver walked out of their schools to protest their mistreatment at the hands of Anglo teachers and college counselors. And then there was the Vietnam War, which Mexican American youth paralleled to their own history once they started to discover it. Mexicans in California, New Mexico, and South Texas were just like the Vietnamese — people rolled over by American imperialism first in the guise of Manifest Destiny and then in the pretense of anti-communism. If the Negro civil rights movement could transform itself into Black Power, then Mexicans could have Chicano Power; if the National Liberation Front would lead the Vietnamese out of colonialism, then the Chicano Liberation Front would liberate Mexicans in the United States who would then have self-determination in Aztlán. (More evidence for Samuel Ramos to claim that Mexicans are mimetic?)

Thus the Chicano came into being, or actually was adapted from a previous categorization. The best story is that the word "Chicano" came from the correct pronunciation of the word *mexicano*. The Aztecs called themselves *Mexica*, from which comes, obviously, the republic's name of Mexico. The "x" should be pronounced as in the original Nahua like "ch," not like it is in either English where it is pronounced as "ex" or in Mexico where it is pronounced as if it were a Spanish "j," which is like "h" in English. If one says "Me*ch*icano" and drops the first two letters, one gets "Chicano," a word thus very much associated with the indigenous peoples of Mexico.

Most likely, though, the word comes from the state name of Chihuahua, a northern, frontier area of the Mexican Republic. The word throughout the first half of the twentieth century denoted someone of lower-class origin, someone rather crude and rustic in their ways. *La Chicanada* refers, north of the border, to recently arrived Mexicans, ones still reflecting *modos rancheros*, or the vulgar, unwashed ways of the impoverished peasantry. The old use of the word is best compared to how middle- and upper-class white southerners might use "cracker" or "red neck" to refer, both somewhat derisively but also often affectionately, to their lower class and uncouth brethren.

The children of Mexican and Mexican American parents took on all of the connotations of these words when they named themselves *Chicanos*. They affirmed their lower class and indigenous origins and not the Spanish roots and the aspirations for acceptance into America that their parents had avowed. Chicanos affirmed the Spanish language (which they often couldn't speak), Mexican folk Catholic spirituality (whose moral codes they often rejected), and praised the lifeways of Mexico (where they were usually called *pochos* and were rebuffed for their being *americanizado*). It was a remarkable effort, like that of the Californios, to self-construct an identity.

They even renamed the place—*Aztlán*. The Aztec origin story told how the Mexica traveled from someplace in the north, a place called Aztlán, before arriving at the immense lake of Texcoco where they would establish their majestic city of Tenochtitlan. Thus it was that Chicanos, avowing their indigenous lineage, lived not in the United States of America but in their ancestral homeland of Aztlán. Chicanos were no longer of immigrant stock like their parents but in their origin place. They had more legitimacy on the landscape of San Antonio, Los Angeles, or Albuquerque than the Euro-Americans who, in this renaming, became the actual immigrants.

In East Los Angeles, nation of Aztlán, the image of La Malinche has provided metaphor for the treatment of Chicano communities at the hands of redevelopers and freeway builders. Through Chicano communities have come the colossal LA freeways, ripping through, splitting neighborhoods, defiling space just like the Spaniards did with Indian women. With Aztlán consciousness it is quite apparent that it is the newcomers, the Anglo establishment, who are engaging in the *chingando* of the Eastside neighborhoods. This makes for militant politics, for identification with the violated Indian.[18]

It is not without some reason that a few Mexican intellectuals have declared Chicanos to be a regional variety of Mexican culture. They happen to speak English, but they do reside in places with names like San Diego, Los Angeles, and San Antonio.

The various community insurgencies surprised the Anglos because they still thought of the Mexicans as the newcomers on the landscape, as the foreigners who should be happy to be in the land of milk and sunshine. It required rebellion to get America to recognize its Mexicans in any meaningful way — people had to reject the American narrative of assimilation and seek not acceptance but liberation from a country Chicanos called racist, imperialist, and culturally colorless. They railed at discrimination, police abuse, second-class treatment in public schools where they judged curriculum to be too Anglo-centered, and having no consequential voice in politics. Most of la raza could agree that these were all legitimate issues because they were part of the lives and legacies of Mexicans in the United States. This shared historical experience of oppression and brutalization is one of the sources of ethnic unity be it of Mexicans, blacks in the American South or South Africa, Serbs, Jews, Palestinians, Armenians, and the list goes on. The assumption, though, is that shared experience will make for shared consciousness and this in turn will make for political unity. This explains Corky González's statement in the PBS documentary "¡Chicano!: A History of the Mexican American Civil Rights Movement" about how "I thought we could have a movement where all the Chicanos would agree."

González's Denver-based organization, the Crusade for Justice, declared Mexican American organizations, and even dissenting Chicanos, to be the enemy because they did not think and envision their future in the way that Corky thought they should. Everyone should think and feel in common because of what they had commonly experienced. Corky wanted Chicanos to have political and cultural autonomy, their own school and justice system — self-determination, in a phrase.

There were also hard feelings between Mexican Americans, especially those who had served in the U.S. military and who had been struggling for acceptance into America, and those who now rejected America, especially its foreign policy. Only César Chávez, the charismatic leader of the United Farm Workers, could draw immigrant Mexicans, Mexican Americans, Chicanos, and even liberal Anglos, to his cause. He was the first and last person of Mexican descent to gain national stature for his union/political efforts, though most non–Mexican Americans could not identify him these days.

This is all even more confused now. The Chicano Movement demanded that Chicano history and literature be taught in the public schools. But now the public schools in neighborhoods where most American-born Mexicans live are full of Mexican immigrant children, not to mention Central Americans and everybody else, who don't speak English and really don't care much about how Chicanos have been struggling for identity in gringolandia. The variety of people we might loosely lump together as of "Mexican-descent" is stunning. And there are more.

It took me awhile to figure out why I had such a difficult time understanding the two Mexicans who tended the yard in a house I rented briefly in Los Angeles. They were Indians. They spoke in that staccato Spanish in which words are cut off before the last syllable and which is so unlike the language of those who take great pride in their Spanish. My high school Spanish teacher, a former opera singer from Panama who loved her mother tongue, taught us "con el labio," to use our upper lips to enunciate clearly our vowels and to roll our "r's." I can't understand these people.

"It is the Indian who for several decades has done most of Mexico's migrating," Ruben Martinez explains, and these Indian people have variously assimilated into mestizo Mexico's national culture. California has as many as two hundred thousand Mexican Indians; many of them speak Spanish, but many don't. They speak Zapoteco, Mixteco, and obscure languages like Chatino and Amuzgo. NAFTA and the New World Order have brought them here. The Indian peoples are mostly hidden away, but in the last 15 years, there have come to be thousands of them in Santa Barbara, Santa Maria, and other places where there is plenty of work in the strawberries and in other fruits and vegetables that Americans have come to assume is part of their cuisine.[19]

Imagine the confounding situation in Wilson County, Tennessee, when two Mixteco-speaking women found themselves in court for allegations of child neglect. The judge could think only to order them to learn English and suggest that they use birth control. We can guess what they are doing—working in service jobs—but what must these Indians be thinking in Tennessee?[20]

In Los Angeles, Oaxacan Indians work mostly in Westside restaurants like the one I fantasized Ramona and I going to. And they have brought their love of basketball to the north where they have organized at least 50 teams into a series of competitive leagues. Sam Quinones tells how the top Zapoteco team in the 1990s called themselves Raza Unida, the same name that Chicano nationalists in South Texas in the 1970s gave to their third-party politics and that Corky González championed in Colorado and which had a brief chapter in Los Angeles elections. Chicanos who identified with the Indian side of their mestizo heritage now find real Mexican Indians (whom I'm sure can't understand their Spanish either) in the parks and high school gymnasiums and playing that most Indian of sports in Mexico, basketball. (Mestizos play baseball and soccer.)[21]

And too many children of Mexican immigrants wanted to be part of America. Not so much the America of Republicans and Democrats, Toyotas and Fords, or the Cleaver family and the Lawrence Welk Show, but what Richard Rodriguez has called the "Protestant I." It's the space to be whatever you want to be and to be a mutable self. Richard has done this well: he's told about how he was once a scholarship boy, then a preppy Stanford student; and now a "queer, Catholic Indian." Lots of Chicanos were mad at him when he opposed affirmative action* and seemed to side with Republican conservatives, and he certainly gave them ammunition, but mostly I think that the Chicano intelligentsia is irate because he discloses to them that in America, unless you're black and/or poor, you can change your identity, your thinking, and your allegiances without too much trouble. It's this "Protestant I" that is such a powerful pull in America. It's not like in Mexico where family and God (recall Octavio Paz) have so much to do with how a self is formed and relates to the rest of the world. If I adopt "the Creed" (which I have mostly) and then succeed financially, if I wanted to I could be a shit-kicker in Austin, a mensch in New York City, gay in San Francisco, Buddhist in Boulder, Latino in Miami, and whatever I wanted to be in Los Angeles.

Chicanismo has reminded Anglo America of several things about

---

* Affirmative action presents some interesting twists in our discussion of constructions of race. If indeed "race" is something people make up to explain things about people and then treat them in certain ways, then it can be argued that affirmative action should be got rid of. After all, recipients of affirmative action receive it because of their "race," and this simply continues the cycle of racial thinking and identification. Supporters of affirmative action can argue that it is necessary to compensate for the harmful consequences of racial thinking by giving victims a "head start" so that they may eventually be able to rid themselves of their social and economic deficiencies, the very ones that become fodder for other people to develop racist ideas about them.

this narcissistic bacchanal of the self. One is that inequality in education, presumptions about Mexicans, and poverty have deprived so many of those with darker skin the opportunity to participate in it; another is that the potency of consumer culture means that most Americans become subjects of the capitalist corporations and what they have to sell, and thus wind up dressing and thinking mostly the same. Ethnic cultures, everywhere that they have not been colonized intellectually and emotionally, challenge the commodification of life and the superficiality of espousing manufactured identities. The contradiction, though, is that when a person of a disparaged group breaks through the social and racial barriers that America has built to keep itself safe from "foreign" contamination — be it by affirmative action, middle-class privilege, or by dint of individual initiative — then one often leaves the parent culture in favor of the "Protestant I." In *Chicano Manifesto* (1971), Armando Rendon exclaimed how the Chicano "has been denied the free expression of his ideas and the unhindered perfecting of his innermost self through the arts."[22] Since then plenty of Chicanos have freely expressed themselves with the outcome that Corky's dream of "movement where all of the Chicanos would agree" is gone forever.

In America, the late Gloria Anzaldúa was pressed to "defend my race and culture when they are attacked by non-*mexicanos*," but she also realized that "for the lesbian of color, the ultimate rebellion she can make against her native culture is through her sexual behavior. She goes against two moral prohibitions: sexuality and homosexuality." This is how Gloria, so magnificently and narcissistically in my view, thumbs her nose at racially chauvinistic gringos and sexually chauvinistic Mexicans all at once. "Being lesbian and raised Catholic, indoctrinated as straight, I *made the choice to be queer* (for some it is genetically inherent)." (Italics are hers.)[23] Nothing could more infuriate Mexican/Chicano nationalists for whom there is some essential nature to maleness and femaleness; nothing could more affirm for Americans the threat of contamination from the south than idol-worshiping, folk Catholic Mexicans like Anzaldúa (whose family goes way back in Texas).

Only in the America of queer, Catholic Richard Rodriguez, the one where the "Protestant I" prevails, could we have Gloria. I could become a patriot.

The Chicano contribution to American and Mexican life and culture is a complex and profound one, at least from Texas west to California, and one that is still unfolding. We have fajitas because of Chicanismo.

The stories on the origin of fajitas vary, but we can be sure that they originated in Texas and that the name derives from *faja*, which means, according to my Spanish dictionaries, sash, girdle, bandage, skirt, and fillet. Fajitas are "skirt steak" or the jowl of the cow. Maybe ranch workers who were paid in kind originated the dish, or maybe it was Mexicans from San Antonio who retrieved the discarded skirt meat from the packing houses, who first made *tacos de fajitas*. It is simply tough meat tenderized in lime juice, sizzled with onions and peppers and rolled into a tortilla and, obviously, was poor people's food.[24]

As with low riders, this is one of the ways that la Chicanada has embellished the landscape by taking something of little use, like an old (American) car or some inferior meat, decorated it, and integrated it as a part of American culture. Of course these days, fajitas are found on lots of restaurant menus, and they are served with guacamole, a concoction of the ancient Aztecs who called it *ahuacamulli*. A staple for the Aztecs, they called the tree *ahuacuatl*, or "testicle tree," because of how the avocados hang from them, in pairs. Fajitas with guacamole are dramatically served on a sizzling platter and are often one of the more expensive items on the menu. I prefer chicken fajitas and I've tried shrimp fajitas. I'm quite certain that neither chickens nor shrimps have jowls, but I am now positive that avocado trees have (many) testicles.

La Chicanada (and readers will realize that I use that term in both the traditional and more recent meanings) has infiltrated America. This blending of things is one of the geniuses of the Mexican people — the legacy of mestizaje. This is also one of the skills of America: here people can take something foreign and suspect like fajitas, then consume, digest, and alter it, and spit out something tasty, but not acknowledge what they have done.

I have eaten fajitas in Mexico. I suspect that Mexicans who have been to America brought them back with them. Is this American food in Mexico?

Imagine when I saw Cheech Marin's *Born in East LA* in my exile in Colorado Springs. It had only recently come out but the theater was rather empty, and I was the only one laughing. There are some magnificent Chicano moments in the movie. Cheech plays the main character, Rudy. His mother tells him to go down to a toy factory to get his cousin, Javier, who is fresh over the border, and who works there. Rudy responds in Chicano-accented English, "Aw come on ma, you know my Spanish is not so good."

The INS raids the factory and Rudy is apprehended. He has left his wallet at home and without identification must somehow convince the *migra* officer that his protestations that "I was born in East LA. I'm an American!" are true. The officer says (and remember it's the early 1980s), "Then, who's the president of the United States?" Rudy responds, "That cowboy guy on TV, that guy who was on *Death Valley Days*! Uh, uh, John Wayne!" "Get him outta here!" goes the migra guy. I'm laughing but nobody else gets it. Of course, the "guy who was on *Death Valley Days*," a weekly drama on 1950s TV, refers to the show's host — Ronald Reagan. Rudy is right on two counts here: the president IS the "guy on *Death Valley Days*," and that John Wayne and Ronald Reagan are in serious ways interchangeable. The migra guy is not that smart. Rudy's deported to Tijuana where he must make enough money to get himself smuggled back across the border. The *coyote* he meets up with, a slightly sympathetic cracker, employs him to teach some Chinese guys awaiting clandestine passage "how to act American." Rudy ties bandanas around their foreheads, almost covering their eyes, and teaches them to say "Órale vato. Whaa's sappening?" in Chicano-accented English. Then he instructs them on how to walk American "in the bad position": "You just lean your head back like you're listening to some hip music that only you can hear; and this hand you put in here (left front pocket); now this hand goes back here, like you just cut one and you want to shoo way the smell."

When this crew finally gets to LA, they come up through a manhole in the middle of a street parade. Rudy's new girlfriend, a Salvadoreña, asks "Whaa's sappening?" Rudy says, "It's a Cinco de Mayo parade." She says "What's Cinco de Mayo?" and Rudy says, "I don't know; we just have a parade every year." There are East LA high school marching bands and Chicanos dressed as Aztecs. In Mexico, everyone knows about Cinco de Mayo (it's more *día de Corona Beer* these days), but no one dances down the streets dressed as Aztecs. The Chinese guys see a cop, they "walk American" like Rudy taught them, say "Whaa's sappening?" and the officer just smiles at these illegal aliens. You see, being "American" is an interesting construct too.

Before this there is quite a scene near the border. Rudy has earned enough money for his stealthy crossing. Loading onto the truck, there is an older woman desperate to join her family in the north but who can't afford the trip. Rudy gives her his place and tells her "vaya con Diós." She, too, will follow in the footsteps of Padre Serra, but in a panel truck with no ventilation.

Rudy walks with determination to a hilltop overlooking the border.

As Neil Diamond's "Coming to America" cranks up, Rudy leads the masses, thousands, and swarms over the hapless border guards, who are helpless to stop their crossing.

Therein lies part of the reason for the demise of Chicanismo. Its stance critical of American materialism and imperiousness is hard to maintain in the face of all those Mexicans dying, sometimes literally, to get here and then to acquire those American symbols of success, a Ford Expedition (as if one who has crossed to the United States needed another "expedition") and Japanese electronics. Chicanos declined the americanos. Now Mexican immigrant kids act more American than Chicanos, what with their low-slung baggy pants, gangsta rap, and visions not of the Virgin of Guadalupe but of Madonna and Britney Spears.

Think of something else that has happened too, something that Samuel P. Huntington doesn't understand in the slightest: Chicano cultural expression represents simultaneously "diversity" AND assimilation. Does assimilation succeed by suppressing local cultural artifacts? Think about the former Soviet Union and Yugoslavia, and then of jazz, blues, or hip-hop in the United States. In good part, assimilation happens when aspects of a "foreign" or "minority" culture — food, music, spirituality — are mainstreamed. How have Italians and Irish "assimilated"? Maybe it's that "Americans" get boozed up on Saint Patrick's Day and eat huge amounts of pasta and pizza. Fajitas, guacamole, and the combination number 3 (the enchilada, taco, beans, and rice that I usually order), have been assimilated into "American" culture. Indeed, they are quite part of the mainstream.

Mexicans' conduct in the United States can be taken as either confirmation of the American project or as a challenge to it. I drive my Volvo with the Rolling Stones on the CD player into the parking lot at El Palenque restaurant in Colorado Springs or the Super A Foods in Highland Park in LA, places where almost all the customers are Mexican immigrants and Spanish is all you hear inside. I'm typically wearing a Tommy Bahama or Nat Nast Hawaiian shirt and running shoes, and I'm rehearsing my Spanish for the meat counter. The lot displays the *rascuache* cars of the poorer ones but also features the hulking Ford F Series pickups and Expeditions that the more successful immigrants so favor. The men wear their polyester shirts and reptile-looking leather boots, and the youth their americano fashion. The scene fairly reeks of the American Dream, of upper-middle-class smugness, and of compensatory machismo.

Such imitation of American consumption patterns certainly confirms America's success at what it does best—purvey consumer goods—though perhaps America's new failure is that it doesn't produce them much anymore. But the recalcitrance of Mexicans when it comes to adopting Huntington's Creed also tenders a challenge. So too does Chicano art.

The self-styled "migrant performance artist" and practitioner of "chicano cyber-punk," Guillermo Gómez-Peña, seeks to redeem America, a place that "is having a very hard time shedding its imperial nostalgia, embracing its multiracial soul, and accepting its new status as the first 'developed' country to become a member of the Third World." Los Angeles, "a concentrated version of the crisis confronting the entire country" is "a city gravely punished by natural and social forces." Mexicans are invisible to Americans, he claims. Dramatically lying on the streets, wrapped in a *sarape*, surrounded by candles, he wants America to "Deal with me! I am here to stay!" he screams. "Fucking deal with me! See my people all around you! See yourself in me, in my people, in our collective pain! Deal with us! We are here to stay!"[25]

"Pobre pelado," I think; he presumes that Americans, and Mexicans, will notice him and give him celebrity status. People are simply much too busy right now.

They are busy fussing about the matters that Samuel P. Huntington broaches, about the traffic, and trying to maintain or achieve something we might call "the American standard of living." And, anyway, Americans are already eating his culture. I'm more absorbed with watching everybody.

I'm more reconciled now with all of these matters than I was during the scene at the Wendy's. In fact I feel quite at peace, even sometimes bemused, watching all these people on the Southern California landscape and the changes they have brought. My love for history also reveals to me that these sorts of experiences of the New World Order are not so unique.

For me a place comes alive when I know about the people who have passed on. In East Los Angeles there is a remarkable boarded-up building on Breed Street just south of Cesar Chavez Boulevard, a street I knew, and my father frequented, as Brooklyn Avenue. Carved on the stile is "Congregation Talmud Torah." I can imagine the Breed Street Shul, once the largest Orthodox congregation west of Chicago, as the majestic and dignified place of worship of the prosperous Jewish people, ones who owned the nice shops once positioned along Brooklyn Avenue, or who held jobs as skilled artisans. They spoke in the Yiddish that they had brought with them from Eastern Europe and that I had always understood from my old neighborhood to be the official language of the Jewish people. I can imagine, in the years between the world wars when more and more Mexicans moved there, the sounds of Spanish and Yiddish mixing on the streets and in the school yards.

What must they have thought of one another, one people from the shtetls of Eastern Europe, by way of Brooklyn, and the other from the pueblos of Mexico? Here were two disparate folk thrown into international migration for very different reasons and then encountering one another in an American city (where they lived separate from any "Americans"). Both of their lives were better in the new place; the Mexicans escaped the disarray of post-revolutionary Mexico and the Jews the horrors of the Holocaust. When they spoke to each other in the public world, it would have been in their lingua franca, English. It's much like now when Mexicans and Central Americans meet Koreans, Chinese, and Armenians (who were there in the 1920s too) in their shops and in the schools.

Immigrants have changed the landscape; they have refashioned it in ways that the designers could not have imagined. The events and daily activities of Mexicans in a place built for Jews in Los Angeles, and now Mexicans in Pilsen, a neighborhood in Chicago that Czech immigrants built, are what make the place. It's not just that Latino immigrants have reinvigorated the storefront economies with their *peluqerías*, *pupuserías*, and *mercados*; it's that they have changed urban space. Some people who have witnessed the changes revel in the diversity and in how once-run-down areas have been brought back to life. Others cringe.

I recall clearly those times in the late 1990s that I took my then-future wife to the ocean fronts at Long Beach, Santa Monica, and Venice. I remember as a kid going in about 1960 with YMCA groups to Pacific Ocean Park and the Long Beach Pike. The counselors drove us in a flatbed truck in which we all stood, restrained only by wooden guardrails. Imagine the lawsuits that that would call forth these days. I liked the truck ride, but I will only reveal now that I thought the rides were much too scary to be any fun. Now those areas are different.

Until the early 1970s Pacific Ocean Park and the Long Beach Pike dominated their respective shorelines. Sailors cruising for tawdry pleasures, even Mexican youth escaping the confines of their families, and teenage lovers straight out of Freddie Cannon songs just seemed to do a lot of walking around, and kids wanted on the scary rides. In the 1920s, midwestern transplants and tourists sat out at the beach in front of huge hotels and in full body cover.

Nowadays the roller bladers, runners, and bicyclists along the cement pathway at Long Beach look at the Mexicans with such derision and haughtiness. Different people hang out at different points along the sand—Chicano and black youth in their NBA regalia; the gays; the Anglo gals, before with their high-cut bikini bottoms, and now more recently the low-slung ones; and the Mexicans just as covered as their midwestern predecessors, but with clothes that came either from Goodwill or Wal-Mart.

In americano culture, the beach is the place for the young to go and get away from their families, a place to smoke cigarettes, and to kiss. For the Mexicans it is a place for the males to go when not working, but better yet for the whole family to go to because it is one of the few places left in America that does not revolve around spending money.

But everyone at the beach is looking at each other and traversing around to get a better view. What the beach is, and what Brooklyn Avenue was once and, like many places in LA, is becoming again, is a "heterosocial" space, a place where everyone goes, where everyone, even if they don't mix that much, even if they fuss about one another, belongs. It's the opposite of gated communities, segregated ghettos and suburbs, Malibu and Disneyland.[26]

Long Beach suffers the cultural complication that some of the Mexicans haven't yet understood—the organization that the americanos have brought to life at the beach. The police give uncomprehending single men citations for having Budweisers. (I have always wondered how fines would be enforced for such people. Likely, it is for situations like this that law enforcement thinks it would be a good idea for immigrants to have ID cards.) On Sundays, after mass no doubt, overweight *mamacitas* would waddle down the middle of the cement path which is divided efficiently and safely into three lanes, one for runners, and one each way for cyclists and bladers. Careening along with long, bare legs, tanned skin, and hundred-dollar sunglasses, those on wheels shake their heads at the squat women who are girdled into austere, calf-length black dresses, and who block rather thoroughly THEIR path. To anyone reared in Southern California beach culture, such attire—nylons swooshing against each other in the heat and leather shoes clunking along the pavement—and having the whole family along, seems ludicrous.

Of course, to anyone reared in Mexican villages such going un-covered (and in the heat no less), unchaperoned, and so fast on a day of rest seems ridiculous if not infamous and disgraceful. I imagine that the heavy women's distant stares — only apparently ignoring the sleek ameri-canos on wheels and indeed oblivious to the way they violate the division of the space — seek to avoid sight of all the bare skin, as if they can refrain from knowing what their grandchildren see, and what, in America, they might become.

I am an American at the beach: I have been with my parents nearly half a century ago and go with my children, but I cherish the feelings of freedom I had at the beach as a youth; I jog along the shoreline in a vain effort to keep slender; I wear as little as possible. Most people run faster than I do, including my beautiful sweetie whose backside I admire as she runs ahead of me. From behind my own expensive shades, I survey, mostly, the americano women and the Mexican men. I've watched girls at the beach for too long to stop now, and anyway it's intrinsically a place for watching, or so I tell myself.

The beach, like so much of Southern California, is spectacle. There is ritual drama here, dynamic interaction between viewers and performers, except that everybody is a viewer and everybody is a performer. People watch and react and create ideas about one another, much like Indians, Californios, and Americans did in centuries previous.

My pace yields plenty of opportunity for observing and contemplat-ing the spectacle. Unlike the dutiful men who walk with their mothers-in-law along the bike path, many of the single men swagger along, their Buds hidden or already consumed, three or four abreast. I could not contrast more with them: me in my rueful little Speedos, this desk jockey running to stay physically fit; they in their long jeans and stripped poly-ester shirts ambling along the beach, relaxing after a week of strenuous physical labor. All of us looking at the women: me, though, subtly and unexpressively, they leeringly with macho aplomb and jokes and mirth. More glares from the americanos.

As my sweetie runs by a gawking squad, one points with one hand, makes a comment to his *compañeros*, shakes his hips in parody, and elicits laughter. I simply smile to myself with some sense of *pocho* superi-ority. My skimpy attire gives the impression that I am a monolingual gringo: as I run by I hear one say of me "ay, puto, puto," barely concealed under his chortling. "If you only knew, pendejos," I think as I briefly increase my pace, and wonder what stories they create about me.

She is so far ahead now and chase becomes so obviously futile, that I imagine the story of these Mexican men, men so different and so the same. They have the bodies of working men, strong biceps and pectoral muscles, and the emerging paunches that come with the plenty of food here in the north, and with watching TV and drinking beer. In Mexico people have barely enough for beans and tortillas. In the United States for immigrants with a job, there is McDonalds with Big Macs two for $3 and Biggie Fries and sodas. It's so cheap because of low wages and the fact that the U.S. government so generously subsidizes the wheat, corn, cattle, potato, and sugar industries. What only the middle class can do in Mexico — go to McDonalds — even undocumented workers in the wondrous United States can do, and their bellies are starting to show it.

Americano and pocho beachgoers wonder why the Mexican gals go into the water with clothes on, actually a tee shirt usually covering either a large bathing suit or shorts and a top. It seems so impractical, and cold, all that sand and wet in one's clothing. Again, difference and strangeness are displayed upon the body.

Americans see these bodies in all of the ways we've been discussing here: as workers who inconveniently stick around, as violators of American space, as representatives of the failure of the Mexican economy, and as out of place and out of sync with this immediate beach environment. I think few realize that these are lonely men, ones whose working bodies have desire. Slender americanas without chaperones must create such confusion and lust.

This matter of the clothed and unclothed body presents us with one of the supreme ironies of Spanish, Native American, Mexican, and American history. Bear with me for a good story about this. I went to a conference of the California Missions Studies Association in 1997 in Loreto, Baja California. A scholar priest gave a ringing endorsement of the missions and missionaries at one of the plenary sessions. This splendid association is made up of Catholic aficionados of the missions (about half), academics (about a fifth), museum, historic site, and architectural professionals (another fifth), and sundry others including a few priests. The good father rambled on about how the Catholic missionaries at great sacrifice brought clothing, food, shelter, and salvation, all lumped together as "civilization," to the poor Indians, and were thus such "great men," a phrase he used over and over again.

Most people nodded, but a few of us in the back snarled and snickered. Of the opinion that no one entryway into the spirit world was any better than anyone else's, well aware that the missionaries depended on the Indians for their initial foodstuffs (think about Plymouth Rock and the first Thanksgiving too) and to build the structures, and that the missions began the doom of the California Indians, we restrained one another from any embarrassing outbursts. I was also thinking about the resort hotel's clothing-optional beach.

To the great chagrin of the conference organizers, and they have affirmed (darn) that no such thing will happen in future meetings, this all-inclusive resort hotel had a nude beach, one that faced the Gulf of California. There were pelicans, dolphins, and whales there, too. Naturally, with complimentary beverage in hand, I spent my free time there along with several other conference participants who had also gone native. I couldn't help but think that here I was returning the place to savagery, or something. Recall Padre Serra's comment about those first Indians he encountered in California: "They were entirely naked, as Adam in paradise before sin."

Running along the beaches of Los Angeles County, spending time at places where gringos and gringas parade in various stages of undress, recalling Loreto and my several trips back there, I am taken with how it is the Europeanized peoples who shamelessly have few clothes on, and it is the descendants of Indians who are quite thoroughly and, in the case of the women, chastely, attired. As I am running I am wondering: "Do these Indian-looking people, the ones who are serving the undressed gringos and manicuring the gardens at the Mexican resorts, know the irony of this situation? Of how they were the ones once naked and called savage and *sin vergüenza* for it?" More likely they just gaze in puzzlement at these crazy americanos who can afford so many fancy clothes and then just take them off.

In an attempt to be more than a pocho tourist on another occasion, I went with some other vacationers — gringas and gringos mostly but at least one other pocho — to a beach where Mexicans go. The chicas in our group got down to bikinis while at least this pocho prepared to show Speedos. People looked. Then we saw that the mexicanas not only had full bathing suits but tee shirts over them. Ooops. I stayed in my long shorts. Going in the water now became impractical.

At the snack bar, still the objects of curiosity, I ordered in my best Spanish, at which point one Mexican woman, there with her daughter and grandchildren, informed me that "nuestras chicas no tienen nada que probar. No tienen que ostentar." To this statement about how Mexican gals don't have anything to prove and that they don't have to show off, I could only say, "Sí. Claro." More intrigue for me about display of the body.

In 1846 the German geologist Ferdinand Roemer, after duly noting that "the Mexicans of San Antonio, moreover, are a lazy, indolent race," observed in that city "a number of Mexican women and girls bathing entirely naked" in the river. "Unconcerned about our presence, they continued their exercises while laughing and chattering, showing themselves perfect masters of the art of swimming," he continued. There are many of these sorts of descriptions of Mexicans' immodesty from the early to mid-nineteenth century, though they usually purport to demonstrate swarthy lasciviousness.[27] The modesty, or maybe shame — I don't think it's lack of anything to prove — that I witnessed at the Mexican beach derives from the mimetic upper middle class in Mexico imposing its priggish views of the body on the rest of society.

I treasure historical knowledge. It explains these enigmatic matters to me. Both by themselves and by outsiders, people are forever being re-described. We've seen that in our previous pages. Readers should not now be so bewildered about what "Mexican," or "mestizo," or "Chicano," or "American" means but understand that these appellations, these designations, are forever changing. There is no better proof of this, I realize sitting on the beach at Loreto and then later at Playa del Carmen in Yucatán and now trying to run along a Southern California beach, than in the phrase "naked savage." In those places, especially Yucatán, Indians, who are falling increasingly away from the Catholic Church in favor of evangelical Protestantism, dress modestly and serve variously undressed Europeans and Americans. Those tourists engage in bacchanals that would outdo the wildest inventions of the mission priests who used those fantasies to impugn the Indians and justify their spiritual conquest. By early evening and with all that complimentary tequila, many of the tourists are witlessly imitating the dolphins and the Juaneño dancers that Padre Boscana introduced us to in our chapter about the missions. Who has vergüenza and who is sin vergüenza, concepts to which we were introduced in our discussion of the missions and the Californios, has now been reversed.

There is so much written on the body, clothed and not, so much spectacle which animates our imaginations in peculiar ways. I watch the immigrant teenagers. With only money enough to dabble in americano fashion, the boys wear their pants baggy, low pitched, their boxers mercifully covering their butt cracks. I see the girls with their low-slung pants, their midriffs exposed and eroticized, their butt cracks on the cusp of infamy. Others of the boys wear their NBA regalia; I imagine these youth to be the ones who play in the Oaxacan basketball leagues. When one comes to live in a metropolis one finds liberation from the confines of clan, community, and the narrowness of the village (or even the modern suburb), but one also finds confusion, loss of identity, often loneliness — the very feelings the traditional society protected one from. Of course, this tension has provided much of the stuff for the history and literature of the city; clothing also reveals this ambiguity, and more.

Wearing clothes as an expression of oneself, even for sexual allure, was one of the most potent appeals of modernity. It was part of the "pursuit of happiness" that went along with "life and liberty" that was everyone's natural right in the modern world. As work and private life became more separated in the modern world, people came to assume that in the same way they could choose political leaders, religion, reading matter, and spouses, they could also choose how they would appear. The self, not the clan or village, would be arbiter of all such tastes. The appeal of modernism derived in large part from its promise of release from the various confines of the traditional, pre-industrial past. In many ways, the Mexican Americans and Chicanos we have been discussing can be seen as excitedly emerging, and manifesting in their politics and appearance, from the pre-modern culture of their Mexican ancestors.

The Mexican youth I see, on both sides of the border, do not seem to make these choices about appearance. The promise and the exhilaration of modernity and its options (their disappointments and anxieties notwithstanding) have been replaced by the penetration of commodity culture into so many of the nooks and crannies of North America. Where in Mexico it hasn't, the young men who journey north have brought it back. Referring to the Indian town of Cherán, Rubén Martínez observes that "each migrant who goes north and returns adds another layer of Americana. . . . All the things we associate with the Indian past (the Purépecha language, the ancient rituals like herbal medicine and sorcery) are here, coexisting with MTV." Martínez offers another description about what I'm saying: "Cherán is an Indian town with one foot in pre-Columbian times and the other leaping toward the twenty-first century."[28]

Such people were never "modern." This is what I see written on their appearance: they consent not to "the Creed" and citizenship but to the dictates of post-industrial capitalism. In linear history they were sup-

posed to have emerged from their traditional societies, the ways of thinking associated with México profundo, into the world of the individuated
self. The tantalizing images that the satellite dish (which on the roofs of
Cherán is a clear marker of who has been to the North and who has not)
and fiber optic cable bring have captured them into webs just as binding,
maybe more so, than the customary restraints of the peasant village.
Through freedom of speech and the press, the liberal arts, and enlightened child rearing and psychotherapy, modern culture, though often
unsuccessfully, tried to train and develop a self capable of making good
choices. I see people who have never had this preparation.

I think of my encounter with Nestor, the ex–Mara Salvatrucha, the
one whose grandparents had been assassinated and who came looking for his mother. "Everybody in Central America knows MacArthur
Park," he said of what is indeed "little Central America" in Los Angeles.
"One thing I knew, find MacArthur Park and my Mom'll be there." (She
was but it was a disappointing reunion.) I asked him if he knew who
MacArthur was. He didn't. I asked him why people didn't go to Buenos
Aires or Costa Rica to escape Guatemala. "This is the dream country,"
he exclaimed, "where the dollars are! You get five (he gestures emphatically with five fingers) quetzales for a dollar!" He'd seen America on
TV: "Rooms with carpets, Puff Daddy, Hollywood." Global capitalism
has penetrated everywhere, even pre-modern (I prefer the phrase "non-
modern") societies such as Nestor's, and drawn such non-modern peoples into its cultural and ideological orbit of consumptionism. "I believe
in saints," Nestor states, and "when I go out there I pray to my saint to
protect me." He is not "modern"—there is not much of an (however
delusional its virtue) individuated self here—but instead part of the postmodern world of global capitalism but with a non-modern spirit worldview. A picture card he carries depicts his saint—la Santa Muerte.

And much is written on what bodies do. In a hotel or a restaurant
in Southern California, I watch Central Americans and Mexicans (and
know that many of both are Indians) do all the drudge work. In my
neighborhood in Colorado where I used to hear the sounds of Arrowsmith and Metallica entertaining scraggly-haired Anglo young men putting on roofs, I now hear conjunto and Mexican pop music sustaining
the work of Mexicans pouring hot tar and hammering down three-tab
shingles. It's effectively obscured from most shoppers at the supermarkets, even health food stores, that Mexicans plant, tend, and harvest our
food, and slaughter and process our chicken, beef, and pork. It is they

who are so central to the satisfying of Americans' most basic needs and sometimes most dubious wants. This situation, more creative destruction, has to do with the labor market and the race to produce with the lowest wages, but it also has to do with the disparagement of work.

One never sees workers — people whose labor creates, repairs, maintains, and actually produces material goods — on prime-time TV, cable TV, MTV, and certainly not in the movies. Americans, of all stripes, know that sweat-expending labor is for chumps and losers, and Mexicans. Here's some more irony: when the missionaries came, when the americanos came, they both exclaimed that the Indians and Mexicans did not engage in disciplined labor. Part of their civilizing mission, then, was to get these primitives to engage in clock-disciplined labor.

Now it is that very spectacle of hard work that makes Mexicans, and the ones who are really Indians and whose Spanish I can't understand, such objects of disregard. Physical labor in early American culture was something that fulfilled people and demonstrated their virtue; affirmation of hard work, even communal labor, was understood to create solidarity and community. Great pride and gratification would come from the satisfaction of human wants by fashioning with one's hands and tools what other people needed to live. And now what do Americans think when they see (if they choose to look) a crew of Mexicans putting on a roof, tearing down a house, rubbing on cars, cleaning the rooms of a hotel? Would they be aghast at crews of Mexicans harvesting infinite tons of strawberries, avocados, and lemons, let alone butchering millions of chickens, cows, and pigs? What was once a sign of their lack of civilization — disciplined physical labor — has become the sign of mestizo and Indian Mexicans' disgrace. Redescription is complicated and challenging.

Redescription also comes from the immigrants themselves. Most people were taken aback at the tenacity with which largely immigrant janitors won union contracts in Los Angeles in 2000. It didn't occur to them that Mexican immigrants, often undocumented, were deserving of family health care, better pay, and paid vacations. The strike actions of these janitors, and laundry, health care, and garment workers, initially confused people accustomed to taking for granted the low-wage services of these workers. They became worthy of moral consideration not because of the preachings of ministers, academics, or liberals but because of what they did themselves.

While events associated with 9/11 and the war in Iraq have assumed center stage, it is appropriate to assume that matters having to do with immigration from south of the border will continue to bewilder and disconcert not only Californians but people in, say, Eagle County in the Rocky Mountains of Colorado, which is now 30 percent Mexican (think ski and tourist industries), or Dalton, Georgia (think carpet factories), which is 35 percent Mexican. Of course Mexico experiences these sorts of changes quite differently but just as profoundly.

You will have noticed that my entire discourse about America and what agitates it, and how it will necessarily but unpredictably change, has evolved around issues emanating from south of the border. America has understood itself within an east to west paradigm. The narrative of the Westward Movement has figured hugely in the American mythologies of individualism, adventure, the civilizing mission, and the infinity of second chances for success. Then, too, as Frederick Jackson Turner, Perry Miller, and Louis Hartz have argued, the West and the Wilderness have given America its distinctive democracy, relationship to nature, entrepreneurial spirit, and a radiant future unencumbered by the gnarled and weighty past of European-style feudalism. These are all disputable legacies of the West, but certainly the American discourse about democracy, opportunity, nature, the self, and so on have all taken place in the context of westward movement.

Now what presses us to think about matters, even Samuel P. Huntington, comes from south of the border. This is not an east to west country anymore, but one where the movement of peoples, beliefs, and challenges — which, like the old frontier, present both opportunity and peril — goes from south to north. The New World Border and NAFTA have changed WHERE we are. Running along the beach, or dining in a Rocky Mountain restaurant, and thinking about the changes the New World Border have brought, I realize that I'm not in the West anymore. I'm in the North.

Western Union and its telegraph wires once trumpeted and embodied America's east to west trajectory. Now Galavisión advertises "Western Union Futbol" in its television programming, and it is via Western Union and cyberspace that Mexicans "wire" their cash home. Now Western Union is about sending money from *el norte* to the south, to Mexico.

In Brooklyn a priest has started a clinic to aid immigrants from Mexico with their health care and social welfare. It is called the Tepeyac Association, named for the hill just outside of Mexico City which was home to the Aztec goddess Tlazoteotl, goddess of fecundity, sexual love, and steam baths, but of course is where the Virgin of Guadalupe appeared to San Juan Diego on December 12, 1531. "Los mexicanos," the majority of whom are actually Mixtec-speaking people from Oaxaca, are saving the money they earn in Brooklyn to fund the relay of a torch being carried from the Basilica of the Virgin of Guadalupe to Saint Patrick's Cathedral in New York City to arrive on that momentous day in December.[29] Now the spirit of the Great Mother blessing the emigrants rides not on wagon trains headed west in a painting by Emanuel Leutze but in a sacred flame coming from the south to the north from the sacred Tepeyac.

Places like New York and Los Angeles are simultaneously ones of great mixing and rigid segregation. Actually, the economic segregation in neighborhoods, schools, and some restaurants figures more profoundly in the differences between people than does the spatial commingling of people on the freeways, in the parks and beaches, and in some other restaurants. That people then imagine their city in myriadly distinct ways derives from this spatial and economic segmentation. That California is the West or the North; that Los Angeles is a paradise lost or a place where there is much *trabajo*; that the city is a place of menace or relative law and order, or a place of opportunity or an overpriced dead end, or a place of impending calamity and doom, or the harbinger of America's future are all different imaginings of place that correspond to the spatial and economic niches that people occupy. Different people in different circumstances imagine Los Angeles, Chicago, Dalton, St. Louis in different ways.

I think about Mexico in these ways too. I remember back to the family trip to my father's homeland in the early 1960s. Mexico was all about its immortal Indian past. Both tourists and the Mexican government celebrated the National Museum of Anthropology in Mexico City, the grand pyramids at Teotihuacán, and the stunning remains of Chichén Itzá. Mexico looked south to those immutable Olmec, Toltec, and Aztec faces eloquently carved into stone for its identity and for its solace. Now Mexico looks north. It is a country that would collapse financially and whose towns and villages would become destitute and desperate without the remission, often via Western Union, of so many millions, indeed billions, of dollars. Now Mexico's Indians are in Fresno, St. Louis, Ohio, Tennessee, Brooklyn.

Vicente Fox, former president of Mexico, has referred to those who migrate north and send all that good money back as "national heroes."[30] It used to be that los Niños Héroes, the six cadets who martyred themselves trying to hold off the U.S. Marines when America invaded Mexico City in 1847, were Mexico's champions, albeit in defeat. They echoed Cuauhtémoc, nephew of Montezuma, who the Spanish mercilessly tortured and hung after he led a legendary, hopeless rebellion against the European invaders. And so too Emiliano Zapata and Pancho Villa who, once killed and their partisans pacified, Mexican politicians lionized, in part, as defenders of Mexico against the avaricious gringo. Now Mexico's heroes go north, again in defeat, to work for the blessed gringo.

I look at all these people, and I think "everything and everybody is different now." Most of the time that the word "Mexican" appears in newspapers and magazines, or out of the mouths of nativist pundits, it refers to illegal immigration and/or the drug wars. As the word becomes increasingly vilified, it becomes better and better for Mexican Americans to favor the classier label of "Hispanic" or the more cool one of "Latino." One could be Chicano but that grows increasingly difficult as more and more Mexicans debouch onto the American landscape and seem to attract all of the attention.

But this has been my point all along about how people are changing all the time both in the matter of who they think they are and in the matter of whom others think they are: how people construct, name and re-name themselves and others. My goal here has been to share with my readers a new set of descriptions, new metaphors, by which they can understand and accept who and what they see on the landscape. I remain fascinated with this issue, but I have learned not to let it aggravate me anymore.

In the Footsteps of Padre Serra

I think about the irony of my grandparents, the ones who lamented that they never followed the footsteps of Ramona and Felipe back to Mexico, at the Evergreen Cemetery in East Los Angeles. I don't believe the common Mexican notion that the spirits of the dead hover around the *campo santo*, the graveyard, or even that souls are in Heaven or Hell. If their spirits were present there, would they feel at rest? The gardeners there, of course, have followed in the footsteps of Padre Junípero Serra to California from Michoacán or Zacatecas. My grandparents' spirits, likely to their great annoyance, would be hearing the sounds of Mexico as the gardeners' boom boxes blasted bad Mexican music and they spoke of their travails in the north. Mexico has come to my grandparents.

I think of my grandfather Jesús's hopes and dreams, of how he fought in a revolution so that Mexico could succeed not simply as a nation but as a humane place and that people could live in peace. I don't know about which to be more sad: that his hopes and dreams for our two peoples have been disappointed, or that our two peoples don't even have those hopes and dreams anymore.

As I have visited these stories of immigrants, of Mexicans who become Mexican Americans and Chicanos, of Padre Serra and Woodrow Wilson, of Ramona, and of scenes at the beach, I realize that perhaps the main thing that distinguishes me from all of these people is that I have never been tempted by either the Devil or God.

I am one of those Californians who, in the process of blending ethnicities, didn't lose faith, but rather just never had it. When I was young I never believed in the Church and not really in God. After the Church condemned Jesús and long before I was born, the González-Monroys never went to Church, though Noni always had statues of the Virgin around the house. My mother ignored religion with Yan-kee sangfroid.

As a boy I believed in Zorro and baseball, as a teenager in "Whenna" on the AM radio, and as a youth in John Lennon, the Stones, and Otis Redding, and in all of the wonderful things in books. Zorro in the salmon *chaleco* is unbecoming (which reminds me of my arriving to the Super A in Highland Park with the Volvo and the Stones on and all of the inelegance of that scene), but I am still drawn to his sense of justice. I am disappointed in baseball, and in both America and Mexico, but I still have belief in those other things. I have never suffered traumatic loss of faith, at least not as regards religion.

There are many Californians like me, products of this conflicted landscape, who really haven't been captivated by the Devil or God. We came to understand that the pleasures of the senses were quite good and certainly not immoral, and that religion was not the pre-requisite to virtue. California has always been the best place to have these sentiments.

The problem for us is that we know that when we would die, we would not live in any way after that. This is why we want to have a good life, in this place, now.

I have mostly written this book in that cause. But I also think that I have written for some immortality.

Oh, and I've gotten over all that foolishness about Ramona.

It's been about the stories, about inspiration and compassion, about crossing borders, and seeing things in new ways. At least I hope that has been the accomplishment of this book. In discussing how Mexico and America are so intertwined, I know I have likely alarmed and pained some people. Others may have found none of this surprising or upsetting and indeed have had validated what they suspected was true all along.

Smug in our knowledge that the New World Border is about "cre-ative destruction" and, as with the Industrial Revolution, that we will someday get through it and experience fuller lives will not satisfy ulti-mately, and this is the best-case scenario. Indeed, it may be that present policies will only intensify our other paradigm for the New World Bor-der, that of "developing underdevelopment," and that matters in Mexico will only get more desperate and class division in America all the more decisive. What happens if there comes to be too much pain and unhappiness and then anger and destruction? Human explosions have scarred Los Angeles before; I can't imagine they won't again.

For many, life in California has been more like a paradise. This is why so many are doing everything they can to get there and then live a good life. As it becomes too expensive and too crowded, more and more Americans are re-creating the California lifestyle of sprawl, California cuisine, mobility, and various entertainments in other places. It's not just the lifestyle that extends; so too spreads that which supports it: service workers who don't count in our moral consideration, or else who are disgraced and disparaged; huge imports of consumer goods from low-wage countries; big motor vehicles to take us wherever we want; whatever kind of food we want whenever we want it. The price of this paradise, maybe pseudo-paradise, has been made clear in these pages.

Ultimately, I am less disturbed by the superficial changes in the California landscape than I am by the prospect that the human and environmental cost of all this will not be sustainable. Maybe there is some limit to the amount of fossil fuels we can consume and still have air to breathe and peace in the world; maybe there won't be any more neighborhoods that will allow themselves to be carved up for freeways and then one day the big one will happen, the big gridlock, and we will all be permanently stuck in our cars. It is unlikely that California, and America, can continue at an increasing rate to use people up in the agricultural fields, packing plants, and hotels and restaurants and then simply discard them; when those groups of people — the fixed class of service workers and those permanently unemployed, or more likely their Americanized children who won't do those jobs anymore — revolt against their exclusion from paradise, they will not create a revolution of new ideas and justice, but as in the Rodney King rebellion, they will loot and pillage for commodities symbolic of the California lifestyle.

Places in California are becoming more and more like Third World cities. No more is a place like Los Angeles a great middle-class metropolis where even blue-collar workers, some of them even black or brown, could afford a home and a car, but it is now a place of tremendous disparities of wealth. There are plenty of very rich people, but not so many middle-class people, and millions of both working and unemployed poor people. The class structure no longer has a wide middle but is more like a pear with a small top and a large bottom. This is like Lima, Bogotá, Mexico City. Many other writers, Mike Davis and David Rieff to name only two, have pointed this out.[1] The future of America, one might think, may follow in California's footsteps.

At the same time, and this is what forecasters of doom forget, people with skills, talent, education, and capital strive fervently to get to California. Especially for those from Latin America, the Pacific Rim, and the American Midwest, California is still the land of economic and social opportunity. Neither freeway jams, earthquakes of the geologic or human character, housing prices, state government insolvency, or anything else will keep the tides back. Prosperity and privation, optimism and distrust, and exuberance and fear portend the future of California.

Many things distinguish so-called First and Third World countries: the matters of development and capital accumulation, distribution of income and consumer spending, and whether or not ownership of resources and productive capital is domestic or foreign. This is all true, but people who have lived, even traveled, in Third World countries know that the most obvious difference is that in the First World, things work. In Lima traffic signals no longer function; the first one to honk in an intersection has right of way. In Managua there is no money to replace the grates covering the drains in the streets and people fall in. In Mexico corruption at Pemex is so great that much adulterated gasoline makes it to the pumps and then into cars, which wrecks engines. Nowhere do faucets dispense drinkable water, nor do toilets function reliably. America is like Disneyland for Third-World immigrants: everything works.

I'm starting to think that what divides Americans more than anything else — more than race, more than Liberalism versus Conservatism, more than family values versus the prerogatives of individuals, more than religion — is that there are some who accept the complex structure of the reality of the world and there are those who resist it. There are those who think of racial identity as something fixed, of the ordering of society as unalterable, that the free market increases human freedom, and that right and wrong are ordained. Then there are those who think in opposite ways: that race and identity are human constructs, that one can combine a sense of irony about present predicaments with optimism about the future, that individualism and freedom are ambiguous concepts, and that truth and justice are often situational. For some, borders and boundaries are what is important. For others, it's *fronteras* and ambiguity.

Neither Mexicans who idealize a venerable traditional family, nor Americans who fantasize an exceptionalist America in which consensus about the American Creed prevailed will find the future intelligible, let alone very satisfying. People, capital, and commodities will pour back and forth across the border. This will challenge the family in terms of geographic integrity, the authority of the fathers, and the allegiance of the children — on both sides of the border, but especially in Mexico. Both countries will experience the contamination that "foreign" people and products inevitably bring.

Many people on both sides of the border, maybe even most of them, will rely on the fixed premises that history bequeaths them. The key will be to develop politics, and to carry on our lives, in ways that acknowledge complexity, celebrate life, and limit pain. Successful lives and politics will be the ones that affirm the borderlands conception of frontera and ambiguity.

Mostly, though, politics and portrayals of these matters emphasize victimization. Americans perceive their country to be overrun, their resources depleted by swarming immigrants, their familiar sights and sounds replaced with foreign noises and smells. Immigrants know that they are being exploited and that they are maintaining the American standard of living for so many, that they are blamed for ills not of their making, that they are in America for reasons usually not of their making, and that their hard work goes unappreciated. Perhaps the issue is not who is right or wrong, but that this pervading sense of victimization on both sides precludes any empathy, any effort or willingness to know one another's stories.

People will continue to pour out of Mexico and into the north for several reasons. The U.S.–Mexico border is nearly unique in the world in that it separates the wealthiest country in the world, measured in gross domestic product and material standard of living, from one of the poorest. Except for Spain's border with Morocco and Germany's with Poland, there is really nothing remotely like the line dividing the United States and Mexico when it comes to separating a rich place from a poor one. Nowhere do the First and Third Worlds abut so dramatically. Likely, this is the most fundamental situation for understanding the power that American economic institutions command over life in Mexico, and why more and more people will migrate from the poor place to the rich place.

Such south to north migration has been the historical trajectory for centuries, and a few policy initiatives are not likely to change that. Imagine, if you will, a hand in the interior of Mexico with four fingers extending northward. The index finger points up to the San Antonio region which the Spanish first missionized (including the infamous San Antonio del Alamo) in the early eighteenth century. The next finger to the west marks the route to the Rio Grande Valley where the expedition of Juan de Oñate of 1598 commenced the efforts to convert Puebloan people and make such settlements as Santa Fe. The next finger over directs us to the Tucson area, the place where Padre Eusebio Kino, a Tyrolean in service to the Spanish Crown, founded the magnificent San Javier del Bac in 1600. The westernmost finger points up the California coast, the place where the Spanish founded that most famous string of 21 missions beginning in 1769. The nineteenth century witnessed constant migration back and forth between the interior of Mexico and Southern California, Tucson, Albuquerque, and San Antonio. In the 1920s a million Mexicans, fleeing the chaos of revolution and its aftermath, migrated to the United States to assume jobs in the burgeoning railroad and corporate agricultural fields. In response to the manpower shortages of World War II, hundreds of thousands of Mexicans journeyed back and forth across the border to work in agriculture and did so for two decades under the auspices of the federally sponsored Bracero Program. Really, then, the dramatic and difficult migrations to which we are now witness are part of a larger historical trajectory. Immigrants to California actually follow in the footsteps of Padre Serra.

There is no reason to think that this strong historical trend will reverse itself; indeed, pessimists make good points about how immigration will only intensify. The population of Mexico increases at an annual rate of about 2 percent, or about two million per year; at present, 40 percent of its population is under 15. Mexico already suffers unemployment of about 25 percent, its subsistence farms are floundering and will face more and more calamity as more cheap food imports come from America's agri-business heartland, and the recurring peso crises highlight the failure of its economy to grow substantially. It is unlikely, in other words, that this young population will become workers or farmers in Mexico's failing economy. They will become migrants.[2]

The first thing that comes to many Americans' minds is birth control and family planning. It won't happen. Condoms cost a lot more than tortillas and hungry families will spend what little they have on the latter. It is one of the saddest aspects of the increasingly theocratic hold that the Catholic Church exercises over Mexico, and that right-wing Christianity holds over the United States, that even if it didn't include abortion rights, money for government birth control programs in Mexico will not be forthcoming from either the United States or Mexico.* The population in Mexico will continue to grow faster than the economy can create jobs.

Ideologues only advocate their familiar. Free marketeers will only intone their mantra of opening markets and increasing trade. They will tout the jobs created in the maquiladoras without acknowledging that only young, unmarried women get them. The economic bustle and building booms of Sinaloa and Monterey will evidence the positive effects of capital investment from the north in Mexico but ignore the fact that so much of the Mexican capital involved in those places derives from the drug trade. They will recount the statistics showing the expansion of exports of food from the United States and imply that Mexicans thus have more to eat. We know that in Mexico it is these very imports that are driving people from their farms and that they have few resources with which to buy food. Living in a free-market society does not make one free. The so-called "free market" results in hunger and compulsion for Mexicans, not freedom. Free trade will only intensify Mexico's woes and the historical trend of migration from south to north.

As with this ambiguity about "freedom," there is grim irony in Mexico's recent turn to "democracy." Elections, with three distinct parties no less, only mean that investors cannot know if Mexico will follow the Partido Acción Nacional (free trade), the Partido de la Revolución Democrática (government support for workers and peasants and enforcement of environmental standards), or the old Partido Revolucionario Institucional (old-style corruption). Predictable one-party states like China or Vietnam are much more desirable investment sites. America prescribes electoral democracy for places like Mexico. Elections, because they might empower workers, make Mexico less advisable for investment.

Advocates of an open border need to go to Tijuana and see the mass of desperate, often degraded, human beings hungering to cross into the United States. Unless it were suddenly converted into a nation of Mother Theresas, America could not/would not absorb these millions of resourceless people who, lemming-like, would take the dire leap across.

---

* In defense of the Church's position on birth control it should be pointed out that if people used condoms or any other "artificial" forms of contraception, they would then be engaging in sexual intercourse not for reproduction but for pleasure, which is, of course, a sin. Thus the Church, by opposing birth control, is saving Mexicans from sin and damnation.

Advocates of government leadership, be they liberal or conservative, will only rattle off tired nostrums, or only ones that have worked in the United States. Part of the genius of the American economy has been its ability to cast away its rhetoric of laissez-faire and decentralized power and then to utilize a strong national state for development. Whether it was granting federal lands to the railroads, protecting the steel industry with tariffs, pumping the economy with military spending, or negotiating NAFTA, an activist federal government has advanced American capitalist development.

Policies associated with New Deal Liberalism put money in consumers' pockets so that they could buy the products of American industry. Support for unions, and programs like the Civilian Conservation Corps and the Works Progress Administration, both of which took idle people off the streets and rails, increased consumer spending. Though they are reluctant to admit it, because of these programs, capitalists had more customers. It might make sense for Mexico to have some of these sorts of programs. To do so would require Mexico to get loans to fund such programs. Mexico can't, and shouldn't, get more loans because they have way too much debt already, and anyway, neither individual nor lending institutions would loan them any money since they are always on the verge of defaulting on their present loans and because the peso is chronically in trouble.

There is no way to get development funds directly to farmers, workers, or even entrepreneurs. All such funds would have to go through the intransigently corrupt Mexican state. The more money the state controls in Mexico, the more patronage and corruption the Mexican political system will experience. Which is a large part of the problem.

We may be mistaken when we understand disparities of wealth, development, and immigration as a "problem." Recall from our first chapter that we are witnessing not so much a disorder but a well-functioning system. This system operates neither rationally nor humanely, but it satisfies both economic and psychological needs: in America, labor markets are supplied, bureaucracies are funded, and people get to feel victimized by foreign immigrants; while in Mexico, excess population is syphoned off, financial ruin is avoided, and political discontent is ameliorated. In America it's not just the gas pumps and the toilets that work but, in often-mean and very shortsighted ways, the whole economic system. In this context, effecting reform is improbable.

In Europe, consciousness of borders seems to be disappearing. The exception is Spain and Morocco where Moroccans, actually Africans, enter into Spain, actually into Europe. Marijuana and hashish, Morocco's only viable export besides its people, also cross into Europe in huge quantities through Spain. In many ways, Morocco is "Europe's Mexico." Indeed, surveillance of non-Spanish-looking peoples — read Africans — and a tightening of the border have proceeded ahead.[3]

In America, concern about the border seems to increase as that very border becomes less and less of a meaningful divider. The fact that the border has moved, that Mexico is now in the Pilsen district of Chicago or across the tracks in Dalton, Georgia, complicates this. Americans become more and more conscious of Mexico and Mexicans as the spectacle of people so yearning for trabajo — sometimes wearing the stigmata of desperation, sometimes joyfully filling the parks and the schools — all dramatize the deficiency of the Mexican nation. It's this pageant of Mexicans in America that makes Americans so aware of Mexico. Because it is more of an apprehension than anything else, Americans will want to maintain borders around the place about which they are increasingly uneasy; they will want to remain clearly separate while with each passing day the two countries become more intertwined.

This foreboding, I fear, will only incline Americans to retreat into comforting beliefs about an immutable past: about how the Puritans founded the country and the culture, about the Founding Fathers and what they intended the nation should be, about the unmitigated heroism of the Westward Movement which entitled them to the land. Now, with the New World Border, things are mutating rapidly.

The familiar is changing swiftly, and forces beyond our control seem to be in charge, or not "in charge" at all. Abstract appeals to tolerance and diversity will not bring peace to the landscape, at least not as long as confusion continues to reign and people respond to their discomfort with an imagined past when everyone lived in homogeneous nuclear families, when borders and boundaries were clear, and when people adhered, or at least aspired, to the American Creed. We know from the stories we've read here that such a past existed only in the form of people's yearnings. Acceptance of other people will only come when we challenge our (and I use the ambiguous Borderlands sense of "our") own "truths," when we have compassion for others, when we "know with" them their experiences, when we know their stories.

So many opposite things going on at once. Richard Rodriguez writes about the "browning of America."[4] Everywhere one looks there are more Mexican restaurants, more things like the Latino Grammys, more Latino politicians, more intermarriage, more celebration of diversity. Before there were so many Mexicans in Los Angeles, it seemed that local news shows often had one Asian and one Anglo anchor, an African American who did the sports, a white guy doing weather, and a Latino somewhere. An anthropologist from a more monocultural society would watch and think that America was a land of happy diversity. But Americans still want their pork chops, potatoes, and peas all separate on the plate. Their congressional representatives vote huge sums for the Border Patrol.

In Mexico the politics are corrupt and cynical, people hate the government, and the economy is failing. To help keep up my Spanish, I sometimes watch the news on Univision. In Mexico the newscasters have gone blond. So too have the dancing girls on the music shows, and they wear low-cut pants to eroticize the midriff, like the stylish young women in America. When Deputy Musquiz Blanco railed at the "blond thieves" who had stormed ashore when Woodrow Wilson sent his guns to Veracruz in 1914, he had no idea about what his comment presaged. In Mexico, middle-class respectability comes from the purchase of the symbols of American prosperity — Japanese electronics and cars. Mexicans become teary eyed at the mention of the words *la nación mexicana*.

Mexico looks forward to its migrant sons and daughters coming back from the north with some entrepreneurial spirit, some gringo savvy* about business, or at least some work discipline learned in the north. Mexico knows it could not survive without the dollars being sent back from the north. Mexico depends on America.

In America, Mexican and Central American immigrants have revitalized the areas surrounding the downtown sections. Once-boarded-up storefronts are now bustling immigrant businesses; previously idle sidewalks are full of walkers and shoppers; lawns are kept, roofs are installed, cars washed, food harvested, houses and hotels are cleaned, children and the elderly are cared for; they all pay taxes. America depends on Mexico.

And, while Americans are aware of the Mexicans they see, amongst the many things that America does not understand — I think it's a question of denial — about Mexico and Mexicans is that we consume not

---

* I use the word "savvy" very intentionally. It derives from the Spanish *¿tu sabes?* or "you understand?" A gringo asking a Mexican "you savvy?" is a way of telling him what he'd better know.

only the cheaply produced products of Mexican labor in the fields, restaurants and hotels, supermarkets, and construction sites but that we also consume Mexican bodies: the years that the heat, dehydration, and pesticides take off of farm workers' life expectancies are built into our fruits and vegetables. There's more even.

The thorns of a lemon tree prick the fingers of a picker's hand, and the blood drips down into the soil. The sweat falls from a lettuce picker's brow, even little children's, and into the soil. The harvesters urinate and defecate into the irrigation ditches because there is no place else to do so. The fouled water flows into the rows of lettuce and cantaloupes. The earth and the crop roots do not reflect on the economic and political considerations that go into this complex agronomy. They simply build the blood, sweat, and shit of the workers (along with all the high-tech chemical fertilizers) into the beautiful and wonderful produce of the land. This is what Americans eat. This is part of Americas' intimacy with Mexico and Mexicans.

I think we need to know and acknowledge this closeness, this intimacy that history has forged between Mexicans and Americans. We cannot retreat from it.

We cannot turn back because — and these are likely the only things that we can learn from history — actions once taken are irreversible and actions almost inevitably have consequences, many of them unintended. From the decision to missionize California, to Ramona and Alessandro falling in love, to deciding to use low-wage Mexican labor to work in the fields, to NAFTA, we can see that even if we might decide that there was something better to do, there is no retraction, no undoing what has been done. California's, Mexico's, and America's futures are so bound together because of actions taken in the distant and recent pasts.

We can only hope that the future will be a better place. For that to happen we need to take to heart Mexicans' and Americans' stories, the ones about the immigrants and the capitalists, about los Niños Héroes and Ramona, about the Indians and the interlopers, Californios and the Chicanos, and about Woodrow Wilson's guns and Padre Serra.

Notes

Chapter 1

1. F. Scott Fitzgerald, "The Crack-Up," *Esquire*, February 1936, and reprinted in *The Crack-Up*, ed. Edmund Wilson (New York: New Directions Paperback, 1956), 69.

2. Joseph Schumpeter, *Capitalism, Socialism and Democracy*, 3rd ed. (New York: Harper Torchbooks, 1962), 81–84.

3. Richard Rorty, *Contingency, Irony, and Solidarity* (Cambridge: Cambridge University Press, 1989), 192.

4. Ginger Thompson, "NAFTA to Open Floodgates, Engulfing Rural Mexico," *New York Times*, December 19, 2002.

5. Oxfam Briefing Paper, "Dumping without Borders: How U.S. Agricultural Policies Are Destroying the Livelihoods of Mexican Corn Farmers," August 2003, 17–20, http://www.oxfam.org/eng/policy_pape_corn_dumping.htm; Chris Kraul, "Growing Troubles in Mexico," *Los Angeles Times*, January 17, 2000, 1.

6. Peter Andreas, *Border Games: Policing the U.S.-Mexico Divide* (Ithaca, NY: Cornell University Press, 2001), 61–65.

7. Sam Quinones, *True Tales from Another Mexico: The Lynch Mob, the Popsicle Kings, Chalino, and the Bronx* (Albuquerque: University of New Mexico Press, 2001), 11–29.

8. "More Deaths Tied to Drug War," *Los Angeles Times*, February, 6, 2005, A4. (An AP article)

9. Octavio Paz, *The Labyrinth of Solitude*, trans. Lysander Kemp (New York: Grove Press, 1961), 60; Helen Hunt Jackson, *Ramona: A Story* (Boston: Roberts Bros., 1884), 230.

10. Tim Golden, "Mexican Drug Dealers Turning U.S. Towns into Major Depots," *New York Times*, November 16, 2002.

11. Steven Mikulan, "Losing Our Shirts: An Unhappy New Year Looms for American Apparel Makers," *LA Weekly*, December 3–9, 2004.

12. Tyler Marshal, Evelyn Iritani, and Marla Dickerson, "Clothes Will Cost Less, but Some Nations Pay," and "When Fear Follows the Fabric Along the Assembly Line," *Los Angeles Times*, January 16 and 17, 2005, A1.

13. Pierrette Hondagneu-Sotelo, *Gendered Transitions: Mexican Experiences of Immigration* (Berkeley: University of California Press, 1994), 83–86.

14. Hondagneu-Sotelo, *Gendered Transitions*, 62–74.

15. Oxfam Briefing Paper, "Dumping without Borders," 20.

16. *Los Angeles Daily News*, October 28, 2004.

17. Steven A. Camarota, "A Jobless Recovery? Immigrant Gains and Native Losses," Center for Immigration Studies, October 2004, http://www.cis.org/articles/2004/back1104.html

18. Josh Sides, *L.A. City Limits: African American Los Angeles from the Great Depression to the Present* (Berkeley: University of California Press, 2003), 24–26.

19. Douglas Monroy, *Rebirth: Mexican Los Angeles from the Great Migration to the Great Depression* (Berkeley: University of California Press, 1999), chapters 2 and 3.

20. Ginger Thompson, "Mexico's 'Tomato King' Seeks a New Title," *New York Times*, July 5, 2004, A4.

21. Quinones, *True Tales from Another Mexico*, 154, 166, 171.

22. Christian Parenti, "Satellites of Sorrow: Los Angeles, Prison, and Circuits of Social Control," in *Unmasking L.A: Third Worlds and the City*, ed. Deepak Narang Sawhney (New York: Palgrave, 2002), 47–62; Chris Kraul, "El Salvador Comes to Grips With Gangs," *Los Angeles Times*, December 13, 2004, A1.

23. Kraul, "El Salvador Comes to Grips With Gangs"; Chris Kraul, Robert J. Lopez, and Rich Connell, "L.A. Violence Crosses the Line," *Los Angeles Times*, May 15, 2005, A1.

24. Solomon Moore, "Mexico's Border-Crossing Tips Anger Some in U.S.," *Los Angeles Times*, January 4, 2005, A1.

25. Andreas, *Border Games*, 7–10.

26. Andreas, *Border Games*, 38–39.

27. Marc Cooper, "Death on the Border," *The Nation*, October 18, 2004, 8, 26; "Arizona: The New Border War," *The Nation*, July 22, 2002, 20–24.

28. See, for example, Peter Schrag, *Paradise Lost: California's Experience, America's Future* (Berkeley: University of California Press, 1999), and David Rieff, *Los Angeles: Capital of the Third World* (New York: Simon & Schuster, 1991).

Chapter 2

Portions of "Zorro, Cows, Indians, and Dons" were previously published in *Contested Eden: California Before the Gold Rush*, Ramón A. Gutiérrez and Richard J. Ortiz (eds.), © 1998 California Historical Society. Published by the University of California Press. Reprinted by permission.

1. Hubert Howe Bancroft, *California Pastoral* (San Francisco: The History Co., 1888), 360; Alfred Robinson, *Life in California before the Conquest* (1846) (San Francisco: Thomas C. Russell, 1925); Charles Nordhoff, *California for Health, Pleasure, and Residence* (New York: Harper and Brothers, 1873), 160; Josiah Royce, *California from the Conquest in 1846 to the Second Vigilance Committee in San Francisco: A Study of American Character* (1887) (New York: Alfred A. Knopf, 1948); Carey McWilliams, *Southern California: An Island on the Land* (1946) (Santa Barbara: Peregrine, Smith, Inc., 1973), 77–83; Douglas Monroy, *Thrown among Strangers: The Making of Mexican Culture in Frontier California* (Berkeley: University of California Press, 1990), 258–63; and Christina Wiebus Mead, "Las Fiestas de Los Angeles: A Survey of the Yearly Celebrations, 1894–1898," *Historical Society of*

Southern California Quarterly 31 (March and June 1949), 61–113; *Los Angeles Times*, May 7, 1903.

2. Central to any understanding of these fabled people are their own accounts of themselves after they fell from influence—their lengthy *recuerdos* dictated in the 1870s. At once poignant and self-congratulating, aristocratic and pitiful, Californios detailed eloquently and self-consciously their own versions of their lives and times to collectors of autobiographies under the direction of Hubert Howe Bancroft, the true founder of studious California historiography. The testimonies, mostly in Spanish, form one of the centerpieces of the Bancroft Library at the University of California at Berkeley and were important sources for Bancroft's magisterial seven-volume *History of California* (San Francisco: The History Co., 1884).

3. Alex Forbes to Abel Stearns, Tepic, April 18, 1831, Stearns Papers, Box 27, Huntington Library.

4. See, for example, Irving Berdine Richman, *California under Spain and Mexico, 1535–1847* (Boston: Houghton Mifflin Company, 1911), and Nellie Van de Grift Sanchez, *Spanish Arcadia* (Los Angeles: Powell Publishing Co., 1929).

5. William M. Mason, "Indian-Mexican Cultural Exchange in the Los Angeles Area, 1781–1834," *Aztlán* 15 (Spring 1984), 124–44.

6. Randall Millikin, *A Time of Little Choice: The Disintegration of Tribal Culture in the San Francisco Bay Area, 1769–1810* (Menlo Park, CA: Ballena Press, 1995), 220–21; George Harwood Phillips, "Indians in Los Angeles, 1781–1875: Economic Integration, Social Disintegration," *Pacific Historical Review* 49 (August 1980), 396, and Padre Señan is quoted on page 401.

7. Robert Glass Cleland, *Cattle on a Thousand Hills: Southern California, 1850–80* (1941) (San Marino, CA: Huntington Library, 1975), 7–17 (Fages's request is quoted on page 7); Manuel Perez Nieto's "Petition for a Land Grant" is reprinted in John and LaRee Caughy, eds., *Los Angeles: Biography of a City* (Berkeley: University of California Press, 1977), 71–73; Bancroft, *History of California*, 1:609–11, 659–65; W. W. Robinson, "The Dominguez Rancho," *Historical Society of Southern California Quarterly* 35 (December 1953), 343; W. W. Robinson, *Ranchos Become Cities* (Pasadena, CA: San Pascual Press, 1939), 11.

8. José del Carmen Lugo, "Life of a Rancher," ed. and trans. Mrs. G.W. Beattie, *Southern California Quarterly* 32 (September 1950), 187, 216–17; "Edwin Bryant, "What I Saw in California," in *A World Transformed: Firsthand Accounts of California Before the Gold Rush*, ed. Joshua Paddison (Berkeley: Heyday Books, 1999), 289; Fray Santa María is quoted in John Caughy, "The Country Town of the Angels," and in Caughy, *Los Angeles*, 76.

9. In Latin America *criollo* refers to a person born in the New World but of "pure" Spanish parents. The word translates literally as "creole" but has a different meaning than the American usage. A person born in Spain was called *peninsular*.

10. On the secularization of the missions, see the texts and endnotes (for an abundance of sources) in David J. Weber, *The American Southwest under Mexico: The Mexican Frontier, 1821–1846* (Albuquerque: University of New Mexico Press, 1982), 62–68; Monroy, *Thrown among Strangers*, 117–34; Bancroft, *History of California*, 3:301–56; Rosaura Sánchez, *Telling Identities: The Californio testimonios* (Minneapolis: University of Minnesota Press, 1995), 121–39; and Beth Haas,

"Emancipation and the Meaning of Freedom in Mexican California," *Bolitín: The Journal of the California Mission Studies Association* 20, no. 1 (2003); Vallejo is quoted in Daniel Garr, "Planning, Politics and Plunder: The Missions and Indian Pueblos of Hispanic California," *Southern California Quarterly* 54 (Winter 1972), 297–98; Juan Bandini to Eustace Barron, December 8, 1828, Stearns Papers, Box 4, Huntington Library; and Figueroa is quoted in Weber, *The American Southwest under Mexico* on page 64.

11. Angustias de la Guerra Ord, *Occurrences in Hispanic California*, trans. and ed. from the Bancroft Library MS by Francis Price and William H. Ellison (Washington, DC: Academy of Franciscan History, 1956), 25; Sánchez, *Telling Identities*, 110–13, and Alvarado is quoted on page 111; Howard A. DeWitt, *California Civilization: An Interpretation* (Dubuque, IA: Kendall Hunt Publishing Company, 1979), 57–59.

12. Sánchez, *Telling Identities*, and Figueroa is quoted on page 133.

13. For an excellent discussion of how the Indians became attached to the ranchos, see Stephen W. Silliman, "Missions Aborted: California Indian Life on Nineteenth-Century Ranchos, 1834–1848," *Bolitín: The Journal of the California Mission Studies Association* 21, no. 1 (2004), 9–11.

14. Carlos Híjar, California in 1834: Recollections, Bancroft Library MS (1877), 15–17, 35; almost surprisingly given her usual romanticization of the Californios, Nellie Van de Grift Sanchez, *The Spanish Period* (Chicago: Lewis Publishing Co., 1926) discusses briefly the role of Indian labor on pages 432–35.

15. Michael González, *This Small City Will Be a Mexican Paradise: Exploring the Origins of Mexican Culture in Los Angeles, 1821-1846* (Albuquerque: University of New Mexico Press, 2005), 126; Silliman, "Missions Aborted," 7.

16. Silliman, "Missions Aborted," 13–21.

17. *Canku Ota—A Newsletter Celebrating Native America*, October 7, 2000, issue 20; Linda D. Navarro, "The Committee for Traditional Indian Health: A Program of the California Rural Indian Health Board, Inc.," *News from Native California* 14, no. 2 (Winter 2000/01).

18. "Testimony, June 1, 1824," de la Guerra documents, quoted in Sherburne Friend Cook, *The Conflict between the California Indian and White Civilization* (Berkeley: University of California Press, 1976), 108; see also "Fray Antonio Ripoll's Description of the Chumash Revolt at Santa Barbara in 1824," ed. and trans. Maynard Geiger, *Southern California Quarterly* 52 (December 1970), 345–64.

19. Juana Machado, Los Tiempos Pasados de la Alta California, Bancroft Library MS (1878), 16.

20. Argüello is quoted in Robert F. Heizer and Alan F. Almquist, *The Other Californians: Prejudice and Discrimination under Spain, Mexico, and the United States to 1820* (Berkeley: University of California Press, 1971), 17–18; George Harwood Phillips, *Chiefs and Challengers: Indian Resistance and Cooperation in Southern California* (Berkeley: University of California Press, 1975), 47–59; on the Leyva episode see Juana Machado, "Los Tiempos Pasados," 11–15, Bancroft Library; and Sánchez, *Telling Identities*, 144–51, and on page 151 she quotes Alvarado.

21. Cook, *Conflict*, 210–16; Sir George Simpson, *Narrative of a Journey Round the World, during the Years 1841 and 1842* (London: Henry Colburn, 1847), 1:353.

22. Phillips, *Chiefs and Challengers*, 48–51; González, *This Small City*, 122, describes the Palomares attack; Lugo, "Life of a Rancher," 209.

23. See González, *This Small City*, 122–23 for some provocative comments on this matter.

24. Sánchez, *Telling Identities*, 229–31, 237–45; Lisbeth Haas, *Conquests and Historical Identities in California, 1769-1936* (Berkeley: University of California Press, 1995), 36–37; Bancroft, *History of California*, 3:445–57; Weber, *The American Southwest under Mexico*, 255–60.

25. Ord, "Occurrences," 49; Haas, *Conquests and Historical Identities*, 47–49; J. Gregg Layne, "The First Census of the Los Angeles District," *Southern California Quarterly* 18 (September–December 1936), 92–93, 96; Bancroft, *History of California*, 3:633–44n lists those who received grants between 1831 and 1840; Robert G. Cowan, *Ranchos of California: A List of Spanish Concessions, 1775–1822, and Mexican Grants, 1822–1846* (1956) (San Bernardino: The Borgo Press, 1985) lists them all.

26. S. M. Lee, *Glimpses of Mexico and California* (Boston: George H. Ellis, 1887), 71; José Arnaz, "Recuerdos," Bancroft Library MS (1878), 17–18; Paul W. Gates, *California Ranchos and Farms, 1846–1862, including the Letters of John Quincy Adams Warren* (Madison: The State Historical Society of Wisconsin, 1967), 4–9.

27. Tomás Almaguer, *Racial Faultlines: The Historical Origins of White Supremacy in California* (Berkeley: University of California Press, 1994), 45–46; Haas, *Conquests and Historical Identities*, 52–53.

28. José Antonio Pico to Abel Stearns, February 28, 1836, Stearns Papers, Box 49, Huntington Library, places the order for the rebozos and cloth; Sanchez, *Spanish Arcadia*, 39; José del Carmen Lugo, "Vida de un Ranchero," Bancroft Library MS, 86–97.

29. For a fuller discussion of this concept of seigneurialism see Monroy, *Thrown among Strangers*, 100–102, and on the legacy of the missions 3–96.

30. "Prayers, religious verses . . . of José Antonio de la Guerra y Noriega" in Personal Papers file, de la Guerra papers, Huntington Library; Lugo, "Vida de un Ranchero," 75–76, 84–85, 98; Híjar, "Recollections," 9–12.

31. "Petition by Doña Eulalia Callis, the Wife of Don Pedro Fages, Governor of the Californias, that Her Case Be Heard and that She Be Freed from the Oppression from which She Is Suffering (Summary)" in Rose Marie Beebe and Robert M. Senkewicz, eds., *Lands of Promise and Despair: Chronicles of Early California, 1535–1846* (Santa Clara and Berkeley, CA: University of Santa Clara and Heyday Books, 2001), 236–37.

32. *Alcalde* is the Spanish word for mayor, but it derives from the Arabic *al-kadi*, or "village father."

33. Bancroft, *California Pastoral*, 334.

34. Bancroft, *History of California*, 3:417–19.

35. José María Amador, Memorias sobre la historia de California, Bancroft Library MS (1877), 207–8; Bancroft, *California Pastoral*, 588, and see also 333–34, and *History of California*, 2:575; Miroslava Chávez-García, *Negotiating Conquest: Gender and Power in California, 1770s to 1880s* (Tucson: University of Arizona Press, 2004), 29–47.

36. Robert Ryal Miller, *Juan Alvarado, Governor of California, 1836–1842* (Norman: University of Oklahoma Press, 1998), 32–34.

37. Chávez-García, *Negotiating Conquest*, 49.

38. José del Carmen Lugo, "The Days of a Rancher in Spanish California," ed. Nellie Van de Grift Sanchez, *Touring Topics* 22 (April 1930), 22; Amador, "Memorias," 228; Richard Henry Dana, *Two Years before the Mast* (New York: Bantam Pathfinder, 1959), 135–36.

39. Antonia Castañeda, "Engendering the History of Alta California, 1769-1848," in Ramón Gutiérrez and Richard J. Ortiz, eds., *Contested Eden: California Before the Gold Rush* (Berkeley: University of California Press, 1998) 241–42; Miller, *Juan Alvarado*, 181.

40. Helen Tyler, "The Family of Pico," *Historical Society of Southern California Quarterly* 35, no. 3 (September 1953), 229–36.

41. Castañeda, "Engendering History," 241.

42. Híjar, "Recollections," 22; Arnaz, "Recuerdos," 24–25; Sanchez, *Spanish Arcadia*, 273; Ord, "Occurrences," 25; "Duhaut-Cilly's Account of California in the Year 1827," ed. and trans. Charles Franklin Carter, *California Historical Society Quarterly* 7 (1929), 311; Gloria E. Miranda, "Hispano-Mexican Childrearing Practices in Pre-American Santa Barbara," *Southern California Quarterly* 63 (Spring 1983), 308–13.

43. Juan Bandini to Eustace Barron, December 8, 1828, Stearns Papers, Box 4, Huntington Library; Lugo, "Vida de un Ranchero," 76–77; Híjar, "Recollections," 9; Edwin Bryant, *What I Saw in California; Being the Journal of a Tour in the Years 1846–1847* (New York: D. Appleton and Company, 1848), 448.

44. Eulalia Pérez, "Una vieja y sus recuerdos," Bancroft MS (1877), 6; José Bandini, *A Description of California in 1828* (Berkeley, CA: Friends of the Bancroft Library, 1951), 9–19; Nellie Van de Grift Sanchez, *The Spanish Period* (Chicago: Lewis Publishing Co., 1926), 478–79; Florence Connolly Shipek, *Delfina Cuero: Her Autobiography, An Account of Her Last Years, and Her Ethnobotanic Contributions* (Menlo Park, CA: Ballena Press, 1991) provides a remarkable list of medicinal herbs that Kumeyaay people used on pages 45, 83–98.

45. Lugo, "Life of a Rancher," 27; Cleland, *Cattle on a Thousand Hills*, 87–90.

46. See, for example, the precision and relish with which Lugo describes dress in "Life of a Rancher," 219–22; Amador, "Memorias," 216; Bancroft, *California Pastoral*, 373–74.

47. Robinson, *Life in California*, 101, 171; Híjar, "Recollections," 23; Vicente P. Gómez, "Lo que sabe sobre cosas de California," Bancroft Library MS (1876), 8; Amador, "Memorias," Lugo, "Vida de un Ranchero," 116–28, and Lugo, "Life of a Rancher," 233–36 for a translation.

48. Arnaz, "Recuerdos," 14–16.

49. Simpson, *Narrative of a Journey*, 1:387; Híjar, "Recollections," 21.

50. DeWitt, *California Civilization*, 66–67; and Bancroft, *History of California*, 4:455–545.

51. McWilliams, *Southern California*, 21; Castro, Palemón Zavala, *El Indio Cajeme y su Nación del Río Yaqui* (Acapulco, Mexico: Gobierno del Estado de Sonora, 1985).

Chapter 3

"Ramona, I Love You" was previously published in a slightly different form in *California History*, 81, no. 2 (Dec. 2002), 134–55, 171. Reprinted by permission.

1. "Ramona," lyrics by L. Wolfe Gilbert, music by Mabel Wayne. Published 1927 by Leo Feist, Inc., New York.

2. Douglas Monroy, *Thrown among Strangers: The Making of Mexican Culture in Frontier California* (Berkeley: University of California Press, 1990), 264.

3. Carey McWilliams, *Southern California: An Island on the Land* (1946) (Santa Barbara, CA: Peregrine Smith Publications, 1973), 70–77.

4. George Wharton James, *Through Ramona's Country* (Boston: Little, Brown and Company, 1911), 62, 363.

5. James, *Through Ramona's Country*, 60, 273; Helen Hunt Jackson, *California and the Missions* (1883) (Boston: Little, Brown & Company, 1902), 77.

6. James A. Sandos, "Historic Preservation and Historical Facts: Helen Hunt Jackson, Rancho Camulos and Ramonana," *California History* 76 (1997), 3, 181; *The Annotated Ramona*, with introduction and notes by Antoinette May (San Carlos, CA: Wide World Publish/Tetra), 149.

7. James, *Through Ramona's Country*, 94–115; Phil Brigandi, "Rancho Camulos and the Home of Ramona," *Ventura County Historical Society Quarterly*, 42, nos. 3–4 (1998), 3, 4, 15–23; Sandos, "Historic Preservation and Historical Facts," 179–83; William Alexander McClung, *Landscapes of Desire: Anglo Mythologies of Los Angeles* (Berkeley: University of California Press, 2000), 77–78; McWilliams, *Southern California*, 165–82.

8. The quote is from "The Story of Ramona's Marriage Place" (No. San Diego: Ramona's Marriage Place, n.d.), 3. See also pages 5–7 on this matter of ignoring the full story.

9. All quotes from the novel are cited in parentheses. While there have been numerous editions of *Ramona*, I have used the popular Avon paperback edition (New York, 1970).

10. Helen Hunt Jackson, *A Century of Dishonor: A Sketch of the United States Government's Dealings with Some of the Indian Tribes*, rev. ed. (Boston 1893), 459–63; George Harwood Phillips, *Chiefs and Challengers: Indian Resistance and Cooperation in Southern California* (Berkeley: University of California Press, 1975); Monroy, *Thrown among Strangers*, 237–45.

11. McWilliams, *Southern California*, 24.

12. Fray Antonio Peyri to Juan Bandini, December 25, 1828, Stearns Papers, Huntington Library.

13. James, *Through Ramona's Country*, 60.

14. Sir George Simpson, *Narrative of a Journey Round the World, during the Years 1841 and 1842* (London: Henry Colburn, 1847), 1:387.

15. McClung, *Landscapes of Desire*, 78.

16. Nicolas Kanellos, *A History of Hispanic Theatre in the United States: Origins to 1940* (Austin: University of Texas Press, 1990), 44–59, 65–69; *La Opinión*, November 27, 1928; Douglas Monroy, *Rebirth: Mexican Los Angeles from the Great Migration to the Great Depression* (Berkeley: University of California Press, 1999), 44, 169.

Chapter 4

1. *Los Angeles Times*, April 14, 1914; *Diario de los Debates*, April 21, 1914, quoted in Michael C. Meyer, *Huerta: A Political Portrait* (Lincoln: University of Nebraska Press, 1972), 200; Friedrich Katz, *The Life and Times of Pancho Villa* (Stanford, CA: Stanford University Press, 1998), 336–38.

2. *Los Angeles Times*, April 23 and 24, 1914.

3. José Vasconcelos, *The Cosmic Race/La Raza Cósmica*, ed. and trans. Didier T. Jaen (Baltimore: The Johns Hopkins University Press, 1997), 18.

4. This discussion derives loosely from Louis Hartz, *The Liberal Tradition in America: An Interpretation of American Political Thought since the Revolution* (New York: Harcourt, Brace and World Inc., 1955), 3–86.

5. Polk is quoted in Glenn W. Price, *Origins of the War with Mexico: The Polk-Stockton Intrigue* (Austin: University of Texas Press, 1967), 36.

6. Alex Forbes to Stearns, Tepic, April 18, 1831, Stearns Papers, Box 27, Huntington Library; Richard Henry Dana, *Two Years Before the Mast* (New York: Bantam Pathfinder, 1959), 135–36.

7. Pio Pico is quoted in Security Trust and Savings Bank, *El Pueblo*, 81; Alvarado is quoted in Nellie Van de Grift Sanchez, *Spanish Arcadia* (Los Angeles: Powell Publishing Co., 1929), 132; Guerrero to Castro, January 24, 1846, Castro Documentos VI, No. 309 (Bancroft MS,1876) is quoted in Robert Glass Cleland, "Early Sentiment for the Annexation of California," *The Southwestern Historical Quarterly*, 18, no. 2 (October 1914), 151; Juan B. Alvarado, *Historia de California*, 2:133–34 quotes Castro, and Cleland, "Early Sentiment for Annexation," page 151, which quotes Alvarado.

8. Woodrow Wilson, "Address at the Tercentenary Celebration of the Translation of the Bible into the English Language, Denver, Colorado, May 7, 1911," in *Papers of Woodrow Wilson*, ed. Arthur S. Link (Princeton, NJ: Princeton University Press, 1966–1978), 23:13.

9. John Mason Hart, *Revolutionary Mexico: The Coming and Process of the Mexican Revolution* (Berkeley: University of California Press, 1989), 129–56.

10. Hart, *Revolutionary Mexico*, 158–62.

11. John Mason Hart, *Empire and Revolution: The Americans in Mexico since the Civil War* (Berkeley: University of California Press, 2002), 235–73.

12. Quoted in Hart, *Empire and Revolution*, 296.

13. Woodrow Wilson, *A History of the American People* (New York: Harper, 1902), 7:122; *World's Work*, January 1914 is reproduced in Link, ed., *Papers of Woodrow Wilson*, 29:24; Wilson, "An Address on Mexican Affairs to a Joint Session of Congress," August 27, 1913, in Link, ed., *Papers of Woodrow Wilson*, 28:230–31.

14. Ray Stannard Baker, *Woodrow Wilson: Life and Letters, President, 1913–1914* (New York: Doubleday, Doran and Co., 1931), 4:238–43; Friedrich Katz, *The Secret War in Mexico: Europe, the United States, and the Mexican Revolution* (Chicago: The University of Chicago Press, 1981), 305–26, and the quote from the American commissioners on the crisis in Mexico is on page 312.

15. *New York World*, May 19, 1914, in Link, ed., *Papers of Woodrow Wilson*, 30:40; Katz, *Life and Times of Pancho Villa*, 311–12.

16. Carlos Fuentes, *The Death of Artemio Cruz*, trans. Sam Hileman (New York: Farrar, Straus & Company, 1964), 181–82, 185–86.

17. Wilson, *History of the American People*, 7:121–22.

18. Ray Stannard Baker, *Woodrow Wilson: Life and Letters, Youth-Princeton* (1927) (New York: Charles Scribner's Sons, New York, 1946), 1:29, 52.

19. Wilson, "Address at the Tercentenary Celebration of the Translation of the Bible into the English Language," 19; "A Talk at Swarthmore College," Oct. 25, 1913 in Link, ed., *Papers of Woodrow Wilson*, 28:441.

20. Wilson, "Address at the Tercentenary Celebration of the Translation of the Bible into the English Language," 19. The Tennyson poem is "The Princess: Conclusion."

21. Simon J. Ortiz, *From Sand Creek* (New York: Thunder's Mouth Press, 1981), 59.

22. Woodrow Wilson, "An Address on Latin American Policy in Mobile Alabama," Fifth Annual Convention of the Southern Commercial Congress, October 27, 1913, in Link, ed., *Papers of Woodrow Wilson*, 8:451; and ibid.

23. Theodore Roosevelt, *Metropolitan*, March, 1915, 422, and *Everybody's*, January 1915, 144-46, reprinted in *Theodore Roosevelt Cyclopedia*, eds. Albert Bushnell Hart and Herbert Ronald Ferleger (New York: Theodore Roosevelt Association and Meckler, 1988).

24. Guillermo Bonfil Batalla, *México profundo: Reclaiming a Civilization*, trans. Phillip A. Dennis (Austin: University of Texas Press, 1996), 44, 132–33.

25. Manuel Ramos, *Profile of Man and Culture in Mexico* (1934), trans. Peter G. Earle (Austin: University of Texas Press, 1967), 18, 53, 68–69.

26. Ramos, *Profile of Man and Culture in Mexico*, 56–61.

27. Carlos Monsiváis, *Mexican Postcards*, ed. and trans. John Kraniauskas (London and New York: Verso Press, 1997), 15.

28. Octavio Paz, *The Labyrinth of Solitude*, trans. Lysander Kemp (New York: Grove Press, 1961), 20, 128.

29. Paz, *Labyrinth of Solitude*, 23–24.

30. Linda B. Hall, *Mary, Mother and Warrior: The Virgin in Spain and the Americas* (Austin: University of Texas Press, 2004), 246–48.

31. Mircea Eliade, *The Myth of the Eternal Return or, Cosmos and History* (Princeton, NJ: Princeton University Press, 1971), 34–59.

32. Eliade, *The Myth of the Eternal Return*, 34–59; Claire R. Farrer, *Thunder Rides a Black Horse: Mescalero Apaches and the Mythic Present*, 2nd ed. (Prospect Heights, IL: Waveland Press, 1996), 1–4.

33. Gerónimo Boscana, *A New Original Version of Boscana's Historical Account of the San Juan Capistrano Indians of Southern California by John P. Harrington* (Washington D.C.: the Smithsonian Institution, 1934), 43-44; Michelle Stacey, "Clash of the Time Lords: Who Will Own the Measure of Our Days?" *Harper's* 313, no. 1879 (December, 2006), 46–56.

34. Linda Schele and David Freidel, *A Forest of Kings: The Untold Story of the Ancient Maya* (New York: Quill/William Morrow, 1990), 77–84.

35. Arthur S. Link, *Woodrow Wilson and the Progressive Era, 1910-1917* (New York: Harper, 1954), 81, 107.

36. Wilson, "Address at the Tercentenary Celebration of the Translation of the Bible into the English Language," *Papers of Woodrow Wilson*, 13.

37. Pancho Villa in the newspaper *Vida Nueva*, November 21, 1915, quoted in Katz, *Life and Times of Pancho Villa*, 528.

38. Link, *Woodrow Wilson and the Progressive Era*, 107.

39. Hart, *Empire and Revolution*, 306–8; Katz, *Life and Times of Pancho Villa*, 336–37; *Los Angeles Times*, April 14, 1914.

40. Hart, *Empire and Revolution*, 308–11.

41. Hart, *Empire and Revolution*, 308–12; Katz, *Life and Times of Pancho Villa*, 354–58.

Chapter 5

1. Jesús González-Monroy, *Cristianizando* (Mexico, D.F.: Editorial García, 1964), and the quotes are from pages 27–28.

2. Serra to Fray Fermín Lasuén, San Carlos de Monterey, June 13, 1770 in *Writings of Junípero Serra*, ed. and trans. Antoine Tibesar (Washington, DC: American Academy of Franciscan History, 1955-66), 1:xxxviii; http://www.carmelmission.org/mission/laconquistadora.html

3. Maynard Geiger, *Franciscan Missionaries in Hispanic California, 1769–1848: A Biographical Dictionary* (San Marino, CA: Huntington Library, 1969), 30–32, 203–5, 207–8, 266–68; Angustias de la Guerra Ord, "Occurrences," 7–9; Tibesar, *Writings of Junípero Serra*, 1:18–20; James A. Sandos, *Converting California: Indians and Franciscans in the Missions* (New Haven, CT: Yale University Press, 2004), 38–39; Douglas Monroy, *Thrown among Strangers: The Making of Mexican Culture in Frontier California* (Berkeley: University of California Press, 1990), 68–96; Lisbeth Haas, *Conquests and Historical Identities in California, 1769-1936* (Berkeley: University of California Press, 1995), 28.

4. Catherine R. Ettinger, "Spaces of Change: Architecture and the Creation of a New Society in the California Missions," *Bolitín: The Journal of the California Mission Studies Association* 21, no. 1 (2004), 23–27.

5. Carey McWilliams, *Southern California: An Island on the Land* (1946) (Santa Barbara, CA: Peregrine Smith Publications, 1973), 34.

6. Malcolm Margolin, *The Ohlone Way: Indian Life in the San Francisco–Monterey Bay Area* (Berkeley, CA: Heyday Books, 1978), 36–40, 134–39; Brian Fagan, *Before California: An Archeologist Looks at Our Earliest Inhabitants* (Lanham, MD: Rowman & Littlefield, 2003), 263–67.

7. Fagan, *Before California*, 177, 324–56.

8. Lowell John Bean, *Mukat's People: The Cahuilla Indians of Southern California* (Berkeley: University of California Press, 1974), 36–62, 163; Fagan, *Before California*, 298, 312–17; Bernice Eastman Johnson, *California's Gabrielino Indians* (Los Angeles: Southwest Museum, 1962), 42–51.

9. Lowell John Bean and Harry W. Lawton, "Some Explanations for the Rise of Cultural Complexity in Native California with Comments on Proto-Agriculture and Agriculture," Henry T. Lewis, "Patterns of Indian Burning in California: Ecology and Ethnohistory," and Jan Timbrook, John R. Johnson, and David D. Earle, "Vegetation Burning by the Chumash," all in Thomas C. Blackburn and Kat Anderson, eds., *Before the Wilderness: Environmental Management by Native Californians* (Menlo Park, CA: Ballena Press, 1993), 27–149.

10. J.F.G. de La Pérouse, *A Voyage round the World, Performed in the Years 1785, 1786, 1787, and 1788*, 3rd ed. (London: Lackington, 1807), 2:193.

11. Borica is quoted in Ettinger, "Spaces of Change," 38.

12. Diary by Serra of the Expedition from Loreto to San Diego, March 28 to July 1, 1769 in Tibesar, *Writings of Junípero Serra*, 1:62–63; Serra to Don Maria Bucareli y Ursúa, Monterey, August 17, 1775 in Tibesar, *Writings of Junípero Serra*, 2:306.

13. Bean, *Mukat's People*, 146–47.

14. See, for example, Margolin, *Ohlone Way*, 150–54; Florence Connolly Shipek, *Delfina Cuero: Her Autobiography, An Account of Her Last Years, and Her Ethnobotanic Contributions* (Menlo Park, CA: Ballena Press, 1991), 46; Bean, *Mukat's People*, 143–44; Gerónimo Boscana, *A New Original Version of Boscana's Historical Account of the San Juan Capistrano Indians of Southern California by John P. Harrington* (Washington D.C.: Smithsonian Institution, 1934), 21, 38–42.

15. Boscana, *Boscana's Historical Account*, 38–40, 41–43; "Annotations by John P. Harrington" in *Chinigchinich: A Revised and Annotated Version of Alfred Robinson's Translation of Father Geronimo Boscana's Historical Account of the Belief, Usages, Customs and Extravagancies of the Indians of This Mission of San Juan Capistrano called the Acagchemem*, ed. Phil Townsend Hanna (Santa Ana, CA: Fine Arts Press, 1933), 141, 176–77.

16. "From a Letter by Luis Jayme," in Rose Marie Beebe and Robert M. Sankewicz, eds., *Lands of Promise and Despair: Chronicles of Early California, 1535-1846* (Santa Clara and Berkeley, CA: University of Santa Clara and Heyday Books, 2001), 156–61.

17. Serra to Bucareli, May 21, 1773, in Tibesar, *Writings of Junípero Serra*, 2:362–63.

18. Padre Cambón is quoted in Thomas Workman Temple II, "Founding of Misión San Gabriel Arcángel, Part II," *The Masterkey* 33 (October–December, 1959), 159; Toypurina and Nicolas José are quoted in Thomas Workman Temple II, "Toypurina the Witch and the Indian Uprising at San Gabriel," *The Masterkey* 32 (September–October, 1958), 146–49; George Harwood Phillips, *Chiefs and Challengers: Indian Resistance and Cooperation in Southern California* (Berkeley: University of California Press, 1975), 25–26.

19. Hubert Howe Bancroft, *History of California* (San Francisco: The History Co., 1884), 1:249–55; Sherburne Friend Cook, *The Conflict between the California Indian and White Civilization* (Berkeley: University of California Press, 1976), 65–66; Serra to Bucareli y Ursúa, April 12, 1776, in Tibesar, *Writings of Junípero Serra*, 2:412; "Anza's Diary of the Second Anza Expedition, 1775–1776," in *Anza's California Expeditions*, ed. and trans. Herbert Eugene Bolton (Berkeley: University of California Press, 1930), 3:87; "Garce's Diary from Tubac to San Gabriel, 1774," in ibid., 3:339–40; Fray Francisco Palóu, *Historical Memoirs of New California*, in Herbert Eugene Bolton, ed. and trans. (New York: Russell & Russell, 1966, originally Berkeley, CA: University of California Press, 1926), 4:61. Only Palóu believed that the neophyte Indians were largely faithful. Anza, Lasuén, Bancroft, and Cook are all convinced that renegade Christians participated in the San Diego revolt.

20. Sandos, *Converting California*, 75; Bancroft, *History of California*, 1:361–63; Geiger, *Franciscan Missionaries*, 92–95.

21. On the matter of venereal diseases, see Sandos, *Converting California*, 111–27.

22. Lasuén, "Refutation of Charges," 1801, in *Writings of Fermín Francisco de Lasuén*, trans. Finbar Kenneally (Washington, DC: Academy of American Franciscan History, 1965), 2:220.

23. Robert H. Jackson and Edward Castillo, *Indians, Franciscans, and Spanish Colonization: The Impact of the Mission System on California Indians* (Albuquerque: University of New Mexico Press, 1995), 41, 53.

24. Francisco Palóu, *Life and Apostolic Labors of the Venerable Father Junípero Serra*, trans. C. Scott Williams (Pasadena, CA: James Warton James, 1913), 213; Serra to Lasuén, January 12, 1780, in Tibesar, *Writings of Junípero Serra* 3:418; Serra to Bucareli, May 2, 1773, ibid. 1:359–363.

25. Randall Millikan, *A Time of Little Choice: The Disintegration of Tribal Culture in the San Francisco Bay Area, 1769–1810* (Menlo Park, CA: Ballena Press, 1995), 219–21.

26. Serra to Felipe de Neve, Monterey, January 7, 1780, and Serra to Teodoro de Croix, Monterey, August 22, 1778, both in Tibesar, *Writings of Junípero Serra* 3:252–53 and 409–13.

27. Beth Haas, "Emancipation and the Meaning of Freedom in Mexican California," *Bolitín: The Journal of the California Mission Studies Association* 20, no. 1 (2003), 11–22.

28. Ernestine de Soto's presentation at "The Missions of Alta California: A Dialogue," Maritime Museum of Monterey, California, October 13–15, 1995; Beverly R. Ortiz, "A Mission Indian Memorial," *News from Native California*, 10, no. 4 (Summer 1997), 7–10.

29. Doyce B. Nunis Jr., *Hispanic California Revisited: Essays by Francis F. Guest, O.F.M.* (Santa Barbara, CA: Santa Barbara Mission Archive Library, 1996), 139; quoted in Garry Wills, *Papal Sin: Structures of Deceit* (New York: Doubleday, 2000), 239–40.

30. Nunis, *Hispanic California Revisited*, 155, 177, 192.

31. Ibid., 162; Monsignor Weber's presentation at "The Missions of Alta California: A Dialogue," Maritime Museum of Monterey, California, October 13–15, 1995.

32. John R. Johnson, "Toypurina's Descendants: Information from Mission Records and Oral Histories," paper presented at California Mission Studies Conference, San Francisco, February 17, 2007.

33. This discussion derives from Victor Turner and Edith Turner, *Image and Pilgrimage in Christian Culture: Anthropological Perspectives* (New York: Columbia University Press, 1978), 203–7, who quote J. F. Sollier, "Communion of Saints," in *The Catholic Encyclopedia*, C. Herbermann et al., eds. (New York: Robert Appleton Co., 1911); and Rudolf Otto, *The Idea of the Holy: An Inquiry into the Non-Rational Factor in the Idea of the Divine and Its Relation to the Rational*, trans. John W. Harvey (New York: Oxford University Press, 1923, 1958), 63–65, 143–44.

34. Mike Wilken, "Common Ground: A Kumiai/Kumeyaay Summit," *News from Native California* 10, no. 2 (Winter 1996/97), 20; Terra Trevor, "Tomol Trek," in ibid., 10–11; http://www.maidu.com/maidu/ourhistory/photoalbum/photoalbum .html

35. Florence Connolly Shipek, *Pushed into the Rocks: Southern California Indian*

Land Tenure, 1769–1986 (Lincoln: University of Nebraska Press, 1988), 3, 8–9, 91–102. Anthropologists often refer to these bands as "tribelets."

36. Fritz Scholder, "The Cupeño and the German," *News from Native California*, 9, no. 2 (Winter, 1995/96), 4–6; Margaret Dubin, "Introduction," in *The Dirt Is Red Here: Art and Poetry from Native California*, ed. Margaret Dubin (Berkeley, CA: Heyday Books, 2002), xii.

37. Deborah Miranda, "Indian Cartography," in Dubin, ed., *The Dirt Is Red Here*, 32.

Chapter 6

1. Raymond Williams, *The Country and the City* (New York: Oxford University Press, 1973), 131.

2. I should note that as of this writing he is a busboy at a Mexican restaurant in Colorado Springs along with a number of fair-haired Colorado teenagers. Next summer, home from college, he will move up to waiter. His Spanish is so bad he could not possibly be of any assistance should there be trouble in the kitchen.

3. Bernal Diaz del Castillo, *The Discovery and Conquest of Mexico, 1517-1521*, ed. and trans. A.P. Maudslay (New York: Noonday Press, 1956), 32, 66–68.

4. Octavio Paz, *The Labyrinth of Solitude*, trans. Lysander Kemp (New York: Grove Press, 1961), 86-87.

5. Magnus Morner, *Race Mixture in the History of Latin America* (Boston: Little, Brown, and Company, 1967), 57–59.

6. Richard Henry Dana, *Two Years before the Mast* (New York: Bantam Pathfinder, 1959), 135–36.

7. Note by Dr. George Clements, August 25, 1939, Clements Papers, Box 79, UCLA Special Collections.

8. José Vasconcelos, *The Cosmic Race/La Raza Cósmica*, ed. and trans. Didier T. Jaen (Baltimore and London: The Johns Hopkins University Press, 1997), 17–18.

9. Paz, *Labyrinth of Solitude*, 24.

10. Samuel P. Huntington, "The Hispanic Challenge," *Foreign Policy* (March/April 2004), 40, 44.

11. Ibid., 32.

12. D. J. Waldie, *Holy Land: A Suburban Memoir* (New York: St. Martin's Press, 1996), 59, 73.

13. Huntington, "Hispanic Challenge," 31.

14. Bonnie Honig, *Democracy and the Foreigner* (Princeton and Oxford: Princeton University Press, 2001), 74–75.

15. Grahame L. Jones, "Mexico Is Right at Home in Win," *Los Angeles Times*, Feb. 16, 1998, C1.

16. *La Opinión*, June 2, 1945, 7.

17. "De Colores" became the anthem of the United Farm Workers.

18. Raul Homero Villa, *Barrio Logos: Space and Place in Urban Chicano Literature and Culture* (Austin: University of Texas Press, 2000), 111–201; Eric Avila, *Popular Culture in the Age of White Flight: Fear and Fantasy in Suburban Los Angeles* (Berkeley: University of California Press, 2004), 196–215.

19. Rubén Martínez, *Crossing Over: A Mexican Family on the Migrant Trail* (New York: Picador USA, 2001), 30; Fred Alvarez, "Interpreters Give Voice to the Indigenous," *Los Angeles Times*, October 11, 2004, B1.

20. Ellen Barry, "Judge Who Ordered English Lessons Restores Custody," *Los Angeles Times*, April 27, 2005, A10.

21. Sam Quinones, *True Tales from Another Mexico: The Lynch Mob, the Popsicle Kings, Chalino, and the Bronx* (Albuquerque: University of New Mexico Press, 2001), 117-35.

22. Armando B. Rendon, *Chicano Manifesto* (New York: Collier, 1971), 306.

23. Gloria Anzaldúa, *Borderlands/La Frontera: The New Mestiza* (San Francisco: Spinsters/Aunt Lute, 1987), 19-21.

24. http://www.iabeef.org/Recipes/Fajitas/Tips.aspx

25. Guillermo Gómez-Peña, *The New World Border: Prophecies, Poems & Loqueras for the End of the Century* (San Francisco: City Lights, 1996), 5, 21, 64, 82.

26. For a discussion of the destruction of heterosocial spaces in LA, see Avila, *Popular Culture in the Age of White Flight*.

27. Ferdinand Roemer, *Texas, with Particular Reference to German Immigration and the Physical Appearance of the Country*, trans. Oswald Mueller (1949) (San Antonio: Standard Printing Company, 1935), 120, 124-25; Arnoldo de Leon, *They Called Them Greasers: Anglo Attitudes towards Mexicans in Texas, 1821-1900* (Austin: University of Texas Press, 1983), 38-39.

28. Martínez, *Crossing Over*, 30; Perry Anderson, *The Origins of Postmodernity* (London and New York: Verso Press, 1998), 55-57.

29. *New York Times*, July 11, 2004.

30. Ginger Thompson. "Mexico's 'Tomato King' Seeks a New Title," *New York Times*, July 5, 2004, A4.

Chapter 7

1. Mike Davis, *Magical Urbanism: Latinos Reinvent the U.S. City* (London and New York: Verso, 2001); David Rieff, *Los Angeles: Capital of the Third World* (New York: Touchstone, 1991).

2. Robert D. Kaplan, "History Moving North," *The Atlantic Monthly* (February 1997), 22-23.

3. Peter Andreas, *Border Games: Policing the U.S.-Mexico Divide* (Ithaca, NY: Cornell University Press, 2001), 115-39.

4. Richard Rodriguez, *Brown: The Last Discovery of America* (New York: Viking, 2002).

Index

·:· ·:· ·:·

About the Author

Douglas Monroy is professor of history at The Colorado College. A native of Los Angeles and a graduate of Hollywood High School and UCLA, he presently lives in Colorado Springs, though he spends the equivalent of at least two months per year in Southern California. He has two grown children and a five-year-old. A mainstay of the faculty softball team at Colorado College for nearly three decades, Doug also plays tennis and golf.

He is the author of *Thrown among Strangers: The Making of Mexican Culture in Frontier California*, winner of the James Rawley Prize of the Organization of American Historians, and *Rebirth: Mexican Los Angeles from the Great Migration to the Great Depression*, both from the University of California Press. Professor Monroy serves on the OAH Distinguished Speakers Series. For the 2004–2005 year, he was the Ray Allen Billington Distinguished Visiting Professor at the Huntington Library and Occidental College. At Colorado College he teaches courses on twentieth-century U.S. history, the history of the Southwest and its arts and literature, and historiography. He has led numerous workshops and seminars for K–12 teachers on a variety of issues related to his scholarly work.

As a child he was mostly interested in sports; as a college student in the civil rights and antiwar movements and in the world of politics and ideas; and Doug Monroy's values, beliefs, and activities have remained consistent with this earlier socialization. Added to this mix has been a strong dose of neo-Freudian thinking and wrestling with the issue of how to mix pleasures with family, environmental, and social responsibility.